Praise for *Parenting for the Digital Generation: A Guide to Digital Education and the Online Environment*

"At Last! The guidelines parents and teachers have been waiting for. And it's all in one organized, straightforward book. Technology can be such a large, difficult expanse of terms and capabilities that change rapidly. Jon M. Garon will give both parents and teachers the information needed to confidently provide support and instruction for any child's education."—Kimberly Durham, PsyD, dean of the Abraham S. Fischler College of Education and School of Criminal Justice, Nova Southeastern University

"As a child psychologist and a mom, I know most parents have concerns about how to parent in this quickly changing and fast-paced digital world. In this book, Garon provides families with a strong knowledge base for understanding the basics of the digital world, offers examples of the benefits of technology, discusses the concerns, and provides an understandable framework for determining how to maintain balance within the family. The easy-to-read charts that describe developmental stages in relation to media use will become a favorite resource as I support families' goals of finding the strengths in the digital world that will help foster their children's development while maintaining age-appropriate and realistic limits. This book is a must-read for all parents."—Sandra Sondell, PhD, psychology consultation specialists

"As a parent of a twelve-year-old, I have often had questions and fears about my child's access to digital media. Like most parents, I have turned to the internet for answers but have been frustrated by the multitude of contradictory opinions that lack credibility or research. As a psychologist and academic, I know there are more reliable and trustworthy sources. Jon M. Garon's book is the resource

I have been looking for. Both comprehensive and readable, *Parenting for the Digital Generation* is an engaging read from cover to cover and a valuable reference book for my shelf. Every parent should have a copy."—Kurt A. Boniecki, PhD, associate provost for Academic Success and associate professor of psychology, University of Central Arkansas

"Today, children and schools are often more adept at understanding and using technology than parents, leaving them confused and without information or skills. Garon gives parents a clear and comprehensive framework so they can 'get their head in the game.' He teaches terminology, relevant laws and rules, dangers, and safeguards. Garon provides understandable and practical strategies for raising healthy children based on their developmental age. I've never seen anyone else put all the pieces together."—Karen Grosby, EdD, dean, Nova Southeastern University College of Psychology

"As a parent, lawyer, and educator, Jon M. Garon brings unique insights to the effect of today's technology on families and the legal/social structures that both protect and threaten family cohesiveness. He combines deep legal and technical knowledge with practical insight. Here lies an understanding of the social and technological waves buffeting children today with the tools and resources needed to calm the waters."—Ted Claypoole, JD, editor and coauthor of *The Law of Artificial Intelligence and Smart Machines* and author of *Protecting Your Internet Identity and Privacy in the Age of Big Data*

Parenting for the Digital Generation

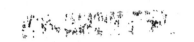

Parenting for the Digital Generation

The Parent's Guide to Digital Education and the Online Environment

Jon M. Garon

ROWMAN & LITTLEFIELD
Lanham • Boulder • New York • London

Published by Rowman & Littlefield
An imprint of The Rowman & Littlefield Publishing Group, Inc.
4501 Forbes Boulevard, Suite 200, Lanham, Maryland 20706
www.rowman.com

86-90 Paul Street, London EC2A 4NE, United Kingdom

British Library Cataloguing in Publication Information Available

Library of Congress Cataloging-in-Publication Data

Names: Garon, Jon M., author.
Title: Parenting for the digital generation : a guide to digital education and the online
    environment / Jon M. Garon.
Description: Lanham : Rowman & Littlefield, [2022] | Includes bibliographical
    references and index. | Summary: "Reviews the broad landscape of legal and
    practical issues facing parents and adolescents when using smart phones and online
    technologies"—Provided by publisher.
Identifiers: LCCN 2021037648 (print) | LCCN 2021037649 (ebook) |
    ISBN 9781475861952 (cloth ; permanent paper) | ISBN 9781475861969 (epub)
Subjects: LCSH: Internet and children. | Computer security. | Parenting—Miscellanea.
Classification: LCC HQ784.I58 G37 2022 (print) | LCC HQ784.I58 (ebook) |
    DDC 004.67/8083—dc23/eng/20211013
LC record available at https://lccn.loc.gov/2021037648
LC ebook record available at https://lccn.loc.gov/2021037649

♾️™ The paper used in this publication meets the minimum requirements of American
National Standard for Information Sciences—Permanence of Paper for Printed Library
Materials, ANSI/NISO Z39.48-1992.

To my children, from whom I have learned all the most important lessons about parenting.

Contents

Preface

The world has gone digital, and there is no going back. Electronic shopping carts have replaced malls and department stores, television has moved to on-line streaming, education has been converted into online portals, and telephone calls have been replaced with texts, tweets, and chats. Changes already transforming the national economy and culture were accelerated dramatically because of the COVID-19 pandemic, forcing this transition on every family in America and throughout the world.

Parenting for the Digital Generation provides a practical handbook for parents, grandparents, teachers, and counselors who want to understand both the opportunities and the threats that exist for the generation of digital natives who are more familiar with a smartphone than they are with a paper book. This book provides straightforward, jargon-free information regarding the online environment and the experience in which children and young adults engage both inside and outside the classroom.

For parents, the digital environment creates many challenges, some of which are largely the same as parents faced before the Internet, but others which are entirely new. Parents have always worked to keep their children healthy, well-adjusted, and engaged in their learning and growth. In the online classroom, however, many children struggle to connect, and they underperform in the absence of the social and emotional support of a healthy learning environment. Suddenly, in addition to serving as the tutor on math, science, and history, the parents of digital students are also called upon to understand copyright law, privacy law, Title IX, and the technical requirements for learning management systems, group chats, Google Docs, and conference call services.

Outside the classroom, parents must also help their children navigate a complex and often dangerous world. Unlike previous generations, children and young adults have far more opportunities to hide their activities from the observations of their parents and other caring adults. For parents, the privacy and anonymity of the Internet complicate their difficult but vital tasks.

At the same time, billions of people spend time on the Internet each day. The vast majority of those interactions pose no threats to the public, and many involve opportunities to connect with others, get work done, learn, play, and engage with friends and family.

This book provides a step-by-step guide for parents seeking to raise happy, mature, creative, and well-adjusted children. The guide provides clear explanations of the keys to navigating as a parent in the online environment while providing practical strategies that do not look for dangers where there are only remote threats.

Introduction

Technology has transformed the way people work, shop, date, and communicate, so it is no surprise that technology has also changed the environment in which people raise and educate their children. While so much change is impacting work, social life, and education, what makes a successful family has not changed. Children still need unconditional love, support, structure, and stability. The modern digital economy is not designed around those goals. Instead, it promotes unlimited and unconstrained access to media, games, and shopping. Social media promotes connections with friends and strangers. But social media also enables trolls, bullying, and stalking. The digital world is one without limits; the successful child's world is one of structure, predictability, and support. Parents and caregivers need strategies and suggestions to harness the digital world in support of their healthy, successful family life.

The digital world has also transformed education. Even before the COVID-19 pandemic, school systems were relying more and more heavily on learning management systems, online experiences, and virtual class sessions. With the global switch to online learning in 2020, these trends were greatly accelerated. Many of these tools and pedagogical strategies greatly supplement in-person learning, but they sometimes fall short when trying to replace the classroom. Parents and teachers have been called upon to rethink their teaching and engagement strategies to make the students' experience as rewarding and developmentally effective in the online setting as in the in-person class. Online teaching takes place in the child's home, making the partnership between parent and teacher more important than ever.

Government, once the censor for television and radio, plays little role in the management of the Internet. Voluntary rating systems so effective in the movie industry and for videogames do not hold sway on YouTube or the thousands of other sites for music, films, videos, and games. Television, once pejoratively called the "boob tube," was often attacked in the 1960s as the great wasteland, a dangerous technology that had a negative influence on children and teens. The radio faced similar accusations in the generations before television. Today, a variety of technologies have earned that scorn, including videogames, mobile phones, and social media.

In this book, *Parenting for the Digital Generation*, parents are offered context to understand the challenges they face in addressing how changing technology requires new strategies to maintain a healthy household. The book begins by laying out a framework for the healthy digital family, one that uses modern technology to supplement rather than supplant what is important for the health and safety of the members of the family. In chapters 1–3, the book provides a strategy for raising children who can benefit from modern technology but not be carried away by the excesses of social media, online shopping, gaming, or the other lures of unlimited online access.

In chapters 4–6, the book explores online and blended education. Chapter 4 provides background so that parents are conversant with the nomenclature and strategies teachers and schools are using to design and implement online learning. Chapters 5 and 6 provide direct guidance on how parents can support their children in online and blended education, as well as addressing issues that arise when technology is used for in-person education. Parents often struggle with communications with their children's teachers, homework assignments, disability accommodations, and other common obstacles to their children's success. These chapters provide suggestions on how to better understand and address those and many other challenges.

In chapters 7–8, the book explores how households can take advantage of the modern technology for the benefit of the adolescents in the household. There are many opportunities created by new digital technology. The people who will be the most successful in the next generation will typically have a strong background using the technologies as adolescents. These chapters help parents understand how best to let teens harness the Internet for their success.

Beginning with chapter 9, the book also explores the concerns that many parents have about the online environment. The book describes the dangers that lurk online for adolescents and their families. Each chapter tries to demystify and quantify these risks, not to diminish them but to provide accurate information about what teens might face regarding threats that may lurk on the Web.

The risks, of course, are real, and Internet users should take care to protect themselves from the risks. At the same time, however, the Internet is not predominantly a wicked den of iniquity designed to steal children and bake them into pies. The Internet is an interconnected series of technologies and communications protocols that allow people and businesses to share information and data of every conceivable type. Like every tool and machine ever harnessed, it can be very beneficial when used carefully and it can become dangerous when misused. Online users need to take advantage of the Internet while using practical precautions to ensure safety.

In most sections, this book uses the term "Internet" as a broad term to refer to the network of computers and technologies necessary to make the Internet operate, the Web which opens the Internet to most general uses, the computers and mobile devices on which content can be found, and the various gaming platforms, social media offerings, streaming platforms, portals, online communities, and Internet of Things (IoT): networked devices that use the Internet as part of their operations. Where necessary to discuss a particular technology or tool, the text will offer precise information regarding the tool being used, but unless necessary, the broader terms "Internet," "social media," or "videogaming" generally suffice.

The final chapters complete the picture of the Internet and its role in a household's daily life, including discussions on ecommerce, privacy, and cybersecurity safeguards. Together, the book provides a roadmap essential for parents hoping to understand the environment in which their children are living, and a set of keys to unlock the world of the Internet that is often locked behind buzzwords and hype.

About This Book

I am a lawyer, so I must also include a disclaimer. The book does not constitute the practice of law or provide legal advice that can be relied upon as authoritative for individual legal matters. This information is general in nature. Where the reader has specific legal questions, the advice in this book should only be used in conjunction with a licensed attorney, familiar with the issues presented by the specific legal matter in question.

This book identifies particular individuals, firms, and companies. Although many of the companies listed are the largest or most visible in their respective fields, the names are used either for illustrative purposes or to provide a starting point for the reader's own research. Conversely, the failure to appear in the book should not be deemed a negative assessment of any particular product, service, or organization. Nothing in the book constitutes an endorsement of these entities or of their services, and the book cannot be relied upon as the legal basis for engaging such services.

Chapter 1

Creating a Healthy Digital Family

All happy families are alike; each unhappy family is unhappy in its own way.

—Leo Tolstoy, *Anna Karenina* (1877)

Most readers of books on digital parenting are not newlyweds thinking about their twenty-year plan to raise a healthy, positive family. Instead, the readers are parents struggling with issues facing their teen's use of technology while often trying to help their children with online classes. Teachers and counselors are trying to implement new technologies which change rapidly and come with a bewildering number of new regulations and requirements. The adolescents and teens themselves are often struggling to keep up with the technology and its impact on their social environment. New apps become popular, then go out of fashion in a matter of months.

The digital revolution has also changed society itself. A child growing up in 2020 lives in a manifestly different world than the child who grew up in 1980, just as that child grew up in a very different America than the child who was raised in 1940. Cell phones and the Internet have reengineered our lives every bit as much as electricity and plumbing did in an earlier era. In addition to providing guidance on how to help raise children in the modern digital era, the advice in this book may also go a small way to help repair the damage to the world created by society's failure to tend to the consequences of the technologies now in use.

A. WHAT FAMILIES NEED

The observation by Leo Tolstoy remains good advice. There are common attributes that make all happy families alike. That is a very good place to start. "The family is one of society's oldest and most resilient institutions. . . . Families—in all their amazing diversity—are the basic, foundational social units in every society."[1]

Healthy families are not defined by a notion of the nuclear family, conceived in the last century, as a mother, father, and 2.5 children. Families often have a single parent, a step-parent, or parents of the same sex. Grandparents, aunts, and uncles often play a critical role in child-rearing and emotional support. Research on healthy families identified twenty-two characteristics, the most important of which is that "[h]uman beings have the right and responsibility to feel safe, comfortable, happy, and loved."[2]

1. Media Is Not a Mirror; It Is Alice's Looking Glass

Modern technology can assist in achieving these goals only in very limited ways. Videoconferencing allows families physically separated to stay in touch and to attend important events in their loved ones' lives. Social media enables people to connect and reconnect with a large circle of friends, sharing birthdays, religious celebrations, and the many highs and lows one experiences through the year. The more distant online connections may become just as emotionally significant as the daily in-person conversations one has with those living in the household. Online friends are not less connected simply because the relationship is mediated through technology.

At the same time, however, social media does not necessarily reflect a true picture of one's friends' real life. When a group of friends on Facebook post only about their exotic trips, their front-row concert tickets, and their romantic conquests, the reader can begin to mistake the highly selective social media feed for a version of life that is much better than the real world can offer. Individual relationships on social media can have the same intimacy and support as in-person relationships, but the aggregate social media experience is not representative of the real world.

Although teens are particularly vulnerable to this glamorization on social media, adults often struggle to separate reality from media idealization as well. The distorting influence of media is not limited to newer social media, but social media has an immediacy and intimacy that traditional television, radio, and print content simply cannot match.

2. Attributes of the Successful Family

In addition to safety, comfort, happiness, and love, there are a number of traits common to successful families. These are five of the most important for building a strong family:

- *Strong marriages are the center of many strong families.* The couple relationship is an important source of strength in many families with children who are doing well. Parents need to find ways to nurture a positive couple relationship for the good of everyone in the family.
- *Strengths develop over time.* When couples start out in life together, they sometimes have considerable difficulty adjusting to each other, and these difficulties are quite predictable. Adjusting to each other is not an easy task. Many couples who are unstable at first end up creating a healthy, happy family.
- *Strengths are often developed in response to challenges.* A couple and family's strengths are tested by life's everyday stressors and also by the significant crises that all of us face sooner or later.
- *Strong families, like people, are not perfect.* Even in the strongest of families we can sometimes be like porcupines: prickly, disagreeable, eager, and ready to enjoy conflict with each other. But we also have a considerable need to cuddle up with each other for warmth and support. A strong family is a work of art continually in progress, always in the process of growing and changing.
- *Strong families tend to produce great kids.* A good place to look for great kids is in strong families.[3]

To be successful in marriage and family life requires all the participants to work on the steps that help reinforce these values. A strong family is built on a healthy, respectful relationship among the parents as well as any of the adults in the family unit, such as grandparents and non-custodial parents. The adults "help each other, keep promises, and show affection to each other."[4] They also model this behavior for the children in the household and encourage the children to do the same.

As a consequence of the family member help and support, members of healthy families "are very loyal to each other, share responsibilities, make decisions together, allow members to make their own decisions with support, and find it easy to trust one another."[5] At the same time, as noted above, strong or healthy families are not immune from conflict and tension. Members of most families will sometimes conflict over limited resources of time, attention, and money. They will react to perceived slights. And each member of the family will have personal goals that are sometimes in conflict with the greater needs of the family.

A corollary of trust and safety is respect. Technology offers a myriad of ways in which one family member can breach the trust of another family member or disrespect that family member. Electronic eavesdropping and snooping undermine trust, particularly if it is done without a person's awareness. Parents should monitor the online activities of their children, with a gradual lessening of supervision as their children age and mature. At the same time, except in extraordinary situations, parents should not conduct such surveillance in secret. Parents should be fostering appropriate behavior and good decision-making by their children. Letting the children know they are accountable for their decisions furthers this goal, while in contrast, spying on the children undermines their trust.

3. The Battle for Time and Attention

Modern technology is not designed to promote healthy families. In many cases, cell phones, games, and online content are mild distractions. For some people, however, these technologies are far worse, promoting values inconsistent with strong families while competing for the time and attention of the family members.

As discussed in the appendices, online content providers make their money by grabbing and keeping the attention of the consumer. A parent's attention is one of the most precious and limited resources in the family. At a minimum, time spent scrolling through newsfeeds or retweeting posts is time not spent on something else. The time adds up. On average, for the year 2020, "US adults spent 7 hours, 50 minutes (7:50) per day consuming digital media, up 15.0% from 6:49 in 2019. . . . Digital time accounted for 57.5% of adults' daily media time in 2020."[6] While many people multitask, such as by watching television while also spending time on mobile games or social media, the total amount of time amounts to a significant part of every day.

In addition to taking time away from the family, mobile devices are particularly good at interrupting the time people spend with others. Incessant text alerts, app notifications, and various reminders tend to go off at all hours of the waking day. Even though devices have some limited ability to set quiet times, the app developers are constantly installing exceptions to these prohibitions. Bluetooth technology could, for example, be designed to set a parent's phone to vibrate mode whenever the device was within the same room as one of the children's phones, or to turn off the ringer when the parent was inside a child's bedroom. Such a design would help remind parents that the time with their children should be uninterrupted by mobile phone distractions. Unfortunately, these are not standard options on cell phones. Instead, the parent has to remember to put away the device manually during time spent with the children.

B. HOUSEHOLD STRATEGIES TO TAME INTRUSIVE TECHNOLOGY

The household environment today may be very different than the household environment from a few decades earlier. Parents generally knew what their children were watching on television because most families had a primary television in a family room. Only the more affluent households had televisions for the children's bedrooms. The adolescents listened to the radio and to records, but both those media were regulated. Through the Federal Communications Commission (FCC), radio and television content were kept quite unobjectionable for most households. Records and CDs were subject to only voluntary content restrictions, but the vast majority of content remained fairly mainstream.

In contrast, as of 2019, "U.S. households own an average of 11 connected devices, including seven with screens to view content (e.g., smartphones or TVs)."[7] These numbers vary significantly depending on the economic status of each household, with some families struggling to have the minimal technology needed to allow children to attend online classes, while other families have significantly more devices. Nonetheless, on average, the technology is ubiquitous. The modern household will often have at least one computer, if not one computer for each member of the household. Most adolescents and adults will have their own cell phone. There will also be televisions, radios, gaming consoles, and smart devices. Family members will experience their games and content each on their own device, wearing earbuds or headphones that block out the rest of the family.

The first step in understanding the digital environment is to recognize the ease with which one can plug into personal devices and tune out the rest of the family. This is true for each member of the household. Although most of this book is focused on strategies parents can use to help their children navigate modern technology, it is important to begin by looking at the family itself.

Children will not respect rules laid down by adults if the adults are modeling behavior that is significantly at odds with what they expect of their children. In addition, parents will develop some empathy for their children's insistence on expecting reasonable and moderate technology limitations if the parents live by similar limitations. Most importantly, however, regaining some of the hours lost to digital media (and television) may strengthen other aspects of the family.

1. Create House Rules

Children crave structure. "[T]he ideal parenting technique would be to give children equal measures of warmth and structure. However, the second-best approach is to prioritize structure over affection."[8] The best advice, then, is for parents to be sure the household is filled with love, warmth, and affection. *Mister Rogers' Neighborhood* captured the importance of this universal support with its opening song: "There's only one person in the whole world like you. If you think about it for a moment, there has never been . . . and there will never be—in the history of the earth—another person just like you."[9] Mr. Rogers' sentiment emphasized the innate value in every human being. His show exemplified the best in modern media by promoting empathy, compassion, and a profound understanding of the emotional lives of his audience. Healthy households will emulate those attributes.

Mr. Rogers fought a war against modern television and technology, which it unfortunately lost. Distractions from online devices make it harder to stick to routines and undermine the normal rhythms of the household. The first step to overcome this tendency is to reinforce the family structure, building time into each day and each week for the important aspects of the household.

As a daily matter, morning routines designed to get each member of the household out of bed, washed, fed, and ready for school or work should be designed with enough flexibility to avoid conflict and a state of continual crisis. This may include a prohibition from cell phones at the breakfast table, or a limit on email, texts, games, and social media until after all the required washing, cleaning, dressing, and eating have been completed. The conditional permission also makes online usage a reward for efficient completion of the other steps. Although this has the unintended consequences of turning online time into a reward for other chores, it has the practical benefit of creating an incentive system that is easier to enforce than an outright ban. A similar strategy can be used for homework and the dinner routine.

The bedtime routine should likely have the reverse schedule. As will be discussed in the next chapter, the use of screens and devices can have a very disruptive impact on sleep. Children, in particular, should be unplugged at least an hour before going to bed. For young children, a regular routine that includes being read to before bedtime provides the best combination of structure, warmth, and safety. As children get older, this should evolve into quiet reading time, but the reading should be entirely offline. For many people, the relaxation is maximized using printed books on reading devices, but this depends on the person and the person's reaction to electronic screens.

Increasingly, families are also introducing mindfulness techniques, yoga, and meditation as additional tools to help unplug from media bombardment and the anxieties of the day. There are many resources that can help parents identify age-appropriate techniques to supplement the afterschool and bedtime routines to help all family members improve their management of stress.

In addition to the daily routine, there should also be a weekly routine. Religious families often use weekends to find time together through religious traditions such as the Sunday church service, the Friday night Shabbat dinner, or the family Friday afternoon following weekend Islamic prayers. Other religions have analogous traditions.

In contrast to healthy boundaries, families should avoid these situations:

- Having no boundaries at all.
- Setting very strict boundaries (often with threats) but failing to implement them.
- Disciplining children harshly without explaining what they did wrong.
- Failing to have a united front (one parent is overly strict and the other is overly lenient).
- Allowing older children to set the boundaries for younger children.[10]

These examples of inconsistent boundaries reflect the importance of structure and parental authority. The need for rules and expectations helps the child and adolescent develop external values which they learn and internalize. When the rules are inconsistent or go without implementation, the children are left confused and frustrated.

2. Game Night and Family Time Together

A common tradition, which often supplements the religious scheduling, is for a family game night. One afternoon or evening is reserved for games the entire family can play together. Game nights provide that combination of structure and warmth at the heart of strong parenting. Although they are not "about" anything, the time shared in cooperative and competitive play reinforces the most important aspects of family success.

As noted earlier, among the important attributes of strong families are the ways in which they address their conflicts. Members of the family are attuned to the feelings of other family members. They spend enough time together to have fun, laugh, and share positive feelings which help offset the conflicts.

The positive support, in turn, helps each member of the family address the inevitable disappointments in life. The challenges help each member of the family develop coping skills. "Families with healthy well-being tend to be resilient. Crisis brings them closer together and they are supportive of one another. They look for something good from a bad situation and tend to accept the things they cannot change."[11]

Games and other forms of play provide an ideal environment to develop these skills in low-stakes environments. Games often have winners and losers, so teaching all members of the family to be gracious in victory and defeat becomes an easy but essential life lesson. Overcoming losses leads to lessons of perseverance, teaching children about grit and the importance of sticking to a project.

Beyond games, there are also family projects from things as simple as jigsaw puzzles and Legos to more complicated model sets and hobbies. Sports can also be used to achieve similar goals. Like game nights, these activities help build camaraderie among the family members, perseverance, conflict management, and social engagement that are healthy, supportive, and engaging while avoiding reliance on Internet technologies.

3. Establishing Boundaries

In addition to routine, the other important step in building effective family structure is to establish clear boundaries. Individual and family boundaries often begin with the Golden Rule, but because the modern world has become so complicated, there are actually three key variations of this tradition.[12] One is the Jewish tradition. The First Century BCE sage, Rabbi Hillel, taught that "love of one's fellow man" was the essence of Jewish teaching. Asked to summarize the entire Jewish religion, Hillel explained: "What is hateful to you, do not do to your fellow: this is the whole Torah; the rest is the explanation."[13]

Christian theology continued this tradition with the Golden Rule of the Christian bible from Jesus of Nazareth's Sermon on the Mount, where he stated: "Do unto others as you would have them do unto you."[14] The third variation is sometimes called the Platinum Rule: "Do unto others as they would want done to them."[15] The variation by including that you should "do unto others as they would have you do unto them" highlights a tension in modern society between equality and equity. In an equal world, all people are treated the same. But in the real world, not everyone starts from the same place. In the family, younger children do not have the same experience and maturity as their older siblings.

In broader society, issues of endemic racism and structural bias have barred minorities and women from opportunities provided to white men. By treating the other as the other wishes to be treated rather than as how "you" would want to be treated, the Platinum Rule demands additional empathy and generosity which may even sometimes demand unequal treatment to provide equitable outcomes. Again, at its simplest, the Platinum Rule would account for rules in family game night that the younger children get extra do-overs in their turns to help them have a more equitable chance at winning the family game. Hillel's interpretation of the Golden Rule fits very nicely with a positive injunction to do at least as much as you would want done for yourself and, when possible, as much as the other person would want you to do.

The Golden Rule, and its variations, helps set boundaries for individuals and the family as well as a broader code for the use of teaching children how to use technology.

[R]elational boundaries refer to the limits a person has with another person. . . .
In a healthy family system, each person assumes responsibility for their part

in keeping the system balanced and safe. For example, a parent might set a boundary against unwanted behaviors like cursing, hitting, or stealing. A spouse might request that his partner doesn't share his private information with outside friends. A mother might ask her daughter to call her when she arrives at her friend's house.[16]

While the Golden Rule provides the general framework for all the family boundaries and expectations, two particular areas are impacted by modern technology: Individual Privacy and Effective Communication.

Individual Privacy

Individual privacy is one of the key boundaries that has been impacted by the Internet. For the adults, all emails, texts, and communications should be private and read by another party only with permission. Older teens should be afforded a similar degree of privacy unless certain other boundaries have been violated; for example, unwanted behaviors such as stealing, sneaking out past curfew, or sexual impropriety require a loss of privacy as a consequence for the boundary violation.

Individual privacy also includes not posting private content to social media. Pictures of teens and adults should not be posted without the permission of those in the picture. What a parent finds cute might be mortifying to a teen, and the teen's perception of their privacy should be respected.

Effective Communication

Many of the challenges within families—and throughout society—stem from a lack of effective communication. Some of these problems are caused by technology, while others are exacerbated through technology. Of course, some problems with tone, attitude, or behavior have little to do with technology.

Effective communications are those that clearly and accurately inform the other person of both the content that one wishes to share and any emotional and metacognitive information the person needs to impart. The communication must share not only its message but also its importance to the sender, timeliness, and expectations of ongoing dialogue.

Sharing a recipe might provide a useful analogy. At a minimum, a recipe must list all the ingredients. If the person sharing a recipe leaves out any ingredients, the recipe will fail. But unless the recipient is a seasoned baker, the recipe will be incomplete without an explanation of the steps needed to use the recipe. Even the list of steps may not reflect the techniques that would be clearer if the parties were speaking in person. Photos that illustrate the steps and the finished item help the recipient visualize the steps and results of the recipe. The photos replace some of what is lost by not sharing the recipe in person. Finally, in cookbooks and magazines, recipes are typically introduced with background stories to provide context and increase the emotional connection of the recipe to both author and reader of the cookbook. When sharing a recipe among friends, the sender will often ask for feedback and to learn how the recipe worked, closing the communications circle between the parties about the shared recipe.

Each of the details expanding the recipe from a list of ingredients to a story and pictures helps the recipient understand more fully about the communication. Without that detail, both the facts and the importance of the communication can get lost. A string of text messages or tweets tends to strip the communication of context and meaning, creating the opportunity for misunderstandings and conflict.

Not every communication needs this level of detail, but communication breaks down when too little information is shared or there are not common expectations between the parties to the communication. Written communication is highly inefficient. It is often stated that "55% of communication is body language, 38% is the tone of voice, and 7% is the actual words spoken."[17] These data overstate the nonverbal importance somewhat and they apply more accurately in some situations than in others,[18] but they reflect the significant importance of nonverbal signals to understanding each other.

In emails, the choice to include third parties in the communications can often be used to change the two-way communication into a way of tattling on another party. At work, it is a common act of aggression to copy a person's boss on an email with a complaint about the person. The same may occur in the family setting, where one child copies a parent to get a sibling in trouble. Emojis and acronyms go only a short way to distinguish between lighthearted, supportive humor and biting sarcasm.

In the family setting, the use of technology to share important communications should be conducted with clear boundaries. Family members should avoid angry emails, texts, and tweets. As soon as an online conversation becomes heated, it should be tabled and reserved for a time where the conversation can take place in person. If an in-person conversation is not possible, then a phone call or videocall is still a much better alternative than overlapping emails.

Both oral and written communications should have boundaries that restrict shouting or its (ALL CAPS) written alternative; require listening to each other in full before responding; avoid silent treatment and nonengagement; and emphasize techniques to share one's own feelings rather than to blame the other party. For example, one such technique is to only speak in the first person, avoiding use of any second-person language. "I felt . . ." and "I am upset because . . ." are examples of statements that reflect the thoughts and feelings of the speaker. When the speaker switches to "you said . . ." or "you didn't . . ." the tone becomes one of blame, triggering defensiveness on the other party.

These communication basics should be part of each family member's shared commitment to each other. Together with the application of the Golden Rule to eliminate sarcasm and criticism, members of the family will find that these simple techniques will help build the harmony and structure typical of a happy family.

C. RAISING CHILDREN FOR SUCCESS

The goal for every successful family is to raise healthy, happy, empathetic, and successful children who will go on to lead fulfilled lives and build strong families of their own. The definition and criteria for what constitutes a meaningful life, a fulfilling life, and a successful life are all well beyond the scope of this book. As a practical matter, however, many of the attributes essential to build lives of meaning and fulfillment will correlate with skills that employers generally prize among college and professional school graduates. The use of employment skills is not a cop-out or reductionist approach to fulfillment. Business success does not necessarily define personal success. They are universal. In *The Little Prince* (*Le Petit Prince*), there is a phrase to explain these values: "L'essentiel est invisible pour les yeux; What is essential is invisible to the eye." The attributes and skills to make one healthy, happy, and productive at work carry over into a person's volunteer commitments, personal relationships, and family life.

1. Grit and Resilience

One of the most common concerns is that the instantaneous nature of the digital age has undermined an adolescent's grit or resilience, the ability to overcome obstacles, and persevere in the face of challenges. Next-day delivery, instant messaging, and always-on communications tend to encourage short-term thinking. Success takes perseverance and an expectation that there will be struggles which must be overcome.

Grit translates into a number of career competencies as well:

- **Positive Attitude**: Approaching work with a positive attitude and displaying this to co-workers and customers alike. . . .
- **Initiative**: [Seeking out new challenges, determining the steps to be taken on projects, and engaging in those task without being told.]

- **Flexibility**: Recognizing that change is a normal part of work, and understanding how to accept change gracefully and participate in change efforts. . . .
- **Work Ethic**: Being productive, reliable, diligent, and loyal to organization's purpose, mission, and values. Includes a personal work ethic assessment.[19]

Parents can foster grit and resilience in their children by encouraging them to engage in activities that have long-term rewards such as sports and arts; by participating in ongoing volunteer activities, particularly those that focus on the social welfare of others; by engaging in group activities; and by working part-time in non-menial activities. Parents can also emphasize long-term thinking by creating opportunities for their children to earn privileges or expensive items they desire.

2. Personal Competencies

In addition to the resilience needed to overcome the inevitable challenges of life, there are many competencies that have been identified by the National Association of Colleges and Employers and similar associations. These competencies are not tied to the subject majors of college degrees. Instead, they focus on the approach graduates take toward meeting in the workplace and in their lives. Not all of them are related to the approaches parents take to addressing online media and digital technology, but many of them are.

- **Critical thinking/problem solving**: Exercise sound reasoning to analyze issues, make decisions, and overcome problems. Ability to obtain, interpret, and use knowledge, facts, and data in this process, and demonstrate originality and inventiveness.
- **Oral/written communication**: Articulate thoughts and ideas clearly and effectively in written and oral forms to persons inside and outside of the organization. Public-speaking skills, ability to express ideas to others and to write/edit memos, letters, and complex technical reports clearly and effectively.
- **Teamwork/collaboration**: Build collaborative relationships representing diverse cultures, races, ages, genders, religions, lifestyles, and viewpoints. Ability to work within a team structure, and negotiate and manage conflict.
- **Digital technology**: Leverage existing digital technologies ethically and efficiently to solve problems, complete tasks, and accomplish goals. Demonstrate effective adaptability to new and emerging technologies.
- **Leadership**: Leverage the strengths of others to achieve common goals, and use interpersonal skills to coach and develop others. Ability to assess and manage one's emotions and those of others; use empathetic skills to guide and motivate; and organize, prioritize, and delegate work.

- **Professionalism/work ethic**: Demonstrate personal accountability and effective work habits (e.g., punctuality, working productively with others, and time workload management), and understand the impact of nonverbal communication on professional work image. Ability to demonstrate integrity and ethical behavior, act responsibly with the interests of the larger community in mind, and ability to learn from mistakes.[20]

These same skills are at the heart of an adolescent's development in their schooling and extracurricular activities. Another skill or value prized in the workplace and home is that of empathy, the ability to understand the feelings and emotional experiences of another. Empathy is the ability to step into the shoes of another. The Golden Rule cannot exist without empathy. Nor can customer service, effective parenting, or a harmonious marriage. The professionalism and work ethic described in the preceding paragraph is largely a professional manifestation of an employee with empathy for the individual's peers. Parents can use these competencies as goals for their children's engagement in online activities. Even the most frivolous online game can be used to promote time management, flexibility, or teamwork. By using these attributes, parents can take time wasted online and repurpose some of it to be part of the more important developmental lessons of parenting.

Chapter 2

Managing Online Engagement

A. USING AGE AND DEVELOPMENTAL MILESTONES TO GUIDE ONLINE ENGAGEMENT

The use of tablets and smartphones by small children has become one of the most divisive issues in child development since the introduction of the baby bottle. In earlier eras, parents were patronized for using the television as a babysitter. Today, that criticism has shifted to debates over screen time.

The rampant criticism of screen usage does not match the behavior for many families. A 2020 survey from Common Sense Media conducted just prior to the COVID-19 stay-at-home orders found that "nearly half of 2- to 4-year-olds and more than two-thirds of 5- to 8-year-olds have their own tablet or smartphone."[1] Usage has likely increased significantly since the study was completed.

At the same time, the usage varies considerably from family to family. As the Common Sense Media survey explains, "in any given day, nearly a quarter (23%) of 0- to 8-year-olds don't use any screen media, while a similar proportion (24%) spend more than four hours with screens. Watching television and videos continues to be the main reason children use screen devices, accounting for nearly three-quarters (73%) of all screen time."[2]

1. Children under Five

The American Academy of Pediatrics (AAP) promotes a strategy that limits screen time. For children under fifteen months, the AAP notes that "infants and toddlers cannot learn from traditional digital media as they do from interactions with caregivers, and they have difficulty transferring that knowledge to their 3-dimensional experience."[3] The AAP recommends against any use of tablets and phones for children of this age, with one exception. The AAP recognizes that many parents are now using videoconferencing to connect their young children with distant family and friends. The report, however, emphasizes that the interaction requires parents to be engaging along with the children to understand what they are seeing. Although the use of videoconferencing with family is not discouraged, the AAP emphasizes that the engagement works primarily because it is mediated by the parent or caregiver.

For children between two and five years old, the advice is more mixed. There are some very useful apps that can be used to stimulate the child's engagement and exploration. Digital tools exist to promote creative game play similar to virtual Legos or Lincoln Logs. There are apps designed to promote learning and engagement, including Peg + Cat Big Gig, I Can Animate, AlphaTots Alphabet, LEGO App4+, The Monster at the End of this Book, and perhaps even the wildly popular Animal Crossing: New Horizons. Additional educational games include Toca Boca, Monkey Preschool Lunchbox, ChromaKids, and Daisy the Dinosaur. Most research agrees that limited use of interactive apps for small children is either harmless or has some modest developmental benefit.

Most of the time young children interact with tablets and phones, however, they are watching videos, which is far less developmental. For young children, passively watching videos has little positive development effect, and excessive time spent watching videos can interfere with child development. "Language development expands rapidly between 1½ to 3 years of age, and studies have shown that children learn language best when engaging and interacting with adults who are talking and playing with them."[4] The time spent holding a cell phone or tablet wastes time each day the child should be developing. "There is also some evidence that children who watch a lot of television during the early elementary school years perform less well on reading tests and may show deficits in attention."[5]

Nonetheless, even the AAP has recognized the value of *Sesame Street* and other programs that have been developed to promote literacy, social outcomes, and cognitive development. When carefully selected, a limited amount of video screen time can promote healthy development. Such use, however, should be for children over three years old, and still limited to carefully selected educational content. YouTube has been sued by the Federal Trade Commission (FTC) for its failure to provide appropriate control in place for online content and generally creates an unhealthy environment for children.[6]

In addition to using the technology, the interaction also allows preschoolers to learn about technology. Through play, the children develop familiarity with keyboards, mouses, touchscreens, and similar components of the computer. Children develop a working vocabulary for the basic components of a computer system. Scholastic suggests, for example, that children entering kindergarten—

- Have a basic working vocabulary of common technology terms, such as "digital camera," "iPad," "computer," "Internet," "mouse," "keyboard," and "printer."
- Have been exposed to common technology terms in the natural context of everyday conversation, such as "on/off," "Internet," "browser," "software," "hardware," "computer," "mouse," "monitor," "keyboard," "digital camera," "printer," "battery," and so on.
- Have taken their first digital photo.
- Find the numerals on a QWERTY keyboard.
- Type their first name on a QWERTY keyboard.
- Understand the basic functions of a browser, including how to open or close windows and use the "back" key.[7]

Since technology is pervasive in modern society, preschool children who learn more about how to master it will likely have stronger technology skills as they mature. This development has the potential to create a positive cycle for long-term success.

2. Children Five to Twelve

As children get older, the majority of children significantly increase the amount of video and media content they consume. Children average more than two hours of television each day and may consume as much video, social media, and other online content in addition to the television content. The nearly five hours of media time spent per student per day does not include the use of online classroom instruction. As parents provide appropriate structure to their family routine and establish the expected boundaries for their children's behavior, parents should pay close heed to the health issues associated with excessive use of digital technologies.

For children in this age range, they are likely to use some combination of television, videogame consoles, cell phones, tablets, and laptops or desktops. Family affluence will largely determine access to various devices. Excessive use of these technologies may correlate with problems of obesity, difficulty sleeping, and mental health issues.

Studies suggest that watching television for more than 1.5 hours per day is associated with increased obesity. This is triggered both by the sedentary nature of watching TV and the high-calorie snacks that are often eaten when watching television.

Children who watch television in their bedrooms or who go to bed with their cell phones often have increased problems with sleep. There are a variety of studies pointing to both the devices and to the content consumed by the children. For example, "exposure to light (particularly blue light) and activity from screens before bed affects melatonin levels and can delay or disrupt sleep. Media use around or after bedtime can disrupt sleep and negatively affect school performance."[8]

Beginning at this age, children begin to engage in social media and the development of their online presence. Although the Children's Online Privacy Protection Act (COPPA) should limit this access, most children can easily circumvent the lightweight age restrictions on most sites well before they become thirteen. The failure of many age restrictions means that behaviors typically moderated by adults in the "real world" can continue unchecked when online.

A small number of children may become obsessed with their online presence. As noted by the AAP, "the prevalence of problematic Internet use among children and adolescents is between 4% and 8%, and up to 8.5% of US youth 8 to 18 years of age meet criteria for Internet gaming disorder."[9]

To address the concerns that might arise for children who are watching television and online content in this age range, there are a number of important steps that parents should consider.

- Work with each child to develop a reasonable, healthy schedule for television, videogaming, and online usage. Put the use of technology into the context of the child's weekly routine rather than singling it out.
- The schedule should limit the use of technology immediately before bedtime. Much of the content viewed online is not conducive to rest. eBook reading may be appropriate before bed, but if the ebook is on the cell phone, there may be challenges keeping the child focused on the books.
- Distinguish educational and developmental activities from online leisure activities to encourage children to develop their skills and stem knowledge of math, science, computing, and technology. There is an incredible array of games, tools, and projects that children can explore online. Like music and language lessons, these activities can be built into the child's routine.
- Children under twelve are not ready for much privacy. Parents should have access to their accounts, passwords, and devices. These should be checked regularly to ensure the usage remains age appropriate.
- Children should not be provided personal accounts on sites that promote (or fail to screen) offensive, adult, or inappropriate content—as defined by the parents in discussion with the children.
- Utilize parental controls on all devices, including the devices owned by each child.

- Watch for emerging negative behavior. If an online user begins to evidence behavioral issues, intervene early. Watch for changes in sleeping habits, mood, or other activities.
- Be as engaged as possible with the content actually being used by each child.

There is an overwhelming diversity in the type and quality of online content. No parent can plan in advance for what a student might find. Instead, by managing the amount of time each child spends gaming, watching TV, and surfing the net, by using the parental controls built into hardware and software, and by discussing the online activities with each student, a parent can create the best environment for the pre-teen.

3. Teens and Young Adults

As children become teenagers and young adults, the average screen time continues to increase substantially. Another study by Common Sense Media finds that the average teenager spends nearly nine hours each day consuming television, videogames, and online media. Time spent listening to music is not included in these nine hours, nor is time online for class or homework assignments. Another study reports that "approximately one-quarter of teenagers describe themselves as 'constantly connected' to the Internet."[10]

The 2015 Common Sense Media study noted that there are "six distinct types of media users among tweens, and five among teens, according to the patterns of their media use."[11] The teen categories in the report were light users (32 percent), readers (13 percent), gamers/computer users (20 percent), social networkers (10 percent), and heavy viewers (26 percent). In the five years since that report, the percentage of social networkers has increased significantly. A 2020 study shows that by age fourteen, 85 percent of teens own a cell phone and engage on social media.

The recommendations for helping teens manage their online presence do not really change from that for their younger siblings, but parents may face a much more difficult time instituting that advice. Unlike younger children, teenagers are keenly sensitive to issues of privacy. Parents generally need to respect this growing independence, which makes monitoring of media usage much more challenging.

Many concerns focus on the nature of the online content or the negative impact that some online activities can have on mental or behavioral health. Each of those topics is addressed separately in the next section. Setting aside those two significant concerns, parents should talk with their children to address the appropriate use of media and entertainment content.

The key to managing technology and media usage is to be sure that the use is part of a balanced overall lifestyle. High school students often become highly focused on their favorite musicians, TV shows, videogames, or social media influencers. As long as that behavior does not interfere with their schoolwork and outside activities, there is no evidence that such focus has any short-term or long-term detriments.

When a teen begins to spend too much time with screens, the behavior can have a very negative impact on sleep patterns, obesity, and social development. Rather than focusing on the amount of time spent online, parents and teens should instead focus on how time is spent more generally.

Teens are occasionally the targets of criminal online behavior. Many of these risks are detailed in Part IV. Parents need to remind their children frequently that anything sent online is public and permanent. Whether it is a racist joke or sexually explicit photograph, once it is posted, there is a risk that the statement or image will go viral and be used against the student throughout the student's entire teen years and adulthood. Teens know better than anyone that relationships are fickle and best friends can become bitter enemies. Sending a nude photograph to one's boyfriend or girlfriend can easily get posted on social media.

Some additional suggestions may be beneficial:

- Work to reduce the priority of online activities by ensuring there are real-world priorities as well.
- Establish limits on the use of social media and online reading just prior to bed. Keep the phone out of the bedroom at night.
- Talk with teens about the sites they frequent, the social media they follow, and the nature of what they read.
- Intervene early when negative content, comments, or behaviors begin to emerge.
- Establish household rules about the teen's privacy and its limits. Many parents continue to monitor the posts, photos, and other activities of their teens.
- Help teens develop digital literacy (discussed in chapter 3), helping them learn to read more than tweets and headlines. Teach them to understand factually supported information and to distinguish facts from opinions and to be wary of ungrounded falsehoods.
- Talk openly about the benefits and harms of online behaviors.
- Expect that the teens will demand the same behaviors of their parents. Parents who doom-scroll at dinner will not have much credibility telling their children to stop following negative content.
- Promote healthy uses of technology, including creativity tools, audiovisual editing software, and games that promote knowledge and learning.

All these recommendations emphasize the collaboration between parents and their teens to be sure that the parents are involved. By encouraging teens to show their parents what they are reading, posting, and playing online, parents can help guide their teens while helping their teens steer clear of the online dangers.

B. FROM IDIOT BOX TO TROLLS

Commentators began to call televisions idiot boxes in the 1950s, soon after television's popularity began to soar. In a famous 1961 speech, FCC chairman Newton N. Minow characterized television programming as a "vast wasteland" of mindless content. "[W]hen television is bad, nothing is worse . . . I can assure you that what you will observe is a vast wasteland. You will see a procession of game shows, formula comedies about totally unbelievable families, blood and thunder, mayhem, violence, sadism, murder . . . [and] endlessly, commercials—many screaming, cajoling, and offending."[12]

In many ways, television has not changed, and the Internet has adopted more of the same. There are examples of brilliant, thought-provoking, and powerful storytelling. There are many more examples of excellent educational programs along with apps, games, and websites that educate and inspire. But there is also a tremendous amount that falls into the vast wasteland of mindless, senseless, violent, crass, and endlessly commercial.

Value, of course, is in the eye of the beholder. But the structure of media has changed in the half-century since Minow delivered the vast wasteland rebuke of the broadcasting industry. Television has become less regulated and the Internet is hardly regulated at all. As a result, there are far deeper and darker corners to the media of today than ever existed when the vast wasteland was first identified.

1. Children's Television Act and Other Age Protections

The Children's Television Act requires each broadcast station to air content that meets the FCC definition for fulfilling the educational and information needs of children. Each station is required to air a minimum of 156 hours of core programming each year between the hours of 6:00 a.m. and 10:00 p.m. The core children's programming requirement also limits the advertising in these shows. Programs intended for an audience of children twelve years old and younger can only air 10.5 minutes of advertising per hour on weekends and 12 minutes per hour of advertising on weekdays.

These regulations are the government's efforts to stop the practice of creating episode-length commercials for children's products. *Hot Wheels* had a successful and highly lucrative television series in the 1960s; *Strawberry Shortcake* became a billion-dollar breadwinner in the 1980s, later joined by

He-Man, *My Little Pony*, *Transformers*, and many others. Critics of the regulations note that even *Sesame Street* generates millions of dollars in licensing revenue from Elmo and his castmates. Fred Rogers summed up the media's attitude to children: "In this country, the child is appreciated for what he will be. He will be a great consumer someday. The quicker we can get them to go out and buy, the better."[13] Few media providers outside Public Broadcasting have ever done anything other than exploit children as consumers-in-training, or worse, malleable shills to promote the consumer spending by the children's parents.

The structure of the Children's Television Act aims to eliminate the worst tendencies of the toy and cereal companies. Children's programs must clearly separate out the ads from the episode's content. In addition, the episode cannot serve as a commercial promotion for the product. As a result of these rules, *Hot Wheel* and *Barbie* movies, for example, would likely run afoul of the FCC rule and be treated as wholly commercial rather than educational programs.

As part of a family's effort to establish structure and develop boundaries, it is very helpful for parents to discuss the nature of television and video characters with their children. Once children are old enough to understand the purpose of advertisements and to recognize that advertisements may not be truthful, it becomes essential that children develop a healthy skepticism about the products being sold. This might begin with simple understandings that the figurines sold in stores cannot fly the same way the characters do on TV, online and in games. As they get older, they should learn that the influence of characters and brands should not control their choice of clothes, makeup, toys, or hobbies.

There are no comparable regulations for online advertising. In addition, social media uses influencers and home-made videos to expand the role of media influence on consumer behavior. Again, it then becomes critical that families openly discuss how purchasing decisions and brand preferences may be manipulated by what members of the family watch online and what Internet sites they use.

In addition to content regulations, the FCC has also mandated certain content restrictions. Beginning in the 1970s, the FCC required that the first hour of evening broadcasts (8:00–9:00 p.m. Eastern and Pacific time, 7:00–8:00 p.m. Central time) be dedicated to family viewing. The Family Viewing Hour was also endorsed by the National Association of Broadcasters. In 1975, however, this short-lived regulation was declared unconstitutional. In addition to the Family Viewing Hour, additional FCC regulations prohibit "indecent" content from being broadcast between the hours of 6 a.m. and 10 p.m. Under the regulations, indecent content is "language or material that, in context, depicts or describes, in terms patently offensive as measured by contemporary community standards for the broadcast medium, sexual or excretory organs or activities."

The FCC has fined networks for the use of swearing and flashes of nudity during prime time. Although the fines have generally been overturned by the courts, the indecency guidelines continue to inform the behavior of most broadcasters.

2. No Regulation for Videogames

Videogames are not regulated by the FCC. Many states and municipalities attempt to create local laws to govern certain aspects of videogames, with a particular focus on reducing the highly graphic violence and sexism depicted in some games. The Supreme Court, however, has ruled that all such laws violate the First Amendment rights of the videogame producers.

To help address the concerns about content in videogames, the Entertainment Software Rating Board (ESRB) provides voluntary guidelines that parents can follow. The ESRB requires that videogame retailers adhere to its ratings standards and regularly audits retailers to be sure they do not sell games to children who are younger than the suggested age rating. The ratings are advisory, of course, and parents are free to purchase games with any rating for their own children. In addition, with the expansion of downloadable games and online shopping, the control of the retail store has decreased considerably, and younger children can typically get access to games intended for adults or older children.

Despite the considerable limitations of a voluntary rating system, parents can generally rely on physical retail stores such as Target and Walmart to enforce the ratings and restrict sales to children younger than the age suggested on the packaging. The same is generally true for major game retailers such as GameStop. Unfortunately, copyright piracy means that nearly every game title (as well as every song and most movies) can be found for free through illegal downloads and file sharing. As a result, parents cannot rely exclusively on what titles they permit their children to purchase. Instead, families should have clear boundaries and limitations on illegal downloading and the use of unauthorized content in the household. As discussed in chapter 13, illegal downloading also creates a significant risk for compromising the household's privacy and cybersecurity efforts. Illegal downloading sites are a common source of computer viruses and malware. As a result, for very practical reasons as well as for ethical concerns and content control, the family's tolerance for such activity should be established with clear guidelines and expectations.

3. Little Regulation for Cable and Online Services

Unlike broadcasting, the FCC does not impose a similar obligation on cable networks, satellite, or Internet streaming and hosting services. The FCC does prohibit obscene content from appearing on cable and satellite, but given the First Amendment protections for speech, establishing that pornographic material is obscene is very difficult to achieve. Efforts by Congress to enact legislation regarding the content on the Internet have failed.

As a result, the content available for children and teens online is only limited to the extent the parents directly control the content available to their children. In particular, YouTube has commercialized the children using its service to promote advertising and sales of goods. A tremendous amount of the content presented to children online is little more than episodic commercials. In addition to the shows featuring action figures and toys as principal characters, YouTube also features young children "unwrapping" their recent purchases. These videos feature children being excited to get a new toy, experiencing the joy of the gift, and extolling the virtues of the product.

4. Worse than Commercial—the Sea of Harmful Content

In recent years, YouTube has also been under pressure to remove hate speech, harassing videos, and other content harmful to children from its channels, including those directed at children. In 2017, for example, YouTube was accused of "'infrastructural violence' against children due to its role in the creation of vast quantities of low-quality, disturbing content aimed at preschoolers," according to the *Guardian* (UK) newspaper. Disney characters, Peppa Pig, and other characters have been stolen and used in low-quality videos aimed at young children that feature acts of violence, cruelty, and offensive language.

In response, YouTube moved away from its exclusive reliance on algorithms, hiring thousands of human reviewers to augment the ineffective YouTube Kids filters designed to keep violent and harmful content away from these channels. While this is an important step, it reflects only a modest effort by one of the online media platforms to restrict the content targeted at small children. Most of such content is still being produced and distributed.

The failure of the video-sharing services to restrict the content on children-focused channels is just one of the many content problems. Social media platforms abound in commentary that can be sexist, racist, and otherwise highly discriminatory.

Through the use of anonymous online forums, comments sections in video-sharing platforms, anonymous Twitter accounts, and other areas, users can post hate speech and bullying comments to attack online users. There is no empathy demonstrated in most online comments. Since the 1990s, this behavior has been labeled Internet trolling, and the trolls use the anonymous nature of the online environment to promote racist, antisocial, and harmful content.

For young children, the commentary pushed by the trolls may be the first time they are exposed to these comments or this language. Tweens and teens may take advantage of the anonymity to post their own trolling content.

Unlike children's television, parents cannot simply assume that the content produced for their children is benign. Commercial streaming services such as Disney+ and Netflix have expanded their age-appropriate content. Public Television is available on tablets, and other broadcasters are improving their efforts at providing children's content. These services provide something of a safe harbor. The broadcasters may have too many ads, but advertising is far less harmful than hate speech.

When children and young adults access Internet content, parents must be vigilant to supervise what they are watching. Parents need to be comfortable asking to see what their children are watching and reading online. Parents must also be quick to address the hurtful nature of trolling behavior when their children are exposed to it.

Children need their parents to reinforce the inappropriateness of the posts pushed by trolls, and to help children who are upset by the content deal with their response. Parents also should be proactive to ensure that their own children understand the harmful consequences of trolling behavior to discourage them from joining in.

Many parents adopt a simple approach to the problem. If the language would not be tolerated around the dinner table, then it should not be posted online. A "troll jar" might help in much the same way some families use swear jars. By monitoring the content children watch and read, and by setting clear standards of appropriate behavior in the family, parents can mitigate some of the worst content seen online.

By setting clear boundaries regarding the content that members of the family consume online, the parents can both educate their children on appropriate behavior and help avoid conflict over watching particular clips or channels. At the same time, the children's tolerance for challenging material will grow as they mature, so no set of rules or boundaries will eliminate these conflicts. Nonetheless, establishing clear boundaries may help provide a method for addressing conflicts over particular content as they arise in a constructive manner.

C. MENTAL AND BEHAVIORAL HEALTH

Helping a child develop and maintain healthy behavior is a priority for all parents. Many people assume that the use of technology can harm the mental health of children and teens who spend too much time online. While that is true for some people, the use of online resources also can be a significant resource to help teens improve their health and wellness. Parents can encourage the appropriate use of digital technology to reduce negative health consequences and facilitate their children's use of technology to address mental health and well-being issues as they arise.

1. Digital Technology's Mental Health Impact

Although there have been widespread concerns about the impact of the Internet and digital technology on the mental health of children and teens, particularly among teenage girls, a recent report from the University of California, Irvine's Connected Learning Lab refutes those claims, explaining that "systematic reviews of evidence in the health sciences do not support these claims, and they suggest that the accompanying fears are largely misplaced."[14]

The report and other studies make clear that there are significant concerns about tween and teen depression, anxiety, and other mental health issues. The incidence of mental health issues, however, occurs in students across all levels of digital technology usage.

> Multiple factors determine mental health outcomes. . . . Factors that can contribute to stress during adolescence include a desire for greater autonomy, pressure to conform with peers, exploration of sexual identity, and increased access to and use of technology. Media influence and gender norms can exacerbate the disparity between an adolescent's lived reality and their perceptions or aspirations for the future. Other important determinants include the quality of their home life and relationships with peers. Violence (including harsh parenting and bullying) and socioeconomic problems are recognized risks to mental health. Children and adolescents are especially vulnerable to sexual violence, which has a clear association with detrimental mental health.[15]

Although technology is not the trigger for mental health and behavioral issues for adolescents, it continues to play a significant role. The research emphasizes that children who experience bullying, for example, are likely to experience it both in person and online. The same is true for children suffering from social isolation. Race-based harassment is well documented in both online and in-person contexts. Racially motivated harassment correlates with higher levels of depression and suicide, increasing the likelihood for minority teens above that of their Caucasian counterparts.[16] Technology is part of the problem, but it tends to reflect the realities prevalent in society rather than any unique to social media, videogames, or particular platforms. Technology can be used as a tool for harassment and social media can serve as an easy platform for harassers to reach their victims.

To protect against these risks, parents need to watch for signs that the normal range of teen moods, stresses, and behaviors do not become severe and lead to untreated mental health issues. These are a few of the warning signs:

- Disengagement with friends, social activities, school activities, missing school days, or not completing school assignments.
- Sleep issues, such as a lack of energy, oversleeping, insomnia, or nightmares.
- Loss of concentration, inability to sit still, mood swings between no-energy and hyperactivity, or other attention issues.
- Harmful behaviors, ranging from cutting oneself, pulling hair, picking at skin, having suicidal thoughts or actions, or engaging in manic or high-risk behaviors.[17]

This is not a complete list, and many of these warning signs are common among teens. Nonetheless, if an adolescent is exhibiting these and other harmful behaviors, then it is important to get the individual medical help. Many of these situations can be addressed through counseling, while others will benefit from a combination of drug treatment and counseling. Since many of these triggers are based on social isolation and the teen's peer environment, adolescents often respond very well to peer counseling and organized therapy sessions.

Technology may also be part of the solution. Increasingly, apps and online communities are available to help provide assistance to teens with depression and other behavioral health issues. The online services may help get reluctant teens to take the first steps in addressing mental and behavioral health concerns.

2. Using Technology to Promote Well-Being

Parents need to recognize that not all apps are created equal, and not all time spent online is wasteful. One example of this is the availability of apps and online services focused on helping teens and adults improve their mental health and well-being. For adolescents struggling with these issues, parents can be proactive by educating themselves regarding the resources available and helping their teens explore these options.

In an article published in the Frontiers of Public Health, researchers focused on the use of technology to help teens address mental health and well-being issues. The research noted that "among all teens, 42% had searched for fitness and exercise information online and 19% had searched for information on stress and anxiety."[18] Other studies suggest "the rates are significantly higher, putting the number at 87% of teens and tweens [who] have gone online for mental health information, 64% have used a mobile health app, and 39% use the online space to seek out others with similar conditions."[19]

Teens use digital technology to provide them direct access to information on mental health concerns, sexual education, weight control, nutrition, exercise, medication management, and many other aspects of their well-being.

Other research has highlighted the potential for digital technology to provide access to suicide prevention and outreach services. The studies note that participants are wary about their privacy in online sessions regarding mental health, and suggest that tools such as this would be best if it were integrated with peer sessions and in-person assistance.

> Adolescents' online risks often mirror offline vulnerabilities. Much of our existing knowledge related to the core principles of how to promote healthy development among young people should translate into an evolving digital landscape. Just as interventions to prevent bullying within school settings have proven effective for reducing cyberbullying, parenting and support strategies that are effective in offline spaces may translate well into supporting adolescents' healthy online experiences.[20]

There are a wide range of apps that help users manage their well-being. Happify, Sanvello, SuperBetter, Mood Tracker, Mood Gym, and Breathe2Relax, for example, offer different strategies for managing stress and building resilience skills. PTSD Coach helps those suffering from post-traumatic stress to track and manage symptoms. Calm, Headspace, Mindful Gnats, and Worry Knot emphasize mindfulness and meditation. There are many apps to assist with recovery from eating disorders or alcohol misuse.

For many teens, mental health issues are one of the key sources of their anxiety and depression, creating a spiraling loop of anxiety and worry. The easy access to these apps can help break that pattern, allowing teens to address their wellness needs directly and heading off more negative situations.

Apps provide only one tool that might help tweens and teens struggling with mental health concerns, but they can play a useful role. Early intervention can often keep a situation from expanding from normal stress into clinical depression, and the ease with which parents and their children can access the apps may provide a useful first step for some situations. The apps may also reinforce the positive behaviors that counseling helps foster, adding to the effectiveness of the medicinal and therapeutic treatment being provided to those with diagnosed medical conditions.

3. Visibility and Positive Reinforcement

One of the unique aspects of digital media is the ability to become visible by posting original content and reposting the content of others. Posting original content can take many forms, from sending a short tweet to dropping an entire musical album or feature-length motion picture. In 2021, the most popular platforms included Facebook, Instagram, Twitter, TikTok, YouTube, WeChat, WhatsApp, Tumblr, Reddit, and others. Twitch and Discord are generally categorized separately, but these also play an important part on the online social experience.

Most of these popular platforms favor short material, and most teens tend to produce short content. Both the posting of original user-created content and the resharing of other people's content play an important role in a person's well-being.

Research highlights that teens (and likely all people) feel support and affirmation when their work is reshared by others. On each digital media platform, there is a mechanism to reshare, promote, like, or highlight the work of others. By doing so, the original author is promoted and everyone who participates in the content's promotion feels part of the community. To create a positive, healthy household of engagement, parents can take advantage of this visibility to support their children and promote the identity they seek to project in the world.

The support networks built by being active online can create a powerful sense of identity. Parents will do their best to encourage their adolescent children to use these tools in a modest, but powerful manner. For example, if a child is a musician, writer, or artist, the parents can encourage the child to share their works with family and friends. If the work receives positive reinforcement, it can be shared more widely on social media. Despite concerns regarding trolls and abusive online responses, in actuality, most comments will be positive. If the works get reposted by others, the engagement will produce a strong sense of empowerment and encouragement for the young adult. The same is true for videoclips of athletic events, presentations at afterschool programs, and religious events.

Of course, this only works if the parents are supportive of their children's choices surrounding their identity. For example, "LGBTQ+ youth will post specifically LGBTQ+-related content in an effort to make their identities intentionally visible, thereby expressing support for others and affirming their own identities."[21] The same is likely true for tweens and teens in every other self-identified community. In contrast, Lesley University reports that "25%

of teens are forced to leave their homes after coming out to their parents and 68% of teens have experienced family rejection after coming out to their family."[22] Such ostracism and rejection, of course, are the antipathy of creating a healthy family. Families struggling with these issues should seek out resources to help maintain a supportive relationship.[23]

For adolescents fearful of their family's reaction, the online visibility provides them a safe place to receive support from people outside of their households. These children are likely to use pseudonyms to hide their identity from their parents and peers while building a network of support within their affinity community.

By engaging with their children, parents can send a powerful message of support to their children and help their children promote their sense of identity and well-being. When the content posted is created by the teen's engagement with productive activities, the online posting has the benefit of reinforcing the activities that are healthy and rewarding to the teen. In this way, a careful use of social media can have a strong, positive influence for the participants.

4. Age Restrictions for Online Content as Privacy Protection—COPPA

Unlike film, television, videogames, and music, there is no government regulation or rating system to assist parents in determining which online content is appropriate for the maturity age of their children. In 1999, there was an effort funded by Microsoft to operate the Internet Content Rating Association (ICRA), but that program never gained support and was closed down in 2010.[24] The closest that Congress has come to a rating system on the Internet is a privacy law aimed at protecting minors under the age of thirteen.

In the absence of content regulations and voluntary ratings, Congress looked to the other aspect of the online experience that it could constitutionally regulate, which was the duty to provide minimal privacy protections. Spurred on by findings by the FTC that few companies were voluntarily developing privacy protections for minors and a White House call for action, Congress passed the Children's Online Privacy Protection Act of 1998 (COPPA).[25] The legislative history of COPPA provides an outline of its central goals

(1) to enhance parental involvement in children's online activities in order to protect children's privacy;
(2) to protect children's safety when they visit and post information on public chat rooms and message boards;

(3) to maintain the security of children's personal information collected online; and

(4) to limit the collection of personal information from children without parental consent.[26]

Congress gave parents or guardians the right to control their children's personal information on the Internet. The law provided a general requirement that websites and online services directed to children obtain verifiable parental consent prior to collecting, using, or disclosing children's personal information. Congress then assigned the duty to create and maintain regulations to the FTC. COPPA extended the FTC's broad authority to prohibit unfair and deceptive acts or practices through the use of fines and civil penalties.

The COPPA Rule was promulgated by the FTC the following year, becoming effective on April 21, 2000. With the growth of social media, the Internet of Things (IoT), and mobile devices, the FTC found that certain aspects of COPPA had grown out of date, and the Commission updated the COPPA Rule in 2013. In the 2013 expansion of the COPPA Rule, the FTC expanded the definition of children's personal information to add online cookies, geolocation tags, and information contained in audiovisual content, including videos and shared photos.[27]

Congress and the FTC have designed the COPPA rules to discourage the collection of personal information regarding children under the age of thirteen and improve the privacy notices used to inform parents about the collection and use of their children's personal information. In doing so, Congress also gave parents more control over the data collected about their children than that which parents have over their own data. The law did not significantly address the common practice of children under thirteen, who frequently use social media and other services designed primarily for adults, but the law has helped with the tracking of young minors and the targeting of children with advertising.

The COPPA Rule uses broad language to cover web companies and service providers that collect personal information from children under thirteen or otherwise allow children under thirteen to make their information publicly available. The rules are very different under COPPA for information collected about children under thirteen by organizations that are not schools or do not fall within the Family Educational Rights and Privacy Act of 1974 (FERPA) (which is discussed in chapter 4). Personal information under COPPA includes the following:

- First and last name.
- A home or other physical address including street name and name of a city or town.

- Online contact information;
- A screen or user name that functions as online contact information;
- A telephone number;
- A social security number;
- A persistent identifier that can be used to recognize a user over time and across different websites or online services;
- A photograph, video, or audio file, where such file contains a child's image or voice;
- Geolocation information sufficient to identify street name and name of a city or town; or
- Information concerning the child or the parents of that child that the operator collects online from the child and combines with an identifier described above.

The COPPA Rule requires the commercial operators of websites and online services to comply with a series of detailed obligations. The failure to meet any of these obligations is unlawful, subjecting the operator to fines or civil penalties. Some of these obligations, such as the duty to employ appropriate security measures, have a very broad application, while obligations regarding parental approvals are quite specific to the children protected by COPPA.

COPPA is not designed to act as a censorship law. Nonetheless, it does have provisions that are intended to separate out web content directed to children under thirteen from sites designed for users thirteen and older. While this separation is very different than other ratings systems, it does provide a modicum of protection for children and pre-teens. There is no bright-line test to determine whether a site is directed to children. Instead, the FTC looks at an array of factors. The FTC

> will consider its subject matter, visual content, use of animated characters or child-oriented activities and incentives, music or other audio content, age of models, presence of child celebrities or celebrities who appeal to children, language or other characteristics of the Website or online service, as well as whether advertising promoting or appearing on the Website or online service is directed to children. The Commission will also consider competent and reliable empirical evidence regarding audience composition, and evidence regarding the intended audience.[28]

Many social media sites include terms of service that prohibit the service from being used by children under thirteen. This allows the site to avoid any duty to comply with COPPA. Most companies that offer content and services for children under thirteen avoid collecting the types of personal information covered by COPPA. Only a small number of services for young children actually go through the process of complying with the parental consent requirements of COPPA to collect information about the children.

In 2019, the FTC fined Google and its YouTube subsidiary $170 million for activities related to the way it commercially exploited content aimed at children. YouTube supports many child-directed channels. YouTube marketing to advertisers touted the platform for access to children. As the FCC explained, "YouTube told Mattel, maker of Barbie and Monster High toys, that 'YouTube is today's leader in reaching children age 6-11 against top TV channels' and told Hasbro, which makes My Little Pony and Play-Doh, that YouTube is the '#1 website regularly visited by kids'."[29]

The fines were not for the commercial advertising directed at small children. As noted earlier, neither the FCC nor FTC has any regulatory authority over YouTube's content. Instead, the fines were focused on YouTube's failure to adhere to the COPPA requirements limiting the collection of personal information about the viewers of the child-directed marketing.

Parents of children under thirteen should use the COPPA guidelines and the obligations of the website operators as something of a parental rating system to assess which services their children are using online. The FTC has summarized the statutes with this outline of duties. Under the COPPA Rule, an operator must

- Post a clear and comprehensive online privacy policy describing their information practices for personal information collected online from children;
- Provide direct notice to parents and obtain verifiable parental consent, with limited exceptions, before collecting personal information online from children;
- Give parents the choice of consenting to the operator's collection and internal use of a child's information, but prohibiting the operator from disclosing that information to third parties (unless disclosure is integral to the site or service, in which case, this must be made clear to parents);
- Provide parents access to their child's personal information to review and/or have the information deleted;
- Give parents the opportunity to prevent further use or online collection of a child's personal information;
- Maintain the confidentiality, security, and integrity of information they collect from children, including by taking reasonable steps to release such information only to parties capable of maintaining its confidentiality and security; and
- Retain personal information collected online from a child for only as long as is necessary to fulfill the purpose for which it was collected and delete the information using reasonable measures to protect against its unauthorized access or use.[30]

To ensure that the parent has approved the use of the child's personal information, the COPPA Rule requires that the operator obtain verifiable consent from the parent regarding the use of the child's personal information. The COPPA Rule requires an opt-in assent by parents, which must be obtained prior to the operator collecting any information from the child under thirteen.

The challenges to the verifiable parental consent made these provisions largely aspirational when the law was first passed. In the 2013 revisions to the COPPA Rule, these provisions were significantly updated to make them more practical and enforceable.

The FTC lists a number of acceptable parental verification methods:

- Providing a consent form to be signed by the parent and returned via U.S. mail, fax, or electronic scan (the "print-and-send" method);
- Requiring the parent, in connection with a monetary transaction, to use a credit card, debit card, or other online payment system that provides notification of each discrete transaction to the primary account holder;
- Having the parent call a toll-free telephone number staffed by trained personnel, or have the parent connect to trained personnel via video conference; or
- Verifying a parent's identity by checking a form of government-issued identification against databases of such information, provided that [the site operator] promptly delete the parent's identification after completing the verification.[31]

Each of these compliance steps is burdensome, dissuading companies from implementing data tracking systems and discouraging parents from completing the verification. Of the standard options, the credit card requirement was generally considered to be the most practical and reliable. Minors under thirteen, it was assumed, would not have their own credit cards. By charging a credit card, went the thinking, an adult was sure to be part of the transaction. This form of verification has some obvious limitations. After all, it is never clear that the holder of the credit card is a parent rather than an older sibling or other person. In addition, the child under thirteen may have access to their parents' credit cards, which they can use without their parent's consent. The transaction is unlikely to appear on a bill, and if it does, it will show that it was almost immediately reversed. Still, the credit card verification provides reasonable compromise to the problem of obtaining verified parental consent.

COPPA highlights the limits on governmental protection of privacy. Very few companies have been fined for their COPPA Rule violations, and clever children can easily evade the limitations to use the Internet services designed for adults. At the same time, COPPA does discourage certain types of online behavior, much more than advertising targeted to children under thirteen. As such, COPPA has at least some impact on the free speech rights of children.

5. Managing Harmful Use and Addiction

While the use of digital technology can keep adolescents connected, engaged, and entertained, there can also be too much of a good thing. A small percentage of tweens and teens suffer from obsessive or compulsive behavior regarding some aspect of their digital technology. For tweens and teens who suffer from these obsessive or compulsive behaviors, their online activities can interfere with their daily obligations and their well-being.

Within scientific circles, there is some debate whether excessive use of social media, gaming, podcasts, or other online activities constitutes a diagnosable illness. Although some researchers insist the term addiction should be restricted to substance abuse involving drinking, drugs, or cigarettes, many others use the term more broadly to include obsessive behaviors toward computers, sex, shopping, food, gambling, and other activities.

The psychological literature varies considerably regarding the nature of these addictions. While drug and alcohol addiction can lead to physical damage to a person's organs, dangerous behaviors such as high-risk sex, and self-destructive activities such as losing jobs or needing to steal money, the comparisons for "gaming addiction" include nutritional deficiencies, poor hygiene, lowered school performance, and impacted interpersonal relationships.

There has not been a true medical classification for the range of behavioral addictions involving gaming, Internet usage, or social media. The research also recognizes "excessive Internet use as a symptom of another disorder such as anxiety or depression rather than a separate entity."[32] "Other scholars have suggested that most cases of [Internet addiction] might operate more like an impulse control disorder wherein people take risky actions, not because they are repeatedly compelled to seek a risky reward, but simply because they lack foresight about such risks."[33]

Studies disagree over the percentage of online adolescents who suffer from some form of Internet addiction from as little as 0.3 percent to over 38 percent, further emphasizing the lack of agreement about the formal disorder.

For parents and teachers, it may be more reasonable to think of excessive use of digital technology as a symptom rather than a distinct disease. As one study puts it, the students "are 'addicted on the Internet' as opposed to 'addicted to the Internet'."[34]

By doing this, the parents and schools will focus on the triggers for mental health issues more broadly, rather than merely treating the symptoms associated with excessive online behaviors. Treating Internet addiction as a consequence of broader wellness issues does not take away from the serious consequences for those who suffer from these behaviors, but it may provide better resolutions to the problem.

As with other mental health and well-being concerns, parents need to watch for those behaviors that distinguish normal adolescent activity from those which are harmful. Red flags regarding addictive use might include

- preoccupation with the game, social media platform, or online activity;
- an ever-increasing amount of time needed to achieve satisfaction with the activity;
- an inability to control the amount of time spent on the activity;
- behavioral problems, including irritability, moodiness, or depression when trying to control the activity;
- interference by the activity with the user's personal relationships, school work, school attendance, or other social activities; and
- hiding the activity and lying about the time spent in the activity.

These are not necessarily clinical tools to diagnose a compulsive behavior, but they all suggest that the online activity has transformed from a source of the teen's enjoyment to a potentially harmful experience.

Even if the behavior has not become a compulsion, it might be interfering with other aspects of the teen's life. Modern adolescents often struggle to keep up and manage their time. Online social media and gaming can easily eat into the limited time the teens have outside of school, extracurricular activities, family, and work obligations. Parents can reduce the likelihood an online activity becomes an obsession by providing clear structures to the household's daily routine. Games, play, and online social engagement should not be precluded, but homework, extracurricular activities, housework, family time, sleep, and other obligations all need to be built into the plan.

Medical research also suggests various steps that can be taken to help manage harmful, obsessive behaviors. "There is a general consensus that total abstinence from the Internet should not be the goal of the interventions and that instead, an abstinence from problematic applications and a controlled and balanced Internet usage should be achieved."[35] The suggestions have not been clinically evaluated, but they are generally consistent with other interventions that help with both addiction and with anxiety and depression disorders. These approaches include the following:

- Set goals for the amount of time permitted in the activity.
- Take a break from the activity and reintroduce it after some weeks away.
- Use outside prompts (or external stoppers) to identify when it is time to stop the activity.

- Introduce physical activities to create the endorphins and other biochemical stimulation.
- Engage in family therapy.
- Enter a support group.
- Explore other therapy options, including equine therapy, art therapy, recreation therapy or others.[36]

In addition, some adolescents who have had severe issues controlling their Internet activity may benefit from medical treatment. The heavy use of online activities may have biochemical feedback that makes medical intervention appropriate. For many others, excessive Internet usage is part of a broader health issue involving anxiety and depression or impulse control. By addressing the underlying health issue, treatment such as counseling and/or medication can also help with the excessive Internet usage.

Whether excessive Internet use is a distinct medical issue or a symptom of a broader health concern, it is important that the consequences to the adolescent are recognized and the family support the teen to get treatment.

Chapter 3

Information and Digital Literacy

A. INTRODUCTION

The first two chapters provide general guidance on how a household can manage competing demands on time, attention, and priority. In this chapter, the focus shifts to the nature of online content and the skills needed to navigate in the sea of online information. To be successful, the consumer of online content needs to be informationally or digitally literate—a skill set unnecessary for prior generations, but essential for the modern age. This chapter provides parents and teachers the basic background information they need to help teach their children and students how to be informationally and digitally literate as well as privacy aware.

Information literacy and digital literacy are two terms that together describe the core skill set for children and adults working in the modern economy. The American Library Association offered this definition for information literacy: "Information literacy is a set of abilities requiring individuals to recognize when information is needed and have the ability to locate, evaluate, and use effectively the needed information."

Digital literacy is a set of abilities to find, evaluate, and utilize tools to create media and digital content. The two sets of skills are closely associated, but a person who is highly digitally literate can produce content across a wide variety of media platforms using text, audio, video, imagery, and software.

In earlier eras, the daily newspaper stood apart from other information because its content came from a unique source and was delivered in a unique format. If a person trusted the local newspaper, then the format of the newspaper helped signal the credibility of the content. As television news gained ascendency, the nightly news, delivered by trusted anchors such as Edward R.

Murrow, Walter Cronkite, or Tom Brokaw, had an inherent measure of trust for the public in the content.

Those external signals used by the public to help establish the trust and validity of content are largely gone. In the modern information economy, children and adults are bombarded with information. It comes in the form of textual content, visual images, animations, and videos. The content is pushed to cell phones, tablets, computers, and televisions without strong indicators as to the source of the content or the nature of the content within the source. Print newspapers continue to separate out the "news" sections of the paper from the "opinion" sections. Those same publishers, however, do little to separate news from opinion in their online journalism. Worse, the news feeds pulled from those publishers to fill social media make no attempt to distinguish news from opinion or to prioritize fact-based research from wild speculation.

Information literacy emphasizes the ability to find information, select and discern from various sources, and apply that information to one's knowledge or to one's writing. Digital literacy applies these skills beyond words and texts to the wide variety of digital media and technologies used to communicate and build the modern information society. Although information and digital literacy include both skills to consume content and to produce content, information literacy is primarily focused on a person's ability to become an informed citizen in their own community. Digital literacy, in contrast, tends to emphasize the skills to communicate and produce content in the digital environment.

For young adults entering the modern workforce, both skills are essential to achieve personal and economic success. Unfortunately, neither information literacy nor digital literacy has been embraced as a fundamental goal for K-12 education. While many schools make efforts to promote these skills, there is not yet a comprehensive strategy to do so.

There are other analytical and critical thinking skills sets that complement and overlap with information literacy and digital literacy. Other sources distinguish media literacy from digital literacy to emphasize the role of mass media's influence in personal information. In addition to the forms of literacy discussed in this chapter, other research focuses on privacy literacy, cultural literacy, scientific literacy, financial literacy, statistical literacy, emotional or interpersonal literacy, and many others. Each field emphasizes the need to be able to understand the information provided, to contextualize that information, to critically analyze the information, and to then be able to use that information for the person's own benefit and for the benefit of others.

B. INFORMATION LITERACY SKILLS

Students in grades K-12 need the basic skills to be able to locate, evaluate, use, and share information that together comprise the information literacy skill set. They must also be able to filter, control, evaluate, and contextualize the information that is pushed on them from advertising, blogs, social media, mass media, and environmental sources. From an early age, young children are inundated with trademarks, brands, and messages that they must evaluate. Even before children are able to read, they are expected to be able to critically understand the lessons of the parables and meanings from their literature. The critical thinking skills associated with children's books and stories is another important aspect of their informational literacy.

Much of the literature concerning information literacy focuses on the importance of information literacy for academic research and independent analysis by students in higher education. Many information literacy educational models emphasize that information literacy provides a framework for researching information. A person identifies a problem to be researched, and using the person's knowledge of authoritative primary sources and trusted secondary sources, the person conducts a search for the information about the topic. The person would then compare the information gathered against the trusted sources, weigh any biases that the sources might have, review the available primary information, and build a hypothesis based on this combination of literature review and empirical testing.

While this model is accurate, it unduly limits information literacy to the realm of academic research. The model can be applied much more broadly to the public's everyday media consumption. A simple model for understanding information literacy has three elements: evaluating the source of information; analyzing and integrating that information; and producing new information that incorporates the information learned.

1. Sourcing Information

Information literacy begins by assessing the source of information. Is the information provided in a commercial, a vendor's marketing material, or other paid content? Practical informational literacy starts with *caveat emptor* or buyer beware regarding the content one receives. The public generally distrusts commercials, but unlike print ads and TV commercials, it may be much harder to tell if the content has been paid for in online settings.

The FTC requires that ads and sponsored content be identified to help protect the public. Influencers and celebrities often receive high payments for their promotional activities. Beyoncé is reported to receive $1 million for each sponsored Instagram post. Selena Gomez earns more than $500,000 for her Instagram posts. Portuguese football player Cristiano Ronaldo and Argentine football player Lionel Messi earn in this same league, as do Ariana Grande, Dwayne "The Rock" Johnson, and some members of the Jenner/Kardashian clan. Less-famous celebrities receive much smaller payments, but their posts are still directed by the sponsors. The same is often true of blogs, social media, mass media, and other content sources that are funded through advertising or direct payments.

When parents discuss what their children watch, listen to, and read, parents should reinforce the importance of understanding the source of information and influence. Between the ages of six and ten, children learn to understand how advertising is designed to influence them and that advertisements may be highly biased sources of information. They will need to be educated that social media posts are often paid advertisements, and that many of their idols actually maintain their online social media presences to promote products and services of advertisers, as do less-famous influencers. Although the FTC mandates disclosure regarding online advertisements, these guidelines have not made it easy for the public to see how much of online content is truly sponsored advertising.

Beyond commercial sponsors, students should be trained to look to the historical veracity of the sources for their content. Some news sources invest heavily to fact-check their content, while other sources are little more than the speaker's opinions. The term "fake news" has become a common phrase in the past few years. The term highlights that news and information sources have an editorial approach to the information they choose to present. When a student used to use the school library as the start of their information search, the student could rely on the library to have vetted the content on its shelves. Search engines do not rank results by accuracy, only by popularity or payment.

The skill of sourcing information also includes the ability to know where and how to seek out accurate information. Beyond merely googling for information, astute researchers know how to conduct specialized searches, use library and academic resources, and select primary resources wherever possible. The primary source for information is the source that actually published or produced the original information. For research, the use of primary sources is essential.

Parents and educators need to remind students that information literacy goes well beyond research. It requires a critical analysis of the news and entertainment content offered by the digital media in the nonstop, 24/7 media streams. When a person relies on a news feed, it becomes much harder to evaluate whether the source from which the feed was copied had been a reliable source, paid content, or intentionally biased opinion. Younger readers, who may never have had prior experience reading only primary news sources, may find these distinctions even harder to make.

Despite the hardship that newspapers have felt in the past decade, there are still nearly 1,300 daily newspapers in the United States (though this is down from the 1,750 that were published in 1970). These newspapers, along with ABC, CBS, NBC, Fox, and CNN, all fund news departments that conduct investigative journalism to gather original information as the basis for their stories. PBS, NPR, Bloomberg, AP, UPI, and Reuters all provide original investigative research content as well.

Even with these sources, unfortunately, the reader has to be careful. Most of these sources produce both independent journalism and a myriad of other forms of content. Opinion pieces and guest opinion columns or segments do not have as rigorous a requirement for fact-checking as the journalistic content. The talk shows and entertainment divisions of these publishers may have little or no fact-checking requirements at all.

For example, according to the lawyers for Tucker Carlson, his nightly show on Fox is a work of fiction. In defending a defamation lawsuit, a federal district court found that Carlson "is not 'stating actual facts' about the topics he discusses and is instead engaging in 'exaggeration' and 'non-literal commentary'."[1] The same court described Carlson's content as "'exaggeration,' 'non-literal commentary', or simply bloviating for his audience."[2] The same is true for most of the talk show hosts on all the networks. While they might use facts as background, they are not required to do so by law or by the policies of their networks.

In addition to the non-news segments from these publishers and broadcasters, many of them also feature paid content from third parties. While the companies make modest efforts to distinguish the paid clickbait from their own media, the design of the sites often makes it hard for readers and viewers to see that it is nothing more than paid, promotional material.

For a growing percentage of the public, the primary source of news has become Facebook rather than any source of investigative journalism. A 2018 Pew study found that 43 percent of Americans rely on Facebook as their primary source of information,[3] a trend that has accelerated in recent years. This is more people than read all the local and national newspapers combined. Over 77 percent use the Internet to get their local news. Most interestingly, nearly one-third of the respondents to the Pew study acknowledged that they sometimes click on stories they think are made up.

Facebook, of course, is not alone. Google, Facebook, LinkedIn, Twitter, Instagram, WhatsApp, YouTube all fail to invest any resources to validate or qualify the content they provide to the public. In response to overwhelming public pressure, these companies have flagged the most flagrantly untrue information about COVID-19 vaccines and 2020 election results, but in general, there is no meaningful validation of the content provided through social media. These services occasionally remove inaccurate content, but only in the most politically charged and rarest of situations. What little editorial responsibility is offered often comes days after news stories have gone viral. Nor are there mechanisms for these companies to publish retractions or updates to inaccurate stories. Instead, fact and fiction are intermingled and published amid advertising content.

Similarly, there is very little validation regarding the people who are alleged to be posting social media content. During the 2016 presidential election, thousands of user accounts were created to produce and distribute false information about the position of the candidates. Presidential candidate Hillary Clinton, in particular, was targeted by a Russian-backed strategy to disrupt the U.S. elections using access easily obtained through Facebook and other social media platforms.[4] Facebook and Twitter have since improved their efforts to restrict foreign accounts for electioneering. The 2020 election was not marred by these foreign efforts because of the attention paid to the concern, but beyond the election content, there remains a tremendous amount of misinformation published every day on social media.

As a result of the undifferentiated stream of media pouring onto the public's cell phones, tablets, computers, and televisions, informationally literate readers must take the time and effort to know the source of the information they are receiving, the source of the links provided in those sources, and the extent to which the publishers are financially or otherwise invested in promoting particular opinions over accurate facts. Parents and educators must work very diligently to explain the differences between sources of content and educate students on the techniques to read critically and focus on factually credible content.

2. Fact-Checking and Integrating Information

Using thoughtful resources of information is only the first step to ensure the quality of the content. Whether reading for oneself or reading as research for a later project, it is also important to go beyond the source and fact-check the information. Well-written journalism and research will identify the sources for their information. This allows the reader to look at the original sources to see that the use of the original information was consistent with the reporting. The original source will usually have much more information than the news story was able to report. It may have important limitations or qualifiers that provide additional context for the information.

Gathering information is only part of the critical thinking process. The reader must then integrate the new information with the knowledge and understanding already possessed by the reader. If the new information is consistent with what the reader already knows, it is usually quite simple to integrate the new information into the understanding or schema of the reader. If, instead, the new information contradicts the preexisting knowledge for the reader, then it takes much greater effort to integrate the new knowledge into the person's understanding. For most people, their preexisting knowledge is resilient. It takes a significant amount of new information to modify a person's strongly held understanding. By fact-checking carefully and reviewing the tension between the preexisting knowledge and the new information, a person can update their thinking and expand or change their knowledge.

The most informationally literate readers and authors will triangulate their new knowledge by selecting information from multiple sources, including those sources that might tend to disagree with the reader's own point of view. By reading articles from multiple newspapers, the reader gets a much more nuanced understanding of the facts and the context for the information. A story featuring the same basic facts can read very differently depending on the context and perspective brought to the story by its author. Expanding the number of sources will help readers develop their own, distinct understanding of a story. This is a requirement for effective academic research, but reading or listening to the news from multiple sources also helps the informationally literate reader gain a more independent understanding of their world.

For parents and teachers, a great exercise is to ask students to read about a topic in the news from three different news sources. By asking the students to identify the similarities and differences in the coverage from those sources, students will quickly develop an appreciation that the same story can be told in very different ways, depending on the perspective of the source. Developing an understanding regarding the source of content is an essential step to assure that the students develop critical analysis skills.

3. Producing New Information

The third step in the information literacy process is the creation of new information. While this might be as formal as a research paper, it might be as simple as a tweet or a text to a friend. Whenever new information is created, the author should be careful to say or write information that is supported by the facts and, where appropriate, identifies the source for the statement. The nature of the material will dictate the amount of textual support required. In this book, for example, direct quotes use endnotes to provide attribution. Where data comes from particular research or studies, those sources are also identified in the endnotes. To increase readability and limit the number of pages, however, each statement does not have its own source listed. Had this been published as a research paper, then it would include hundreds of additional citations to reflect the research that occurred as part of the writing process.

In blogs and online content, the standard practice is to use hypertext links to allow the reader to simply click on the link to find relevant sources. Hyperlinks enable much more casual writing to include effective sourcing to the underlying material. Using sources also has the benefit of allowing the reader to evaluate the sources used for the information and help the reader critically assess the credibility of the content.

If the new material is produced by a corporate sponsor or advertiser, then the author should clearly identify it as commercial content. If the author has a financial or other personal interest, the author should also disclose that information. This requirement is equally true for the influencer who receives a free gift in exchange for an Instagram post or for a research scientist who receives grant funding from the company who has its products used in a research study. Armed with the information about the potential conflict of interest, the informationally literate reader can use that information to help assess the trust to be put in the post or research project.

C. DIGITAL LITERACY SKILLS

Being informationally literate will help a person produce high-quality content, but to operate in the information economy, the individual must also be digitally literate. Similar to informational literacy, digital literacy involves both the skills of obtaining content and the skills of producing content.

At its simplest, digital literacy requires that person know how to use the basic tools essential to get online. These skills include understanding how to launch and use web browsers and how to launch and use the basic apps on a tablet or mobile phone. Most children develop these skills at an early age. In many families, basic concerns about digital literacy are often focused on the difficulty that the older adults have with technology.

Microsoft has created a digital literacy toolset that identifies six areas for attention, beginning with access to online information and increasing in sophistication to the creation of digital content:

- Access information online
- Communicate online
- Participate safely and responsibly online
- Collaborate and manage content digitally
- Work with computers
- Create digital content[5]

The digital literacy skills for communicating online include the mechanical ability to share information as well as the more complex skills to engage online in a safe and responsible manner. When writing online, authors use hyperlinks to connect their writings to their sources and direct the reader to additional materials. The digitally literate writer understands how the URLs function and is able to create permalinks to ensure the access to content when needed, to embed images and audiovisual files, and to ensure compatibility across various platforms.

Digitally literate students are expected to learn the core functions of the word processing software, produce a PDF, use presentation software, use basic functions in a spreadsheet, and apply basic html coding so that the authors can control the look and feel of the content they create as documents or post to blogs and other Internet sites. These skills are largely end-user skills for the software provided by the software companies.

Underlying the use of some of these technologies is the knowledge of algebraic math and simple statistics. These core skills are the modern equivalent of reading and writing for any employment requiring analytical ability.

Increasingly, the ability to create and edit audiovisual files have also become fundamental skills. Digitally literate students are expected to be able to take photographs, shoot videos, record audio files, and edit the work to create and share video information.

Another important part of basic digital literacy is the ability to curate the content created and received. Each media platform has its own version of how to create, store, and retrieve information. To be digitally literate, the user must understand the basics of how these systems work so that the user can adapt to the unique features of each platform.

The ability to write computer code is generally considered a skill more advanced than basic digital literacy, but being digitally literate is an essential prerequisite to being able to code software. These advanced skills are essential to the digital economy. While not all students need to learn to create software, students should be exposed to the basics of software code in order to understand how computer code informs and influences the products and services available to the public.

Another aspect of digital literacy is an understanding of copyright and the rules and restrictions on using content found online and integrated into other material. Unfortunately, a great many websites get this wrong, making it more difficult for students to learn by modeling their behavior by observing what is online. Chapter 8 provides more detailed guidelines for adolescents who create content for their own websites or for social media sites. Teachers and parents helping out in the physical and digital classroom must also be aware of these obligations.

D. PRIVACY, NETIQUETTE, AND SECURITY LITERACY SKILLS

Some models of digital literacy list safe and responsible online participation as a digital literacy skill, but the scope and importance of this skill dictates that it is understood as a separate skill set. To communicate online, it is not enough to understand how to post content to the Internet, it is equally important to know what to post and what to avoid.

Privacy and security literacy reflects the basic knowledge about the most common harms that occur when engaging in online discourse and adopting strategies to minimize the risk of harm that can occur when engaging with others online. Maintaining Internet privacy and security is much like wearing a seatbelt or locking the front door to one's house. On any given day, the chances are very low that a car will be in an accident or a thief will choose to break into a particular house. But every day, some cars are involved in accidents and some houses are burglarized. Safety and security habits will greatly reduce the risk or scope of harm that might occur.

Google has sponsored a website and resource center for children and their teachers to help understand these basic online practices. The "Be Internet Awesome" site[6] provides slides, classroom exercises and other information for introductory privacy, netiquette ethics, and security framed in language for young children. The advice and tools are simple and clear:

- Share with Care
- Don't Fall for Fake
- Secure Your Secrets
- It's Cool to Be Kind
- When in Doubt, Talk it Out[7]

Google has created student resources and teacher materials around each of these five themes. These five steps provide a useful model for older teens and adults as well.

For older teens and adults, the first step for privacy, netiquette, and security literacy is the security step. Users must ensure that all reasonable steps have been made to use strong security on all devices and sites. Information that is not stored securely will not remain private. All users of digital technology should understand how to use the basic security features of their devices and systems.

- Every device in the home should have firewall protection.
- Each site and device should have its own, unique passphrase.
- Wherever possible, the user should employ two-factor authentication.
- Dormant accounts should be closed and deactivated.
- Devices should be updated regularly to protect from vulnerabilities as they are found.
- Avoid clicking on links from emails or websites where the user does not have a high degree of confidence regarding the origin of the content.

- Avoid clickbait and other lures designed to push inappropriate content or content designed to allow security breaches on the user's system.
- Public Wi-Fi systems may allow others to capture the traffic on those systems, so do not send unencrypted, sensitive information on public systems.
- Update the privacy settings on cell phones, apps, and social media platforms.

Despite the advice to take all precautions, the underlying assumption for using the Internet and digital technology is that every system is likely to be breached. Any picture, video, or document created and stored on a computer remains at risk of being stolen and distributed. This is why banks and credit card companies use two-factor authentication. They know that passwords are often stolen. By requiring that the password only be used on a trusted device, it reduces the opportunity for thieves to have both the stolen password and access to the needed device.

From the initial assumption, the most important lesson is never to create, store, or distribute any file that the author would not want made public. Email is particularly easy to intercept and read. Never send social security numbers, credit card numbers, or other data that can be pulled from emails.

Another important protection involves nude photographs and sexually explicit content. Since it is almost always illegal to create nude photographs of minors (other than for medical purposes), the best practice is never to take nude photographs of minors, including of oneself. Teens should be very careful not to create or share nude images, which might be treated as illegal child pornography by many states. Parents should even be careful how they photograph their infants and toddlers. What are intended as celebratory bath pictures of a parent's young children could be stolen and distributed to child pornography rings. In 2019, the National Center for Missing & Exploited Children received nearly 17 million tips on its Cyber Tipline.

Beyond sensitivity regarding sexually explicit material, parents and teens should be thoughtful about the information they provide to people who are only known pseudonymously online. In the online environment, the people in the chat group or gaming group may not be who they say they are. While these online communities are healthy and often an important part of a person's social environment, they are not vetted. On occasion, predators, bullies, and trolls join these groups. By being cautious about the personal information shared, one can participate in online communities without exposing oneself to the risks of being manipulated or victimized. Importantly, if someone in an online community begins to act odd or in an aggressive manner, be quick to report the behavior and leave the group.

Chapter 4

Online Education Fundamentals

A. INTRODUCTION

Chapter 5 provides strategies and tactics that a parent can use to work with their children, teachers, and school administrations to help ensure the most effective educational experience for their students. But before jumping into the strategies and tactics, this chapter provides the history and educational context for online and blended education. For many parents, online education was not on their radar until the COVID-19 pandemic closed in-person schools and forced school systems to rapidly transition to these online learning platforms, systems that had evolved largely for higher education and professional training uses.

As of the time of this writing, most families are looking forward to the return to in-person education, which is expected for most programs in Fall 2021. For some students, however, online education has become the preferred learning modality. And many school systems are exploring how to use online education as a supplement to their in-person offerings. With these significant changes to the educational system in mind, it is helpful for parents and teachers to have a grounding in the basics of online education before exploring the role that parents and households can have in promoting online educational success for their students.

B. ORIGINS

Distance education and remote learning have existed for centuries. The earliest were correspondence courses for teaching shorthand. Since the early days of printing, published books and workbooks extended formal education from the classroom to the home. An ad in the *Boston Gazette* in 1728 offered to teach shorthand through lessons mailed weekly. In the late 1700s, correspondence programs were already being used by European universities. In 1840, Isaac Pitman introduced his phonetic shorthand system in England. Twelve years later, his brother Benjamin Pitman brought the program to the United States, offering correspondence courses across the country.

The early development of radio was anticipated to be the basis for a profound increase in access to remote education. The University of Wisconsin-Madison is credited with having the first educational radio station, WHA, beginning in 1919. By 1925, there were 171 stations licensed to educational organizations. Although more stations started after that date, by 1937, only thirty-eight remained.

The early stations would typically broadcast classroom lectures over the radio. Enrolled students would listen in and then mail back their completed lessons to the instructor. The general public could listen in to these lessons, as well, but only the enrolled students could gain certification or make educational progress through these programs.

The scope and effectiveness of these programs varied, but they were not considered particularly effective. Nonetheless, they played a role in extending education for students who could not access a classroom due to geographic limitations, costs, or other constraints.

As radio matured, so did the educational stations. In the 1940s, the federal government started supporting public and educational broadcasting. This quickly expanded into support for public television as well. Congress then passed the Public Broadcasting Act of 1967, establishing the Corporation for Public Broadcasting as a private, nonprofit corporation appointed by the president of the United States and confirmed by the Senate.

Although public radio and television have flourished, only a small portion of their content relates to educational disciplines. Television shows such as *Mister Rogers' Neighborhood*, *Sesame Street*, and *The Magic School Bus* had powerful effects on early childhood development. At the same time, however, most of the programming falls into broader categories of general interest.

Although some correspondence courses continued to be print-only, the ability to mail records, tapes, CDs, and DVDs further spurred the expansion of distance education. By 1982, the International Council for Correspondence Education recognized the transition and moved away from "Correspondence" in its name. Instead, the organization adopted the name International Council for Distance Education.

C. DEFINITION AND ATTRIBUTES
OF DISTANCE EDUCATION

Today, online education is another variation in the ways in which distance education has been provided through correspondence programs and other methods. To understand distance education, it is helpful to begin with a working definition. Focusing on accreditation standards, the U.S. Department of Education distinguishes between correspondence programs and distance education programs. It uses the following definition of a distance education program:

> **Distance education** means education that uses one or more of the technologies listed in paragraphs (1) through (4) to deliver instruction to students who are separated from the instructor and to support regular and substantive interaction between the students and the instructor, either synchronously or asynchronously. The technologies may include
>
> (1) the Internet;
> (2) one-way and two-way transmissions through open broadcast, closed circuit, cable, microwave, broadband lines, fiber optics, satellite, or wireless communications devices;
> (3) audioconferencing; or
> (4) video cassettes, DVDs, and CD-ROMs, if the cassettes, DVDs, or CD-ROMs are used in a course in conjunction with any of the technologies listed in paragraphs (1) through (3).

The European Union has adopted this working definition for its funding and regulations:

> [D]istance education comprises those teaching-learning processes in which as a rule teaching and learning are separated in both space and time. Bridging the distance and guiding the learning process is effected by means of specially prepared materials (media) and in the context of an organisation which steers and supports the whole process.

The two definitions together provide an excellent framework for structured distance education. Both definitions stress that the learning instruction does not occur in person and may not occur simultaneously. The definitions also highlight that the instructor is managing or guiding the learning process through regular and substantive interaction. Finally, for distance education that meets academic accreditation purposes, the student–teacher interaction is provided through an educational institution.

1. Synchronous

The definitions of online education include both synchronous and asynchronous forms of education. Synchronous learning merely means that the instructors and the students are in the same place or learning environment at the same time so that the interaction between the two can happen simultaneously. Classroom learning is necessarily synchronous. Online classes using Zoom or other video-sharing technologies achieve a similar result to being in the same room, though as discussed in later chapters, there are also significant differences between sitting together in a classroom and participating together on a video call.

The greatest benefit of synchronous instruction is the ability of the instructor to respond to the real-time feedback provided by the students. As discussed below, synchronous lectures do not add much more to the course than asynchronous videos can offer. Live instruction allows the instructor to interact with the students and the students to interact with each other in real time. By engaging together to understand new material, build on their existing knowledge, increase their confidence, and reinforce their prior knowledge, each class session helps instruct the students and consolidate their prior learning.

Unfortunately, in a demand for efficiency, many higher education courses rely on lectures as a primary mode of instruction. Even if the class is predominately lecture based, however, the instructor can break up the material into small blocks and introduce modest opportunities for interaction to enable the students to increase their repetition.

2. Asynchronous

In contrast, asynchronous courses are separate in time and space. For example, all forms of print correspondence education and those using mailed media utilize instructions that were created and recorded in advance of being delivered to the students. The students read, watch, or interact with the materials upon receipt of the materials, but at a different time than that of their creation.

Advocates of asynchronous education focus on the ability to replace class lectures with videos and similar content that can be more engaging and informative. For noninteractive material, cognitive science experts suggest that people have difficulty paying attention to lectures or videos longer than six minutes in length. (Coincidentally, this was the length of early movie camera film reels, which explains why early cartoons were six minutes in length.)

In an asynchronous class, the live lecture is replaced with prerecorded videos. These videos may have better visual features that enhance learning and be scripted and edited tightly to focus on the content. At the same time, however, unless they are designed with interactive elements, the overall retention will still drop off considerably when the videos are longer than six minutes. Studies suggest that this length can be nearly doubled if the videos are interactive by embedding questions and required responses from the students.

3. Self-Paced

There is a third structure for teaching, known as self-paced instruction. A self-paced course provides all of the instructional materials to the student in advance of the term or unit, and allows the student to move through the material at the student's own pace. Self-paced instruction has the benefit that it allows speedy learners to move quickly through the material without getting bored. Students who move more slowly will feel less pressure from those who are waiting for them to finish.

Well-designed self-paced courses will include additional content designed for those students who are struggling to grasp the concepts. The nature and amount of material to be covered can vary in a self-paced lesson because the students are not required to keep pace with each other, and they are evaluated based on their mastery of the material rather than the amount of time they work on the lesson.

The downside of self-paced instruction is that such programs are not designed to have the students work with each other and learn from the other students. In a typical, synchronous classroom, questions and discussions raised by participants in the class will serve to represent the kinds of questions being raised by many of the students. Instructors adjust their teaching to reflect the questions coming from the group. Just as important, students learn from each other, providing feedback and engagement. The interaction of the students with each other helps build understanding of the material and improves the retention of the knowledge. Self-paced materials rarely can replace this aspect of the learning process. Moreover, self-paced programs lose the social networks and engagement that is an important part of the structured educational experience.

Since so much of the learning that occurs in school is designed around the students' social engagement, most accredited distance education programs limit self-paced lessons. For both synchronous and asynchronous instruction, the programs typically require that the students are kept on the same schedule. Most are designed to promote interaction and collaboration among the students in addition to the students' engagement with the instructor.

D. MODALITIES—FACE-TO-FACE, ONLINE, AND BLENDED INSTRUCTION

There is a wide range of instruction, from individualized tutoring providing a student with a one-on-one relationship with the instructor, to correspondence programs where the students are provided lessons, readings, and audiovisual materials that students complete at their own pace. For most school districts and universities, the three most prevalent forms of education are face-to-face, online, and blended or hybrid.

Traditional education is conducted in a face-to-face setting, meaning that the students and teachers are together in the same physical space at the same time. Also described as live, in-person instruction, the traditional teaching methodology is the standard against which newer teaching methods are evaluated.

Class size is often a significant differentiator for the quality of in-person instruction. The richness of personal attention provided by the instructor and the immediacy of feedback become diminished when the class size becomes too large. In-person instruction also requires management of the learning environment. In elementary and secondary school environments, the time and attention needed to manage the student interaction can become a significant distraction from the instruction and engagement.

In contrast, first-year college courses can have 500 or more students in attendance in auditorium-styled classrooms. Other courses might grow into the thousands by using remote classrooms facilitated by teaching assistants. In these courses, the student–teacher interaction is sporadic at best, bearing little resemblance to the small class, interactive environment prized as the standard for effective education.

In contrast to the face-to-face instruction, online education is typically conducted by the student using a home computer. The instructor provides lesson plans, reading material, audiovisual material, and assessments through a learning management system (LMS) that hosts the content. As discussed above, some versions involve the use of live, synchronous sessions that enable the students to gather in an online class, see and hear each other, and interact with the instructor much like a traditional classroom. In other courses, more typical of adult education, the materials are provided in an asynchronous format so that the students do not interact during live sessions. Students may still engage with each other through discussion boards, group exercises, and other assignments each week during the course, just not as a large group during an in-classroom session.

Many schools and universities are shifting to a blended or hybrid mode of instruction. In a blended instruction mode, students will meet in live classroom sessions on a regular basis, but the instruction will be supplemented with the LMS-based tools. In a blended learning environment, students will use the discussion boards, small group assignments, online assessments, and asynchronous audiovisual materials to engage both inside and outside the classroom. Blended learning models often incorporate aspects of self-paced learning to give the student more direct control over the learning experience as well.

Schools balance the in-classroom experience and the online experience in many different ways. Traditional programs have dabbled with online instructional tools by using the LMS to replace handouts and simplify communication with parents. As a result of pandemic-induced social distancing, other programs have limited students' in-classroom exposure to once per week, and moved most of the course online.

Studies suggest that blended instruction is the most effective form of education. It combines the best attributes of small-classroom, personalized instruction with the ability to use the learning time most effectively. Since lectures are not very interactive, blended courses tend to move lectures online into videos. This frees classroom time for more group work and one-on-one instruction. LMS systems simplify the administration of quizzes, discussion boards, and other opportunities for formative assessment, which further enriches the opportunity for learning.

E. COGNITIVE SCIENCE AND LEARNING THEORY

The debate over online education and the fear that students are falling behind masks a more fundamental debate over what makes good education. The areas of educational theory and cognitive science provide a great deal of evidence for those techniques that promote healthy learning. The strategies differ somewhat for each age group, but the common approaches for learning apply to students of all ages.

In recent years, empirical neuroscience has enabled researchers to take a peek into the mind to understand the application of these strategies in practice. The simplest understanding of memory starts with the process of acquiring information in short-term memory and then storing it in long-term memory.

1. The Mechanics of Short-Term, Long-Term, and Working Memory

Long-term memory is where learning occurs. Long-term memory reflects the store of knowledge acquired through experience and education. Long-term memories can last for the lifetime of an individual.

Short-term memory is the ability to remember a limited amount of information that has not been encoded into permanent, long-term memory. A common example is a person's ability to repeat a telephone number long enough to write it down or type it into a cell phone without the number being encoded into long-term memory for later retrieval. Short-term memory is defined by its extreme temporal decay and limited capacity. The temporal length is typically limited to 20–30 seconds and the capacity is typically described as holding seven chunks of information.

In addition to short-term and long-term memory, the brain also features working memory, the brain's workspace that allows both new information and recollected information to be processed and used. Working memory models are closely related to short-term memory models, but they provide a much more detailed set of explanations on how the system works.

The encoding process of the working memory translates the data into meaning for memory. As schema theory predicts, information that supplements existing knowledge and experience is much easier to store and remember than information that has no context. The encoding process is separated into different categories for visual encoding, acoustic encoding, or tactile encoding—based on the sensory input. Similarly, there are different encoding labels for the mental process, including semantic encoding which emphasizes the context of the information, such as concepts, ideas, and definitions. Elaborative encoding reflects the connection of the new information to the schema of the learner, while organizational encoding reflects the encoding based on the lists or structures of information used by the learner.

The encoding drives the connections among the neurons in the learner's brain. The neuron connections are called synapses. The number, size, and location of the synapses will define the ability of the brain to learn and retrieve information. The more synapses that develop, the stronger the memory and easier the recall.

Learning—the ability to store, recall, and utilize information in a contextually relevant manner—comes from the growth of the synaptic connections. Long-term retention and retrieval come from the ability to maintain these synaptic connections over time.

To explain the biological process, there are three primary approaches to learning theory: Behaviorism, Cognitivism, and Constructivism. There are many variations within these three categories as well as additional approaches beyond the three core approaches, but these reflect the broad understanding of learning psychology.

2. Behaviorism

The behaviorist approach to education was pioneered by B. F. Skinner. Skinner demonstrated that students learn complex skills and knowledge through reward and reinforcement of students' behaviors. The reinforcement technique used to promote effective learning is an example of this behaviorist approach. When students receive encouragement for efforts that approximate the desired skills, the feedback encourages the students to focus on those skills and refine their efforts. Behaviorist approaches focus on practice and repetition to reinforce memory associations, systematic routine, and step-by-step instructions.

3. Cognitivism

The next important development in educational psychology came from Swedish psychologist Jean Piaget. He helped establish that learning involves active construction and, accordingly, learning should itself be active. Students use their existing understanding as the base upon which to build new knowledge. They use "schemata"—patterns of thought or behavior to organize information and understand the relationships among new knowledge—as scaffolding to learn and adapt their understanding. This approach emphasizes the use and contextualization of knowledge rather than its memorization. Students can learn a list of facts more readily if they use the facts in context rather than memorize them in isolation.

Professor Mary Steward provides a list of techniques that build on Cognitivism:

Pedagogies arising from cognitivist research focus on schemata development, catering for individual differences in cognitive style and teaching that supports how the brain processes information. They include:

- Emphasizing not just new knowledge but assimilation with prior understanding building on previous learning and exploring relationships
- Enforcing activities that prevent cognitive [over]loading by creating space for note-taking or discussion and by breaking teaching sessions into manageable chunks
- Activating prior learning through the use of summaries, reading prompts, or questioning
- Adopting strategies such as discussion, note-building, and questioning, which relate new information to existing information to aid assimilation, encoding, and memorization
- Using variety and mixed media in teaching to accommodate sensory preferences
- Presenting concepts in varied ways, for example, in constituent parts and holistically, to cater for different cognitive styles
- "Externalizing" thinking, for example, through the use of lists, concept maps, or flow diagrams to explore relationships between concepts

- Using analogies or metaphors to help attach meaning and assimilate new learning
- Using novelty, surprise, and emotional engagement to capture the mind's attention and help memorization

Pedagogies arising from constructivist studies emphasize student-centered, active learning and the role of the teacher as facilitator, including:

- An emphasis on students being active in constructing their understanding of knowledge
- A focus on discovery, exploration, experimentation, and developing and testing hypotheses
- Project work, research-based learning, problem- and enquiry-based learning methods
- The role of the teacher as a guide, providing "scaffolding" to learning—that is, to ensure the student has the requisite knowledge, skills, and support to negotiate a piece of learning—and prompting the student through questioning or modeling.[1]

4. Constructivism and Other Approaches

The third major approach to learning theory is Constructivism. This approach builds upon the cognitive learning theories of Piaget. Constructivism is distinguished from Cognitivism because it focuses on the need for the student to take in new knowledge based on the prior knowledge and pre-existing schema of the learner. Two equally intelligent students will learn how to fish at different speeds if one has never been to a lake and the other spends time in boats and on the water. The experience of the second student provides her a schema to understand fishing that the first student has not developed.

Constructivism focuses on the schema development at the individual level. "Constructivism is based on the premise that we construct learning new ideas based on our own prior knowledge and experiences. Learning, therefore, is unique to the individual learner. Students adapt their models of understanding either by reflecting on prior theories or resolving misconceptions."[2]

These are only a few of the many approaches to learning theory. Psychologist Carl Rogers and psychologist Abraham Maslow each separately focused on the emotional motivations of students and learning. Adult learning theory emphasizes the learner's agency, highlighting the need for meta-cognition, reflection, and self-awareness of the student's learning process, attributes that work well for students in most age classifications.

F. SUPPLEMENTAL EDUCATION—DISTANCE LEARNING OUTSIDE OF ACCREDITED INSTITUTIONS

The Internet has created tremendous opportunities for learning outside of the structured classroom environment, provided as websites or phone apps. For children and young adults, the most important is Khan Academy, which offers "practice exercises, instructional videos, and a personalized learning dashboard that empower learners to study at their own pace in and outside of the classroom." Khan Academy is a nonprofit organization, providing its services free of advertising. Khan Academy has also expanded into free test preparation for the SAT, LSAT, and Praxis. By offering free test prep, Khan Academy helps break down one of the key financial barriers to college and legal education.

Kahoot! is another very popular app platform designed primarily for young children learning math and reading. The company's portfolio of educational options has grown significantly in 2020, including the acquisition of Drops, a foreign language learning app. Drops competes with Duolingo, another very popular foreign language learning app.

There are also game apps with spelling games, puzzles, and logic games. Players who spend time on these apps become much better at the game. There is no evidence, however, that improving the game play leads to other cognitive improvements. The FTC, for example, fined WordSmart Corporation for false and misleading claims that its apps would help students "learn faster, improve reading speed, or increase grades, IQ scores, or test scores." Jungle Rangers and Luminosity were also fined for misleading claims.

For college-level online learning, there are a number of platforms that provide massive online open courses (MOOCs) designed to harness the capacity of universities and individual instructors to offer distance education free or at low cost to anyone interested in a subject who did not need the academic credential of a university. Coursera, Udacity, Udemy, and other providers typically offer a set of readings and videos. Much like correspondence courses, some of the platforms emphasize self-paced, automated quizzing. MOOCs generally have a very low completion rate among class attendees, reflecting the problems of isolated, self-paced learning and courses that have very casual enrollment. In many ways, the participation in MOOCs looks much like it does for gym memberships, with only 10 percent of the members becoming committed users while the remaining 90 percent are casual users.

MOOCs have largely evolved into professional training platforms, where the value is much stronger, and the participation is much higher. LinkedIn Learning (formerly Lynda.com), Udemy, and other platforms provide very practical skills development modules, including a variety of computer science certifications. Microsoft and Google have added free certification training programs as well.

Most MOOCs have high-quality content. Learning apps vary much more, but the leading companies provide very effective instruction. The popularity of these platforms speaks to the strong interest by students of all ages to learn new skills and study new material. But the small success rate highlights the essential difference between self-paced, self-directed education and school. The vast majority of people need to be in a structured program or schedule of education that sets external deadlines and forces the students to keep pace with each other and the classroom. Without the deadlines to force students' completion of assignments, the positive reinforcement of instructors, and the peer engagement of community, students tend to drop out of educational programs.

G. FERPA—PROTECTING EDUCATIONAL PRIVACY

Well before distance education had become digital, privacy advocates had begun to worry about the role of the computer age on student privacy. A 1974 study by the National Council of Citizens in Education identified a pattern of abuses in student record keeping:

- Carte blanche access to school records by school personnel, law enforcement agencies, welfare and health department workers, and Selective Service Board representatives;
- Lack or denial of the right of parents and students to inspect school records, to control what goes into them, and to challenge their contents;
- Failure to obtain permission from parents before collecting information on students and their families (for example, before submitting students to psychiatric or personality tests);
- Serious abuses in the preparation of student records that follow students throughout their educational careers; and
- Failure to inform students and parents when, to whom, and why others are given access to records.[3]

As a result of the report, an amendment was made to the 1974 General Education Act, creating the Family Educational Rights and Privacy Act of 1974 (FERPA), which has become one of the oldest federal privacy laws available. FERPA applies to all schools that receive funds from the U.S. Department of Education. This includes all public schools at all grade levels, as well as any private schools that receive federal funding for any of their programs. In addition, state educational licensing requirements may further extend FERPA privacy rules to private institutions that do not use federal support.

Under FERPA, educational institutions are prohibited from disclosing "personally identifiable information in education records" without the written consent of the student, or, if the student is a minor, the student's parents. Severe violations of FERPA can result in a financial penalty or the loss of eligibility for federal funding. Violations of FERPA do not, however, create rights to sue the institutions directly.

In addition to the protection from disclosure of personally identifiable information, FERPA also provides students—or their parents if the students are under eighteen—the right to inspect their own educational records and request corrections of inaccurate information.

FERPA also allows for substantial information to be published by the educational institution unless there is an objection by adult students or the parents of a minor student. "Parent" is defined to include guardian. This information is categorized under the term "directory information." Schools once regularly published directories so that parents and students could contact each other. The directory information usually includes the name, address, telephone listing, age, grade-level participation in officially recognized activities and sports, and dates of attendance. This allows a school to promote its athletic teams and publicize the success of its students without seeking permission before every press release and yearbook is published or before its website is updated. A student may choose not to be included in this directory information by informing the institution.

Beyond the directory information, there are also a number of other situations in which student records can be shared. FERPA allows schools to disclose records without consent, to the following parties or under the following conditions:

- School officials with legitimate educational interest;
- Other schools to which a student is transferring;
- Specified officials for audit or evaluation purposes;
- Appropriate parties in connection with financial aid to a student;
- Organizations conducting certain studies for or on behalf of the school;
- Accrediting organizations;
- To comply with a judicial order or lawfully issued subpoena;
- Appropriate officials in cases of health and safety emergencies; and
- State and local authorities, within a juvenile justice system, pursuant to specific State law.[4]

One area of increasing concern is the ability of a school to give educational records, including attendance information, to campus safety officers or law enforcement. Under the FERPA regulations, the information can be provided to police and safety officers provided there is a judicial order or lawfully issued subpoena.[5] However, the school must make a reasonable effort to notify the student or parent about the order or subpoena prior to its compliance, so that the student or parent may seek protective action. This notice requirement will not apply if the subpoena was issued from a federal grand jury or court and the order prohibits that the advanced notice be provided. There are similar nondisclosure provisions for a court order issued as part of an investigation into domestic or international terrorism.

Another area where student records are permitted to be shared is in the context of health and safety emergencies. The basic rule is that a school "may disclose personally identifiable information from an education record to appropriate parties, including parents of an eligible student, in connection with an emergency if knowledge of the information is necessary to protect the health or safety of the student or other individuals."[6] In such instances, otherwise protected disciplinary records may be made available by the school if there is a significant risk to the safety or well-being of that student, other students, or other members of the school community.

The FERPA regulations make clear that when there is an emergency or other significant risk to the health or safety of a student, to other students, or to faculty, staff, or members of the public, then the duty to protect the student records is secondary to the need to protect health and safety. This requires an articulable and significant threat to health or safety. In such an emergency, school officials can provide law enforcement and others with information helpful to cyberbullying situations, school shootings, disease outbreaks, and other situations that put students at risk.

There is also some confusion regarding the right of law enforcement to create and maintain its own records.

> Law enforcement unit records are records that are: (1) created by a law enforcement unit; (2) created for a law enforcement purpose; and (3) maintained by the law enforcement unit. Law enforcement unit records are not protected by FERPA because they are specifically excluded from the definition of "education records" and, thus, from the privacy protections afforded to parents and eligible students by FERPA.[7]

While a law enforcement unit typically means a commissioned police officer or noncommissioned security guard, the definition is much broader. As a result, a school district can designate anyone who meets the criteria that the person is "officially authorized or designated by that school or school district to (1) enforce any local, state, or federal law, or refer to appropriate authorities a matter for enforcement of any local, state, or federal law against any individual or organization other than the agency or institution itself; or (2) maintain the physical security and safety of the agency or institution."[8] This means that some schools designate "a vice principal or other school official to act as the law enforcement unit officer."[9] The records that such a vice principal keeps would then be outside of FERPA limitations and available to law enforcement agencies without any of the procedural safeguards afforded by FERPA.

In addition, while FERPA has had a considerable impact on reforming the manner in which schools maintain student records, it is again worth noting that a school's failure to comply with FERPA could result in a financial penalty or the loss of federal aid if the breach of the FERPA rules was serious and sustained. In contrast, in emergency situations the risks to the schools and their students, faculty, and staff are immediate. It appears that the Department of Education has never actually imposed a financial penalty on any school due to a FERPA violation.

Chapter 5

How to be an Engaged Parent in Online and Blended Education

A. THE KEYS TO EFFECTIVE ONLINE EDUCATION

Experience in the explosive expansion of online education triggered by the 2020 pandemic has also reinforced the critical importance of social interaction for effective learning. The anecdotal evidence suggests that most students crave social interaction with their peers. The absence of social engagement has had a significant, negative impact on the students' learning and development.

In secondary schools, educators constantly struggle to keep students focused on the instructional goals and off their social interactions. Yet, by the time these students have become adult workers, corporations are required to invest time and resources to create team-building exercises, retreats, and community activities to create these social bonds. The corporations have learned that communication and interpersonal effectiveness improve significantly when people come together to share common goals and objectives. This same understanding helps build winning sports teams, acting companies, and social clubs.

The same is true for online education. Online education has many positive attributes, but it is not inherently social. The social aspects of online education help keep students engaged and willing to participate. This both reduces drop-out rates and increases the amount of time and effort students commit to their learning. Structuring the online course to promote interactions among the students is an essential—but often overlooked—component of effective online education.

For parents of students participating in online education and adults participating in their own online education, the keys to success are clear:

- The learning should be interactive, providing peer feedback, social engagement, and social motivation to keep the student engaged in the learning.
- The quality of the skills and knowledge being learned must be of high quality.
- The learning environment must compel participants to proceed at a minimum pace (offering students the ability to get ahead is a benefit, but the design must strongly discourage students from falling behind).
- The instructor must structure the learning to positively reinforce active engagement by the student through games, formative assessments, and exploration of the content.
- The learning must be active, so the student is involved and developing context for the material.
- There must be immediate, effective, and supportive feedback so the student can learn from the experience and incorporate the student's personal knowledge to the learning.
- The skills and knowledge must be developed over time, using spaced repetition, retrieval, and interleaving of the content.
- Students should be reminded that if it feels hard, it is working. Just like physical workouts, learning is a process of challenging boundaries.

For parent and educators, these elements are essential to build effective learning environments. For most K-12 education, the content is well established. Instead, the effort and focus need to be on the context and environment for the students' motivation, learning, and support. This remains equally true for college, even in graduate and professional education.

For parents, this list of the key building blocks of online education will help them partner with their students' teachers and schools to maximize the effectiveness of the instruction and success of the online students.

B. LEARNING IN PRACTICE

Distance education shifts a great deal of responsibility out of the classroom and into the home. This creates significant challenges for parents and learners who receive less direct engagement from their online teachers.

An effective learning environment takes each of the core learning theories into account to develop an environment most conducive to learning. In practice, these techniques should blend together. Deep learning that engenders easy retrieval requires strong synaptic connections. Although it is inaccurate, the analogy to exercising the learner's thinking muscles fits surprisingly well. The more one works a muscle while varying the ways in which it is being worked, the stronger it gets. The same is true for memory and learning. And like developing physical skills, learning improves by varying the exercises and mixing up the strategies to work the learning muscles.

Parents do not need to become cognitive science experts to learn from the evidence presented by the neuroscience and learning theory experiments. Instead, they can build on the conclusions to create better learning outcomes and more positive learning experiences.

- **Great Teachers Motivate**. This axiom is supported by the neuroscience. Repeated experiments demonstrate that synaptic connections improve with positive, emotionally engaged learning environments. When a student wants to succeed, the student will do much better, and external motivations such as pleasing teachers and parents are strong motivators. If a particular teacher is not a motivator for a student, then the parent can provide additional, supportive motivation.
- **Reinforce Success**. Learners want positive reinforcement from the joy of succeeding and from the people surrounding them. In contrast, punishments and more subtle negative reinforcements can discourage all aspects of learning, not just a particular, unwanted behavior.
- Pace. Students can only absorb so much information in any block. Give students time to consolidate and reflect. Instructors should use short pauses and other techniques to break up the learning, engage the students, and encourage interaction. Tasks such as write a paragraph (or draw a picture for younger students), discuss with another student or small group, ask a question, answer another student's question, and others help manage the pace of the teaching throughout the day.
- **Practice, Don't Study**. Students will generally remember information if they have been tested on it rather than if they have been given the opportunity to reread content. The active process of test taking creates a strong cognitive impact on the learning. Rereading, in contrast, offers only a very limited benefit on the student's learning. Parents can make a huge, easy impact on learning by asking their children about what they are assigned to read. Engaging the students in a discussion about their assignments will strengthen the memory and learning about those assignments.
- **Use Spacing and Interleaving**. The brain works harder to remember information and to broaden the schemata used to retrieve the information when the student worked harder to learn the information. Over the length of months and years, students will remember information with which they have interacted multiple times much more effectively than information that they learned deeply and set aside. New material should be interleaved with experience on older material.
- **Engage the Students**. Parents are not expected to be the subject matter experts for their children's learning. By asking the students to write quiz

questions or design projects to learn the material, the students will be
deeply engaging with the materials while reducing the work the parents
need to do to support the children's learning.
- **Collaborate**. Students need constant supervision and strong support. At the
same time, the online learning tools can become a resource for the parents
as well. Parents can share the duties to help the students' learning by part-
nering with the parents of their children's small groups. A class of thirty
could have five parents each agree to be the parental teachers' assistant on a
particular subject. Each parent would be required to do far less than if each
parent were solely responsible for helping his or her own child.
- **Socialize**. The online learning environment risks being highly isolating
for teachers, students, and parents. Collaborations and small group projects create environments that encourage socialization and collaboration.
Emotional success and peer approval are also strong drivers of learning, so
allowing time for some socialization benefits the learning.

C. LEARNING MANAGEMENT SYSTEMS AND PARENTAL ACCESS

Traditional education is largely driven by the selected schoolbooks. For online
education, the learning management system (LMS) drives many of the decisions
about a student's online experience. Every online course and most face-to-face
courses utilize the LMS to manage the interaction of text and audiovisual content. The most popular systems are Canvas, Blackboard, Moodle, or the Google
Classroom, but there are more than 300 platforms being marketed.

The LMS is separate from the videoconferencing software. Zoom has
become the national standard for business, webinars, and classroom use, but
it has many competitors as well. These include Microsoft Teams (which is
replacing Skype), Cisco WebEx, Slack, GoToTraining (the academic version
of GoToMeeting), and even videoconferencing features of social media on
Discord, Facebook Messenger, Google Duo, and many others.

With the explosive expansion of online education in 2020, the LMS
platforms provided increased integration of the videoconferencing features
directly in the LMS. Even though these services are provided by separate
companies, students can now find the links to their class sessions directly
within the LMS.

1. Components of the LMS

Many schools have standardized the LMS navigation so that the student experience is the same from course to course. Standardizing the navigation makes

it much easier for students to find important information. Standardizing navigation is a form of structure and predictability that students appreciate.

A typical LMS navigation would include the following elements:

- Syllabus
- Announcements
- Calendar
- Lessons/Modules
- Discussion Boards
- Assignment Drop Box
- Tests/Quizzes
- Grade Book
- Live Classroom

For online and blended instruction, the LMS becomes the centerpiece of the educational experience. In the K-12 environment, there is an extremely wide range of approaches to the adoption and use of LMS technology. Most have the ability to connect parents to the school district and to each student's courses. The first benefit of using the technology to connect with the parent is to overcome the technological barriers to using an LMS with the students. If the parents are communicating with the LMS, then the parents are likely to be able to help their children with the sites. Parents need to accept that the LMS has replaced the PTA mailing and parent assembly as the source for school information.

2. Communication through LMS Announcements

Parents should be able to receive announcements from the school district, school, and their children's classes through the LMS. Parents should be able to see the grades and feedback for their children, and to use the LMS to submit many of their children's assignments. If the school district has not enabled these services, the parents should insist they do so. If the school district has enabled these services, then it is the obligation of the parents to take advantage of these channels of communication. They are no longer optional.

Since each LMS has a messaging service, it also simplifies email communications between the parents and the teacher as well as the parents and the school. Any announcement posted in the LMS should automatically be sent to the enrolled parents directly.

3. Using the LMS to Encourage Parental Collaboration

The LMS also provides opportunities for the teacher to collaborate with parents more directly. Particularly for online programs, the teacher can send information to the parents to help them work with their students, to provide discussion boards for parents who wish to discuss and collaborate ways of improving their students' engagement, or to share other tips and strategies. Because they are asynchronous, discussion boards have the benefit of permitting parents to log into the system whenever the time is convenient, potentially offering new opportunities for parents to engage with the teacher and with the other parents.

4. Sticking with the LMS Avoids Noncompliance and Learning Curve Barriers

Everyone involved with online and blended education struggles to keep up with the technology. School districts struggle to provide the funds and the IT personnel to support these systems. Teachers are required to manage technology on top of the pedagogy and classroom. Parents are being asked to solve their students' connectivity issues. By focusing on a single LMS, the limited time and funds to learn and use the system can be focused on the single system used by all parents and students.

For those new to online learning, schools should provide tutorials and guides to help use the systems. The initial use of the LMS should provide the users an opportunity to learn the navigation of the course and be able to work within the LMS before the assignments begin. This is equally important for both the students' and the parents' experience.

In an introductory session, for example, students can be asked to provide a brief introduction of themselves to their classmates and take a simple interest inventory. Students will have an early opportunity to explore the technology and to socialize with classmates. The performance on this simple assignment will let the instructor see the students' comfort with the course tools and be able to help struggling students at a stage where there are no graded deadlines.

At the risk of stifling creativity, everyone involved in the design for the LMS should remember that usability is the goal, not aesthetics. The student and parent users of an LMS should be able to move from course to course without surprises in the structure or navigation.

Similarly, it is important to stay with the school district's or university's adopted LMS and videoconferencing platforms. There are thousands of free or low-cost options, and they may have features that a particular adopter might want. But the free and low-cost providers may not be meeting the privacy requirements of state and federal regulations, and they often fail to provide the minimal accommodations required to meet the Department of Education disability requirements for use in the classroom. If a tool is ad-supported, for example, there is a good chance that it is not designed to be used in educational settings.

D. PREPARING FOR ONLINE INSTRUCTION

For students participating in school from home, parents are implicitly part of the instructional team. Some schools will work closely with the parents to make this an explicit partnership, while many others may call on parents to help with the instruction and evaluation without ever explaining their needs or goals.

1. Learning Objectives

When teachers develop a course, they start by identifying the learning objectives for the course. The teachers identify the specific skills they wish to develop during the course, the knowledge they intend for the students to acquire, and the values the course is intended to develop. Every course should have clear objectives for the skills, knowledge, and values. Those three attributes are then used to develop the lesson plans that will take place during the year. In primary and secondary education, the lesson plans will integrate the calendar as well, so that the major events in the year can be incorporated into the lesson plans. Each lesson plan is then created to have its individual learning objectives that help support the desired course-wide learning outcomes.

At a minimum, parents should be provided the learning objectives of each online course, and preferably the learning objectives of each module or lesson being conducted in the course. Understanding the learning objectives will make it much easier for the parents to help with the assignments and to emphasize useful aspects of the project.

Parents should also have access to evaluation criteria used for particular assignments. By knowing the evaluation criteria, parents can give help and reinforce the goals of the teacher. Where individual teachers have omitted this information, the parents should reach out to obtain the information, encouraging the teacher to work with the parents of their students as part of the learning partnership.

2. Structure

One of the biggest changes for online learning is the lack of structure in the day. Schools are highly regimented, and this structure helps many students focus on learning. The structure also breaks the time into small blocks, creating breaks for the students, opportunities to socialize, and physical activities. At home, the structure may be much harder to replicate or maintain.

Structure helps eliminate distractions.

At-home students and workers will benefit from a similar routine both for online class and for homework. Develop a routine that includes healthy sleep habits, good hydration, physical exercise, and consistency. The schedule should realistically schedule class time, homework time, meals, chores, and free time. Schools vary considerably in how much online time is spent during the school week and how much of that time is synchronous. Parents must start with the expectations of the school and then build a home plan to supplement those expectations. Parents should also collaborate with their children to establish the schedule, and then everyone should commit to it. Over time, the routine will reinforce the commitment to homework and study sessions.

Of course, not all students respond to the structure in the same way. Parents can also take advantage of the new environment to help their own students and match the structure to the students' learning behavior.

Students' performance improves considerably when the students get enough sleep. High school students, in particular, are often sleep deprived because school districts often schedule classroom hours based on bussing schedules and fleet availability rather than the health needs of the students. Student learning will benefit from starting formal courses at 9:30 a.m. rather than 7:30 a.m. if a school district can make this shift.

3. Anxiety and Social Isolation

For some students, online learning increases anxiety and social isolation. Even before the 2020 pandemic, nearly one-third of students suffered from anxiety issues, and that number has significantly increased from the stress of COVID-19 health issues, closings, and continued uncertainty.

The first step in addressing anxiety is to acknowledge it. Students may not understand what anxiety is or how to describe it. Parents and teachers should be proactive to address the issue with students who exhibit signs of easy agitation, refusals to participate, concentration problems, uncertainty paralysis, or heavy tiredness, any of whom may be struggling with anxiety.

Parents and teachers should begin by treating the anxiety seriously and respectfully. A person's feelings are true whether or not the person's perspective on the cause of those feelings is accurate. By being supportive, taking the students' concerns seriously, and respecting the students, parents and teachers can help reduce the problem. This means being careful to avoid making students feel ashamed of their concerns, minimizing them, or embarrassing them in front of other students.

Understanding the anxiety can then help develop a strategy to reduce the anxiety's impact on learning. There is a myriad of calming techniques, such as breathing exercises, physical exercise regimes, and yoga. Some students will need help from clinical strategies provided by therapists, psychologists, and psychiatrists.

Online education also has the challenge of increased social isolation. While the use of cameras and audio in class provide some interaction, nonverbal communication is severely diminished in online settings. Filmmakers compensate for this by making dozens of small editorial cuts in each film scene to help capture the kind of eye movement that the viewer would likely make it in person. A film scene will cut to a raised eyebrow, a hand twitch, the look passing between two characters, or to an object in a room that catches the attention of a character. Even with all this work, film cannot deliver the same experience as live theater. The online classroom cannot come close. Videoconferencing provides a grid of tiny boxes, overlapping sound, and pixelating backgrounds.

Group projects may make up for some of this. They can be excellent vehicles for socializing students and reducing the anxiety involved with the online classes. Parents should consult with instructors at the beginning of the term and regularly thereafter to build opportunities for study sessions and collaboration into the class. Parents should remember that the social aspects of the time spent in these exercises is a goal of the collaboration. Provided the work gets done, socializing should not be discouraged.

4. Focus Strategies Based on Age and Development Levels

Although there are many strategies that work for both elementary students and adults, in practice, the nature of the learning exercises should be geared for the developmental level of the student. Concentration and self-direction are key measure of development. Younger children cannot be expected to have the same level of concentration as older students, and younger children will need more active supervision.

As a result of the shift to mandatory online education by many public school systems, a range of guidelines and requirements were produced. The Illinois State Board of Education, for example, issued guidelines limiting the work per day for first- and second-grade students to a range of 45–90 minutes per day provided in units of 5–10 minutes in length. The same recommendations suggested that high school students could be expected to be in class 20–45 minutes per class for a total of 3–4.5 hours daily. Other states have guidelines that are similar, but the particular guidance can vary substantially.

The Illinois recommendations also recognized that there were many informal activities that programs and families could utilize to benefit the students. The suggestions recognized the unique situation triggered by the pandemic, but these items also provided useful ways of developing skills, knowledge, and values outside the classroom.

These suggestions provide activities away from the online classroom that are very effective at developing students' knowledge, skills, and values.

Table 5.1 Engagement activities for mind, body, spirit, environment, and family enhancement

Suggestions for Additional Activities[1]				
Mind	*Body*	*Spirit*	*Environment*	*Family*
• Reading, e.g., independent reading, listening to someone else read, audiobooks • Puzzles, Word Searches • Write a story or in a journal • Count money • Draw a map of your neighborhood • Building with blocks or Legos • Listen to a podcast • Watch a documentary	• Take a walk • Dance • Exercise • Fine/gross motor activities • Stretch or do yoga • Play a sport	• Listen to music or sing • Playing (inside or outside) • Creative arts • Coloring or drawing • Imaginative play • Meditate • Do something you've been avoiding	• Clean up your room • Do age-appropriate chores • Gardening • Fix something broken • Take care of pets or plants • Cook or bake	• Write a letter to someone • Play board games with a family member • Tell jokes or riddles • Build a fort and tell stories in it • Offer to help someone

Board games and card games can also be used to encourage math. Cooking and baking can also be used to reinforce math. Parents can adapt the collection of recipe collections into language and history lessons. Well-selected documentaries and podcasts can be used to expose students to new material. Outdoor walks can be used to learn about nature and the environment. Learning does not need to be confined to the classroom.

5. Video Fatigue and Zoom Bombing

In addition to the potential ill effects triggered by the social isolation of online education, there are other potential negative effects of being online in virtual classrooms. For example, some students are highly self-conscious of their online image. For these students, seeing themselves in Zoom or other videoconferencing platforms each day may create additional anxiety. At the same time, for many students, using the video tools should actually help with the online learning. Nonverbal communication is an essential part of communication and interpersonal relations. Although the Zoom windows are a poor substitute for true in-person communication, they still afford much more context than text alone or even text with voice.

Still, key components are missing or distorted. The missing nonverbal cues include tone and pitch of voice; facial expressions; eye contact; and body language.[2] Teachers and schools vary considerably in their attitude regarding mandatory camera use for online learning. One reasonable model is to require cameras be turned on during class time, but allow students to opt out of the camera usage if they have a good reason to do so. When using this approach, the student rather than the instructor should have the final say on whether the reason to turn off the camera is sufficient, and the instructor should also be clear that the student's mental or physical health are acceptable reasons. Parents may need to encourage schools that apply more rigid policies to give the students more autonomy and respect regarding their use of videos. When applied in this fashion, teachers find that most students will still use their cameras for class.

During the early months of the COVID-19 epidemic and the rapid shift to online learning, instructors also had to address classroom control and the unwelcome phenomenon of "Zoom Bombing" or videoconferencing hijacking.[3] The FBI reported two instances of individuals who jumped into classrooms to yell profanity and to display swastikas. Many similar incidents occurred in school classrooms and in public events taking place through videoconferencing. Instructors and videoconference hosts can limit the ability of uninvited guests to crash their classrooms by keeping the links to the classes private; by using waiting rooms so that attendees can be identified before letting them in; by the host restricting camera-sharing access; and by using the most updated software which has additional privacy settings.[4] In the online environment, instructors are required to understand many skills beyond classroom management and content knowledge, including the settings and capabilities of the software tools they use.

E. HOMEWORK AND TAKE-HOME ASSIGNMENTS

If adopted by the instructor, an LMS can provide parents an easy way to understand the assignments and expectations for the students' progress. The calendar view in the LMS will provide the student and parent clear deadlines for the students' assignments. If the parents have direct access to the assignments, the parents can read the instructions provided to the student to help ensure that the student understands what the task is for the course.

The single most important part of completing homework for online courses is the difficulty in concentrating on the homework. Students—as well as adults—greatly overestimate their ability to multitask. Most studies show that multitasking is synonymous with doing multiple things badly. Multitasking has even been shown to temporarily reduce IQ.

As students and at-home workers have learned from the 2020 pandemic, working at home requires a different discipline than going into work. Getting dressed to go out to work or school, commuting, saying hello, and other morning routines are much more important to a person's readiness mindset.

Even with a routine, the risk of distractions for homework on the computer is much worse than homework in a workbook or notebook. Multiple windows on the computer or laptop mean that music and videos are likely running, email and Discord conversations are popping up, notifications are appearing, and the computer is essentially conspiring against the student from focusing on the assignment.

- **Music should be the only noise in the background**. Other than a limited amount of background music or white noise, all other external distractions should be reduced as much as possible. Pick a space that does not have a lot of other activity. If three or four people are trying to get work done at once, it is much more difficult to concentrate, and the scheduling pressure also becomes a distraction.
- **Eliminate the computer and phone distractions**. On Windows, for example, there is a "focus assistant" that can be used to turn off computer notifications. Turn off the phone or leave it in another room to avoid hearing the notifications. If students have a problem switching to Twitch or Discord every few minutes, consider using multiple sign-ons for the computer. By creating a "Studying" account for the student, that log in can be installed without access to games and pop-ups. It will not eliminate access to web pages, but it can further reduce the temptation of distractions.
- **Establish a concentration mindset**. Stretches, brief meditation, breathing exercises, or other physical training will help improve concentration and help focus on the assignment rather than on everything else going on.
- **Prepare in advance**. Online courses typically have most of the materials needed for the homework on the computer, but if an assignment or project needs textbooks, markers, rulers, or other tools, be sure to pull those in advance. Teachers or parents can help the students by writing out the requirements in advance.
- **Use the LMS calendar and checklists**. The LMS should provide a clear schedule of due dates. The calendar works even better if it is supplemented with checklists. Checklists can be on paper, or they can be apps like Microsoft's ToDo. Checklists are the simplest form of learning "gamification," where rewards are earned by achieving accomplishments. The psychic power of checking off a ToDo list is quite powerful. Parents can also

subscribe to the list, allowing the parents to see the progress on assignments as they are completed. Checklists also eliminate time wasted discussing what is due and when it is due.

- **Pace the work**. Regular breaks to stretch, use the bathroom, check on the phone notifications, and clear the mind are healthy. They should be structured, however, so that the breaks remain around ten minutes for each fifty minutes of concentrated homework. The length of the homework sessions will necessarily vary for younger and for older students, but the approach works for all ages.

Discussion boards also provide a useful way for students to check in with each other on the instructions for assignments and other topics regarding the course. Often classes will make their own discussion groups in non-school apps. These can generally be helpful, but they do not have the instructor or parent moderation. For a discussion on what can happen in social media, see chapter 10 on cyberbullying.

In addition to the concentration and motivation challenges, students may have fewer opportunities to ask the instructor about the assignment. Teachers can help with this by using short videos and handouts that give both students and their parents information about the expectations on assignments, particularly if the assignments are novel or complex.

Over time, online classrooms make it very easy to collect examples of student work from prior years and share those examples as illustrations for students. These make an excellent resource which grows each year. (FERPA restrictions apply, so if the student's name is on a work, the instructor should be sure that the family has not opted out of publishing directory information.)

F. LEARNING BEYOND THE CLASSROOM

There are very different ways to measure the effectiveness of online education. Often, they are measured using standardized test scores. In college, online educational programs will be judged based on the retention and graduation rates of the programs. These numbers will help identify if programs are substantially deficient, but they do not reflect the broader goals of education.

For most people, the important lessons were not learned in the classroom. Problem solving, grit and diligence, interpersonal skills, and many of the most important attributes were developed outside of class in extracurricular activities, part-time jobs, or volunteer activities. Schools struggling to transition to online education or struggling with budgetary constraints tend to leave these aspects behind.

1. Teams, Clubs, and Organizations

For many students, the driving force behind their school experience is their participation in athletic teams, musical and theatrical performances, and school organizations. If a school moves entirely online, many of these opportunities will be lost.

Athletic teams are very hard to replicate online. Coaches can assign workout tasks, ask the students to share stats, and post videos. Of course, such exercise will not replace the camaraderie of competition or even practice. While it is not the same, bringing teams together to run drills and review videos of individual practice sessions will provide missing socialization and motivate healthy behavior.

Artistic programs have a similar problem. Bands and choirs can practice individually, but participating in online live sessions is a struggle, given the latency issues of most videoconferencing software. If a school or club has a sound editor, students can be given a sample track and record their own performance as individual tracks that the sound editor can compile into a complete recording. Orchestras, bands, and choirs can take advantage of these tools. Transforming a school choir into a YouTube music program will allow students to socialize, participate, create, and be proud in their final product.

Student groups can also meet online. The goals for the groups might change considerably, particularly those groups that had been dedicated to hosting activities on campus. Nonetheless, the groups can meet, socialize, and create their own objectives appropriate for their purpose. Student groups can take advantage of videoconferencing to invite guest speakers from around the world to participate in their programs.

When running student organizations, the organizers should remember to focus on participation and inclusion. Taking the time to have everyone give an introduction or brief update on what the participant has been doing helps reinforce the importance of being in the group. Assigning small tasks to each group participant also gives each member a role and sense of belonging that is much more important for online groups than for in-person clubs.

Some school districts may be struggling to add these resources to their schools. Local and national nonprofit or religious organizations can play a useful role adding support for these clubs and activities. Girl Scouts, Campfire, 4H, and BBYO, Urban League, and hundreds of other organizations offer afterschool programs. These programs can drive student engagement to provide socialization and emphasize the interpersonal skills and resilience essential to lifetime success.

2. eSports

Videogaming may also provide some benefits. The term eSports reflects the growth of some videogame platforms into organized competitive videogames with leagues for collegiate players and high-paying competitive leagues for professional eSports athletes. The NBA created an eSports league using the basketball-themed NBA 2K game franchise. In 2020, with many sports leagues shut down, ESPN broadcast the NBA 2K League games. Most league games are live-streamed on Twitch, and viewership has neared 2 million viewers for finals of League of Legends and the introduction of Valorant.

Presently, eSports are not state-sanctioned official sports. For comparison, Robotics teams are state sanctioned in Arizona, Connecticut, Minnesota, and Texas, allowing the state to award state-champion titles and letters for participation. Instead, the schools who offer eSports programs run the experience as school clubs. The leagues are run by national sponsors, including the High School Esports League, the High School Starleague, and Youth Esports of America.

At the collegiate level, eSports are hot. NPR has reported that "more than 170 colleges and universities participate. And there's money on the table—more than $16 million in college scholarships."[5] The story continued, "naturally, high schools have followed suit."

eSports programs add the structure of the high school club to the experience of online gaming. Many students use the online chat during the game play for a great deal of their social interactions. The gaming creates a healthy opportunity for interaction, team coordination, and skill development.

3. Mindfulness

Mindfulness is another important trend that can be introduced by (or for) the family as part of the transition to online learning. Mindfulness is the popularized, Western version of Buddhist meditation and physical exercise designed to promote "the intentional focus of one's attention on the present moment in a nonjudgmental way."[6] Although the term is widely used for a much broader variety of skills development, this definition provides a narrow focus on the key attributes for a mindfulness regime.

Mindfulness is not primarily a school-based strategy to reduce anxiety and promote emotional well-being. Although there are dozens of programs in public schools around the country, mindfulness techniques are much more frequently used by individuals to deal with stress, pain, and emotional health. As such, mindfulness might be the ideal strategy for a family coping with the shift to the online environment.

Mindfulness has also undergone rigorous empirical testing. "Thousands of studies conducted throughout the past 20 years have demonstrated the effectiveness of mindfulness in treating a wide range of disorders, including depression, anxiety, post trauma traumatic stress disorder, eating disorders, chronic pain, and even psychosis."[7]

Professor Thomas Armstrong, author of *Mindfulness in the Classroom,* emphasizes in his book that mindfulness is itself an entirely secular exercise. Many uses of mindfulness are practiced in religious traditions. In public schools, instructors need to be respectful of the strict separation between church and state. When used in the home, families can adapt these practices to the family's belief systems. Professor Armstrong provides a helpful introduction:

> The essence of mindfulness is simple: by attending to the present moment with an attitude of acceptance, openness, and curiosity, we can train our minds, regulate our emotions, control our behaviors, and cultivate healthier relationships with the people and events around us. This process has three components. The first is *focus*. This could be a focus on our breathing, our bodily sensations, our eating, our walking, or any other tangible activity that we're engaged in during the course of the day. The second component is *open monitoring*, which involves the noticing our inner and outer experiences in whatever forms they happen to take, as they arise from the moment to moment within our awareness. The third component is *attitude*, and in particular, having an open, nonjudgmental, curious attitude towards whatever experience comes up as we practice.[8]

In *Meditation In Schools: Calmer Classrooms,* Gina Levete explains that "[m]editation practice can offer students an approach to help address the abstract needs of their inner being. Its discipline, in the best sense of the world, involves stillness and silence. From this position there can be a space for peace, wonder and awe."[9]

Parents can find a wide range of books, websites, and videos helping develop mindfulness techniques for the home. To add structure, during the 2020 pandemic, many people joined online mindfulness sessions to add camaraderie to the process of mindfulness training. Mindfulness is particularly important for online education because the stimulus of the computer screen may have a sensory effect that should be managed.

4. Parental Learning Objectives

As noted above, the student's academic program sets out a set of learning objectives intended to identify the particular knowledge, skills, and value development that the program and each course within the program is intended to achieve each year. The learning outcomes are often tied to the goals of grade-level achievement in primary and secondary education. For graduate and professional education, the learning outcomes are typically tied to the licensure requirements of the field or discipline.

Parents usually have goals regarding the development of their children as well. Parents' goals of skills, knowledge, and values may only loosely overlap with those of the formal educational institution. Despite this, because of the structural control school districts (or private schools) have over children under eighteen, the dictates of the school district generally drive the time and focus of a student's progress.

A small percentage of parents are sufficiently dissatisfied with these outcomes that they choose to home school their children. Others select private schools or charter schools with objectives that align more closely with the parents' desires.

All parents can supplement the learning objectives of their children's schools, but there is a difference when learning moves online. Rightly or wrongly, most public school systems operate as if they have the exclusive control over their students' learning outcomes. In online education, in contrast, the school districts operate with the more accurate understanding that they play a part in their students' education, but they are not the exclusive vehicle for learning.

Parents can seize the opportunity to take a much larger role in shaping their students' educational goals. In the United States, parents, of course, have exclusive control over the religious education and training of their children. The mindfulness training, discussed above, provides another example. Parents also manage their children's skill developments through the choice of which extracurricular teams, clubs, and social organizations they support for their children.

In the online setting, the gaps in the school district programs provide an opportunity for parents to take on additional roles, if they so choose. Classrooms are not particularly good at instilling resilience and grit, essential skills for adulthood. Parents can work with volunteer organizations to engage their children in long-term projects that promote these skills. Parents can bring arts and crafts projects such as sewing or model building, musical instruments, second languages, family history exploration, or robotics into the home to encourage the development of essential skills, important values, and additional knowledge. And as discussed earlier, students need to develop their digital literacy, so reading programs in the house can be used to help students improve their reading and develop the digital literacy skills to be able to qualify the sources from which they are learning their news and information.

Like the school districts and instructors, parents can do this best by creating a set of learning objectives for each of their children each year. Homeschooling resources may help with this. By articulating what is truly important in the household using the annual identification of the skills, knowledge, and values, parents can work with their children to establish their shared priorities.

Chapter 6

Equity and Equality for Online and Blended Education

A. ACCESSIBILITY

Equal access to education is both a form of inclusion and a legal requirement. Parents who have children with short-term medical issues or long-term special needs learn very quickly that the laws protecting their student's rights to education are essential to ensure that school programs provide their children services sufficient to allow their children to thrive in their educational environment. Equal access to education is protected by numerous federal laws including the Americans with Disabilities Act (ADA), the Rehabilitation Act of 1973, and many others. These legal obligations require schools to provide accommodations in order to eliminate the barriers to the student's education.

1. Section 504 Requirements

Section 504 of the Rehabilitation Act requires that students with a disability are entitled to free and appropriate public education (FAPE). The prohibition is very broad: "No otherwise qualified individual with a disability in the United States . . . shall, solely by reason of her or his disability, be excluded from the participation in, be denied the benefits of, or be subjected to discrimination under any program or activity receiving Federal financial assistance."[1] Under the regulations, to be a qualifying disability, the impairment must substantially limit one or more major life activities.

Substantial impairment and the list of major life activities are broadly defined. The regulations provide a non-exhaustive list of examples of major life activities: caring for oneself, performing manual tasks, seeing, hearing, eating, sleeping, walking, standing, sitting, reaching, lifting, bending, speaking, breathing, learning, reading, concentrating, thinking, communicating, interacting with others, and working. There are many others.

Once a student is qualified, the educational institution must provide meaningful opportunities to the student to participate. Common examples of accommodations include note takers, quiet testing rooms, additional time on timed tests, adjusted seating arrangements to see the front of the classroom, digital texts, sign language interpreters, and adherence to the Web Content Accessibility Guidelines (WCAG) 2.0 standards for website accessibility.

The educational institution will typically evaluate the documentation of the disability and then work with the student or student's family to develop the appropriate accommodation.

2. Americans with Disabilities Act

In addition to the Rehabilitation Act, the Americans with Disabilities Act (ADA) also requires that students be provided with accessible classrooms, websites, and other services. The ADA "dictates details in classroom design, teaching strategies, and the use of technological aids. ADA compliance also requires using communications tools, such as captioning and transcription services, to convey important information."[2] Creating an effective classroom for students with disabilities requires more than inclusion, but also equitable focus:

> As an educator, activities, lessons, and instructional techniques in the classroom cannot be geared towards simply reaching a broad group of children. Instead, ADA compliance in education requires you to pay close attention to the needs of students with disabilities. This includes:
>
> • Ensuring all students have the opportunity to take part in and benefit from school programs and services.
> • Providing students with disabilities the same types of opportunities and experiences other students enjoy.
> • Making sure the quality of services and benefits provided is equal to those received by other students.
> • Emphasizing classroom accessibility and providing the proper equipment to increase the student's comfort and chances for success.[3]

Parents are critical partners in helping teachers and schools provide truly inclusive educational opportunities for their children. Each child is unique, and general approaches to accommodation may often need modification to be effective. When the parents collaborate with the teachers on how best to achieve these goals, the students will receive the most robust opportunities for engagement in the classroom or online environment.

Special education covers a much broader category of needs than accessibility resources for students with a sensory deficit. A student who has one or more disabilities is eligible for special education support if the student's disabilities adversely affect the student's educational performance. Students who have needs that cannot be addressed through general education resources, even with accommodations, are then eligible for additional or individualized instruction, though these rules will vary by state.

The Individuals with Disabilities Education Act (IDEA) is the federal program that both requires states to provide free, public education to eligible children with disabilities and helps fund the state costs for the special education expenses. While great in theory, the Department of Education recognizes that the majority of jurisdictions fall below the federal expectation of performance. Educational resources are scarce, and adoption of individualized resources to online education has been a slow, difficult process. Eligible students must first receive a comprehensive evaluation to assess the learning and cognitive development of the student. The results of the evaluations are then used by the school and the parents to develop the Individualized Education Plan (IEP) appropriate for the student's learning.

The goal of IDEA is to promote the access to general education in the least restrictive environment. For in-person education, there is a great deal of focus on the placement of the student into developmentally appropriate classes. Today, through the use of assistive technology and accommodations, most students are successful in general education courses. At the same time, many students need special education instruction during part of the school week, and some students require substantially more individualized instruction.

In addition to the educational assistance, eligible students should also receive related services to assist the student develop the fundamental skills essential to the student's education. These can include transportation services, speech-language therapy, occupational therapy, mental health counseling, social work, and similar services.

Increasingly, the use of assistive technologies can greatly reduce the need for students to enroll in specialized classes. Under the Assistive Technology Act of 2004, assistive technology is a very broadly defined term to mean any technology "that is used to increase, maintain, or improve functional capabilities of individuals with disabilities." These can range from wheelchairs to iPads, including general-purpose tools and machines that can be modified for additional use by people with disabilities.

Readers and remote devices can greatly benefit students with certain needs. Touch screens, signal lights, text-to-speech software, and other devices have been used for many years. Braille keyboards and smartphones, socially assistive robots, and communications tools are beginning to make a difference for some students. Other technologies such as QR codes and LMS links help students access content more easily. As devices enable students to interact with their instructional material using modalities such as body gestures or touch screens, even more students will benefit from the ability to interact with their content.

In the online setting, the use of recorded live classes can create a new way for students to participate in the live Zoom sessions and then receive the needed accommodations outside of the live, online time.

Academic research, however, suggests that some teachers may be reluctant to adopt new technologies based on their own training, the school's technological infrastructure, or the school culture. In addition to having the financial resources to purchase the relevant equipment, effective special education strategies should be sure to include plans to train the teachers, to help build the use of the technology into the lesson plans for the curriculum, and to assess the effectiveness of each technology to ensure that it provides the best tool to address the learning goals of the student. When the student, the teachers, and the families are comfortable with the technology, the potential for its usefulness increases significantly.

3. IEP Requirements under IDEA

In addition to the ADA and Rehabilitation Act, the federal government subsidizes the states' efforts to provide educational opportunities to students with disabilities through IDEA. As the American Psychological Association explains, "Prior to IDEA, over 4 million children with disabilities were denied appropriate access to public education. Many children were denied entry into public school altogether, while others were placed in segregated classrooms, or in regular classrooms without adequate support for their special needs."[4]

IDEA helps states meet the financial demands of providing free education to students with disabilities between the ages of three and twenty-one. To receive the funds, states must meet six criteria:

- Every child is entitled to a free and appropriate public education (FAPE).
- When a school professional believes that a student between the ages of three and twenty-one may have a disability that has substantial impact on the student's learning or behavior, the student is entitled to an evaluation in all areas related to the suspected disability.
- Creation of an Individualized Education Plan (IEP). The purpose of the IEP is to lay out a series of specific actions and steps through which educational providers, parents, and the student themselves may reach the child's stated goals.
- That the education and services for children with disabilities must be provided in the least restrictive environment, and if possible, those children be placed in a "typical" education setting with nondisabled students.

- Input of the child and their parents must be taken into account in the education process.
- When a parent feels that an IEP is inappropriate for their child, or that their child is not receiving needed services, they have the right under IDEA to challenge their child's treatment (due process).[5]

For the purposes of IDEA, the criterion to determine eligibility is whether the disability adversely affects educational performance. If the disability impairs the educational performance, then an IEP is the appropriate method for addressing the situation. In contrast, if a student has a qualifying disability that does not affect educational performance, then the educational institution must still provide reasonable accommodations, just without establishing an IEP to put those accommodations in place. For example, if a student breaks her arm, the reasonable accommodation of a note taker can be utilized without first creating an IEP.

In most cases, using an IEP will provide a more comprehensive strategy to address the disability of the student. At the same time, however, the IEP process is more complex and cumbersome than requesting disability accommodations.

The IEP process begins with the school evaluating the student to determine eligibility and need. Within thirty days of determining the student is eligible (and annually thereafter), the school must meet with the student and parents. The school will use a team of educators and staff to attend the meeting with the parents to determine the IEP. The outcome of the meeting is a written IEP plan. The plan should have learning goals, strategies for the student to meet the goals, and all accommodations to assist the student in meeting the objectives spelled out clearly.

The IEP will include a number of components. It will identify the child's present level of academic performance and achievement to help establish a common understanding about the student's academic, social, and physical abilities. It may include everyday activities in addition to academics. The IEP will also include the proposed individualized instruction plan, the related services to be provided by the school, accommodations in the teaching and learning environment, and other aspects of the plan to assist the student.

Ideally, the plan developed is agreed upon by both the school and parents. In some schools, voluntary mediation is used if the plan cannot be negotiated at the meeting. Parents may also file a complaint with the state education agency, requesting a due process hearing if other efforts at reaching agreement have been unsuccessful.

Once agreed upon, the plan must be followed diligently by the school. The parents should closely monitor the accommodations and adjustments required under the plan to ensure the plan is followed correctly. Despite the federal

funding, schools are often hard-pressed to pay for the individualized accommodations and instructors, and their institutions often look for opportunities
to drop plans or reduce costs. Students need to be protected from losing their
protections under the IEP plans. Special care needs to be taken for students
with continuing plans who turn eighteen, because the student may be asked to
waive the protections negotiated by the student's parent, stripping the student
of the protections that are legally offered until the age of twenty-one.

4. Online Education Accommodations

With the rapid transition to online education in 2020, many families were
caught off guard. Although there are accessibility standards for online education, many IEPs had not previously taken online education into account
because the modality was not a significant part of the student's educational
plan. When the plans changed, so did the importance of accommodating the
students who had barriers to access of the online content.

The standards for website availability were derived from the Web Content
Accessibility Guidelines (WCAG), developed through collaboration between
the Web Accessibility Initiative (WAI) of the World Wide Web Consortium
(W3C), the primary international standards organization for the Internet. The
guidelines have been developed following four key principles for web accessibility: perceivable, operable, understandable, and robust. Perceivable means
that the content must be both visually and auditorily accessible. Operable
requires that websites work with various devices such as text readers, magni-
fier, or pointer devices that help people with disabilities. Understandability
requires that the web should have both the information and the operation of
the website readily understandable by the users. Finally, robust refers to the
requirement that the website is compatible with a wide variety of assistive
technologies and other user devices, and updated so that improvements in the
assistive devices will be able to continue to take advantage of the websites.
While these four principles are straightforward, the WCAG 2.1 standards
have many detailed standards and technical requirements.[6]

Initially, the WCAG guidelines were developed as voluntary, recommended standards. Since then, however, they have been adopted by the
International Organization for Standardization (ISO) as a standard and incorporated into the regulations under section 508 of the Rehabilitation Act and
its technical counterpart, section 255 of the Telecommunications Act. As a
result, companies building websites, apps, and online equipment for education or commerce in the United States should be developing them to be compatible with these standards. The standards have been updated to WCAG 2.1.

There are two steps needed to ensure compliance with accessibility under
WCAG 2.1. First, at the institutional level, the educational institution must

be sure that all technology purchased or licensed complies with the minimum standards required by the Rehabilitation Act and the institutions' obligations to meet IEP objectives and accommodation requests. Many school districts and universities did not initially develop their systems with accessibility in mind, but vendor support and regulatory pressure have brought most institutions into line.

Second, the instructional designers and individual instructors must be diligent to ensure that each file and page added to a course is also accessible. The major commercial LMS systems are all quite adept at meeting the obligations to provide accessibility. But the LMS systems allow each individual instructor to edit and adjust the course website, and this can create many problems.

The University of Oregon has collected an excellent set of suggestions based closely on the WCAG 2.0 and 2.1 Standards.[7] Each instructor should use these guides as checklists when updating their LMS or adding content to their site.

Perceivable—Users must be able to perceive the information being presented. It can't be invisible to all of their senses.

- Add alt text to images and visuals
- Close caption videos and provide transcripts for audio
- Provide sufficient color contrast between text and backgrounds
- Make sure content doesn't rely on color alone

Operable—Users must be able to operate the interface and navigation. The interface cannot require interaction that a user cannot perform.

- Provide clear structure with properly marked headings
- Create descriptive links that make sense out of context
- Provide sufficient time for interaction and response
- Avoid content that can trigger seizures

Understandable—Users must be able to understand the information as well as the operation of the user interface. The content or operation cannot be beyond their understanding.

- Clarify expctations through clear directions and models
- Follow conventions to ensure a predictable and consistent experience
- Use plain language
- Indicate the language of your content[8]

These are all excellent suggestions for instructors, and they provide parents a set of reasonable expectations, if they find their students are struggling with the content being provided to them. At a minimum, instructors should be sure to close caption the videos and use Word, Google Docs, or HTML web pages rather than PDF documents for content. PDF documents can be used if they are checked for accessibility, but unless the instructor has an Acrobat Pro account, it is better to avoid PDFs or to use them as duplicates for HTML web pages. Microsoft PowerPoint also has an accessibility checker built into the software to ensure that the image-heavy use of PowerPoints can be accessed.

B. SPECIAL EDUCATION UNDER IDEA

Special education covers a much broader category of needs than accessibility resources for students with a sensory deficit. A student who has one or more disabilities is eligible for special education support if the student's disabilities adversely affect the student's educational performance. Students who have needs that cannot be addressed through general education resources, even with accommodations, are then eligible for additional or individualized instruction, though these rules will vary by state.

At noted above, IDEA is the federal program that both requires states to provide free, public education to eligible children with disabilities and helps fund the state costs for the special education expenses. While great in theory, the Department of Education recognizes that the majority of jurisdictions fall below the federal expectation of performance. Educational resources are scarce, and adoption of individualized resources to online education has been a slow, difficult process.

Eligible students must first receive a comprehensive evaluation to assess the learning and cognitive development of the student. The results of the evaluations are then used by the school and the parents to develop the IEP appropriate for the student's learning.

The goal of IDEA is to promote the access to general education in the least restrictive environment. For in-person education, there is a great deal of focus on the placement of the student into developmentally appropriate classes. Today, through the use of assistive technology and accommodations, most students are successful in general education courses. At the same time, many students need special education instruction during part of the school week, and some students require substantially more individualized instruction.

In addition to the educational assistance, eligible students should also receive related services to assist the student develop the fundamental skills essential to the student's education. These can include transportation services, speech-language therapy, occupational therapy, mental health counseling, social work, and similar services.

Through ongoing innovation and reduced production costs, the use of assistive technologies can greatly reduce the need for students to enroll in specialized classes. Under the Assistive Technology Act of 2004, assistive technology is a very broadly defined term to mean any technology "that is used to increase, maintain, or improve functional capabilities of individuals with disabilities." These can range from wheelchairs to iPads, including general-purpose tools and machines that can be modified for additional use by people with disabilities.

Readers and remote devices can greatly benefit students with certain needs. Touch screens, signal lights, text-to-speech software and other devices have been used for many years. Braille keyboards and smartphones, socially assistive robots, and communications tools are beginning to make a difference for some students. Other technologies such as QR codes and LMS links help students access content more easily. As devices enable students to interact with their instructional material using modalities such as body gestures or touch screens, even more students will benefit from the ability to interact with their content.

In the online setting, the use of recorded live classes can create a new way for students to participate in the live Zoom sessions and then receive the needed accommodations outside of the live, online time.

Academic research, however, suggests that some teachers may be reluctant to adopt new technologies based on their own training, the school's technological infrastructure, or the school culture. In addition to having the financial resources to purchase the relevant equipment, effective special education strategies should be sure to include plans to train the teachers, to help build the use of the technology into the lesson plans for the curriculum, and to assess the effectiveness of each technology to ensure that it provides the best tool to address the learning goals of the student. When the student, the teachers, and the families are comfortable with the technology, the potential for its usefulness increases significantly.

C. THE DIGITAL DIVIDE

Just as every parent is concerned about their own child's access to educational resources, every community should be concerned that all students in that community have the tools and support needed for its children to succeed. Unfortunately, the data highlight that in most communities, there are significant gaps based on economic and racial disparities. Since the 1990s, the term "digital divide" has been used to highlight the patterns of inequity in access to computers, high-speed Internet connections, training, and other resources. Although the price of computers and mobile devices has dropped considerably from the 1980s, there is still a substantial cost to owning and staying current with the technology used in the classroom. Parents and educators need to understand these systemic barriers in order to make intentional choices to remove the inequities in the digital economy and the system of education.

The National Telecommunications and Information Administration (NTIA) tracked household broadband for households with school-aged children. In 2019, slightly more than 26 percent of household did not have Internet at home.[9]

Adults in management or professional careers have a much greater need for fast Internet connections. Non-hourly employees tend to take work home and prioritize the technology in the household. According to the Federal Bureau of Labor statistics, 54 percent of employed Asians and 41 percent of employed whites worked in management, professional, and related occupations. In comparison, 31 percent of employed Blacks and 22 percent of employed Hispanics worked in this sector, which is the highest-paying occupational category. As a result, both resources and need are separated along racial lines.

Across the nation, most school districts are funded through local property taxes. As a result, in wealthier districts, school systems can afford to purchase and maintain computers for their students. These are the same districts that have a higher median income, meaning the families have greater resources to purchase personal equipment for the home as well. In poorer neighborhoods, there is less money for computers and Internet services and less tax revenue to support the school district's efforts to make up the gap.

"Black and Hispanic adults remain less likely than whites to say they own a traditional computer or have high speed internet at home, according to a Pew Research Center survey conducted in early 2019."[10] Students who have more access to technology in their homes are likely to use the tools much more frequently. Having a single home computer might be sufficient in a home where that computer is not used by the parents for work and most homework is completed in notebooks, but when every member of the household needs to be online, owning a single computer will leave each family member frustrated.

The data correlate quite well with the professional employment data. In total, 82 percent of whites reported "owning a desktop or laptop computer, compared with 58% of Blacks and 57% of Hispanics."[11] The difference among racial and ethnic differences in broadband adoption were substantial, but not as great, with 79 percent of whites, 66 percent of Blacks, and 61 percent of Hispanics using broadband in the home.[12]

Those without home computers or laptops and without broadband are much more likely to rely on smartphones to connect online. Smartphones provide excellent tools for some online activities, but they do not provide a quality platform for using digital texts, writing essays, and studying complex material. In addition, many smartphone plans use metered connections, meaning that the cost for access can become very high with heavy usage.

Students who do not have the resources at home often turn to computer labs in their schools and libraries. During the 2020 pandemic, however, these facilities were often shut down or their hours heavily curtailed. Library staff have reported seeing cars parked near their closed facilities as members of the public tried to piggyback on open Internet connections.

The federal Computers for Learning program is among the largest national efforts to reduce the gap. Begun in 1999, it allows federal agencies to provide their computers and equipment to qualifying K-12 school districts and educational nonprofit agencies for redistribution. The organizations can select equipment from the database of available equipment, provided that the organization can pick up the equipment within fifteen days of the order. Since the schools or nonprofits are responsible for the transportation costs of the equipment, the organizations must have a plan to address the logistical needs of getting the machines. In addition, since these are decommissioned government surplus, the equipment may be less than ideal for the schools or individual students.

In addition to the federal surplus program, a handful of nonprofit charities have begun to address the situation by providing free or low-cost computers to the neediest of families. Generally, a family has to be eligible for an income-based government assistance program to qualify for the machines. This reflects only a fraction of the public in need of computers, and these programs are generally designed to get the first computer into a household. As a result, these programs do not come close to addressing the structural gap created by a lack of technology in the homes of millions of families.

The redistribution of computers is a helpful supplement to the problem, but it does not address the lack of broadband access. Many of the Internet Service Providers (ISPs) offer low monthly rates, often below $10.00 per month. The eligibility restrictions vary by provider. These programs often incorporate speed or bandwidth restrictions. The Federal Communications Commission (FCC) Lifeline program provides a $9.25 monthly discounted rate on online telephone, wireless, or Internet line. There is a limit of one Lifeline service per household. The program is available only for those with income at or below 135 percent of the Federal Poverty Guidelines.

The digital divide, first identified in the 1990s, has not been substantially eradicated. The impact on students during the 2020 pandemic has been profound, and it highlights the need for a substantial reassessment of the manner in which society addresses the inequities of private access to the public need. The effect on educational performance and digital literacy are profound, and these will not change if the public does not have access to the basic tools essential to be part of the modern economy.

D. DIVERSITY AND INCLUSION

As noted above, the digital divide cuts across both economic divisions and racial divisions. For online technology there is also a gender divide, with far fewer female students participating in eSports and other online activities than their male counterparts. The World Web Foundation reports that "men remain 21% more likely to be online than women, rising to 52% in the world's least developed countries."[13] In the United States, both men and women use the Internet in nearly equal numbers, but how they use it and how they are respected online may be significantly different.

Given the challenges of gender, racial, LGBTQ, and economic disparities in the classroom, the educational institution and the individual instructor have a significant challenge creating inclusive and equitable educational opportunities for all their students. Many of these same challenges exist in both online and in-person instruction. Instructors must always be attentive to behaviors from students that would put down other students and create teachable moments out of comments that are insensitive or pejorative. Parents must strive to be collaborative partners with their children's teachers, helping reinforce the importance of inclusion and equity in the classroom.

The Columbia Center for Teaching and Learning suggests five principles that will help establish an inclusive online classroom:

- Principle 1: Establish and support a class climate that fosters belonging for all students.
- Principle 2: Set explicit student expectations.
- Principle 3: Select course content that recognizes diversity and acknowledges barriers to inclusion.
- Principle 4: Design all course elements for accessibility.
- Principle 5: Reflect on one's beliefs about teaching (online) to maximize self-awareness and commitment to inclusion.[14]

Although the guide was developed for college course design, these principles provide a solid framework for academic programs for students of all ages.

1. Recognizing Diversity in the Course Design and Content

Effective course design begins with the identification of a course's learning objectives, in terms of knowledge, skills, and values. Diversity and inclusion should be a universal value in education, along with respect for fellow students, collaboration, honesty, and mutual respect.

In some courses, such as the United States or World History, issues of equality are appropriate as the learning outcome knowledge goals for the course. In other courses, such as math, the subject matter may not lend itself to the same learning outcomes for the knowledge or skills. Where there is an opportunity to make diversity and inclusion one of the learning goals, instructors should be sure to do so, and parents should actively ensure this is done.

In all courses, the choice of assigned content drives most of the learning outcomes, so it is critical that the content chosen for a course reflects the goals of diversity, inclusion, and equity. College faculty have much more flexibility than primary and secondary instructors on selecting the course content, but even in public school systems, there is an opportunity to add readings and assignments that highlight an inclusive approach to the content. Instructors can accomplish this by ensuring diversity in the authors read by the students, by using examples that reflect on a multiplicity of cultures and viewpoints, and by using student assignments that let the students find and reflect on the sources used.

Parents can play an important role as well. Parents can supplement the in-school materials with authors and perspectives of importance to each family's priorities. Even brief discussions during the semester can reinforce these values being taught within the school can highlight the perspectives important to that family and reinforce the priority of diversity and inclusion.

2. Fostering Belonging for All Students

An inclusive classroom begins with a strong rapport between the instructor and the students, and it fosters a strong rapport among students. This begins by reducing anonymity for the students, which serves to reinforce each student's identity and tends to discourage inappropriate, anonymous behavior.

Teaching with the cameras on reminds students that they are visible and active participants in the classroom. Addressing each student by name and using ice-breakers helps personalize the experience and connect with the unique experience each student brings to the classroom. Using discussion boards and other opportunities to let students bring their own experience and worldview into the classroom reinforces the values of each student's unique identity and fosters a sense of pride in the student's personal history.

Teachers often create such opportunities for younger students with exercises that ask the students to provide a history of a grandparent or other relative, using the event to share personal stories and develop understanding. Projects such as this can be adapted to online projects and expanded to explore age-appropriate themes relevant to personal identity and American history.

Teachers should always be mindful to model inclusive behavior. Online texts and materials increase the ability to include a wide range of resources for students. The use of chats in online sessions allows more students to respond to a question. By using the chat function, the online classroom becomes less prone to be captured by students who are the fastest at raising their hands.

For parents, fostering belonging can be reinforced by connecting with the children's teachers and with fellow parents, particularly parents who may not be in the children's social circle. Teachers can consider creating the occasional small assignment that randomly assigns the students and their parents to collaborate as a way to build community and create new connections.

Just like instructors, parents should be mindful of their children's online behavior. If the children are teasing other students, using harmful language, or taking insensitive actions, the parents should be the first to address the situation. When parents set their own expectations of mutual respect, inclusion, and adherence to the Golden Rule, students are much more likely to follow.

Chapter 7

Beyond High School—the Professional Online Presence

A. INTRODUCTION

Many teens develop websites during middle school or high school as projects, and nearly all have accounts on multiple social media sites. They will likely also have public profiles on a variety of gaming platforms. These activities create a public presence for the teen. While the digital media presence for a thirteen-year-old might be cute, it may not reflect the person's growth and development at the time of a college application or application to medical school. Social media and online content do not reflect on the growth and development of their users particularly well.

For a teen looking to enter college or the workforce, the legacy content from earlier online activities might now be embarrassing or harmful to future prospects. As a result, it is very important that teens reassess their digital media portfolio at each milestone in their personal growth.

B. NAVIGATING MODERN SOCIAL MEDIA'S CANCEL CULTURE

Teens and their families must also reconcile that they are coming of age in what has been described as the age of outrage and the "cancel culture." The fracturing of mass media and the use of social media often create what has been described as an echo chamber effect where people have their own points of view reinforced and lose the interactions with those who have different backgrounds and different beliefs.

As the interactions become less direct and personal, social media have increasingly responded with a heightened, sometimes artificial sense of moral indignation for the actions of others. Mass media has followed and reinforced these trends with a spate of talk shows that sometimes appear to be news media, when instead they are produced as cheap entertainment filler designed to substitute for the decline in investigative reporting and professional journalism. The social media outrage and the entertainers holding forth on news channels have reinforced this tribalistic trend.

The tribalism is fueled by the power of social media to publicly shame individuals. This public shaming is often described as "canceling" someone, which seems more palatable than asking the person to wear a scarlet letter.[1]

The *Merriam-Webster* dictionary provides this explanation:

> To cancel someone (usually a celebrity or other well-known figure) means to stop giving support to that person. The act of canceling could entail boycotting an actor's movies or no longer reading or promoting a writer's works. The reason for cancellation can vary, but it usually is due to the person in question having expressed an objectionable opinion, or having conducted themselves in a way that is unacceptable, so that continuing to patronize that person's work leaves a bitter taste . . . Lisa Nakamura, a professor in the Department of American Cultures at the University of Michigan, [explains], "People talk about the attention economy—when you deprive someone of your attention, you're depriving them of a livelihood."[2]

Tribalism and public shaming are not something new. The very structure of the U.S. Constitution was designed to prevent popular majorities from transforming into tyrannies by limiting majority power through a myriad of checks and balances designed to limit any majority's passions of the moment.

In 2015, for example, no college publicly acknowledged that it used an admitted student's social media presence to revoke the student's admissions. Yet, by that time it had become a common practice for colleges to review the public Facebook page and other social media accounts supplied by the student to round out the application. While it might have had an influence on the student's likelihood of admission, the factors influencing decisions were neither made public nor revealed to student applicants.

In 2020, in contrast, Cornell University, Harvard University, Marquette University, University of Florida, Xavier University, and others each rescinded acceptances for students due to their social media posts. In most cases, these schools responded to racist posts by newly admitted students following the murder of George Floyd in Minneapolis, in May 2020. In other cases, the schools responded to social media involving sexist or misogynist content. Additional schools addressed offensive social media posts by using their code of conduct policies or by encouraging the students to voluntarily withdraw. Critics of the university responses noted that the enrollment rescissions served as the perfect example of the cancel culture in action.

Schools concerned about the speech rights of the incoming students chose to address the offensive content rather than punishing the incoming students. Clifton Smart, president of Missouri State University, for example, wrote a blog post to explain why he did not order the rescission of enrollment offers from students who posted highly offensive material. Although he wrote that he was horrified by the posts, he felt the First Amendment rights of the students would be violated. He also explained that it was the role of the university to educate rather than punish. "We cannot expect or require that students come to us fully formed, possessing all of the skills and characteristics that exemplify Citizen Scholars. It is our job and our duty to help them develop these traits through education and exposure."[3]

For teens entering college or the workforce in the current environment, it is important that they recognize the reality of the environment and respond appropriately. Although it has always been important to have a positive social media presence, the harsh language often found in social media fights will have a profoundly different presentation when appended by an institutional representative to a job or college application.

C. HOW EMPLOYERS AND UNIVERSITIES USE APPLICANTS' ONLINE PRESENCE

For both prospective employers and college admissions offices, there is a strong incentive to pay attention to the social media presence of their applicants. While 34 percent of employers had already begun to use social media in their hiring reviews by 2008, by 2013 that number had increased to 77 percent.[4] As a general starting point, applicants should recognize that anything made publicly available online is available to prospective employers and collegiate admissions offices. Or to steal from the famous Miranda warning given to criminal suspects, "anything you say can and will be used against you."

1. Employers

Employers must be mindful of their obligations under antidiscrimination laws not to use access to social media as a way to learn information that legally cannot be used in the hiring process.

Companies are concerned that if adverse material information about a potential hire is readily available on the Internet and overlooked, then the company could be subject to public embarrassment and potential liability. To avoid such risks, employers will screen out those candidates who post inappropriate photographs, drug use, discriminatory comments, false qualifications, confidential information, or disparaging comments about their current employer.

At the same time, the information on social media can disclose a candidate's religious affiliation, age, gender, sexual preference, veteran's status, disabilities, and other attributes that cannot be legally used in the decision to hire the person, set pay, or determine the terms and conditions of employment. The online information may not be used to discriminate without violating the Federal Equal Employment Opportunity Laws (including Title VII of the Civil Rights Act of 1964; the Equal Pay Act of 1963; the Age Discrimination in Employment Act of 1967; the Americans with Disabilities Act of 1990; the Rehabilitation Act of 1973; and the Civil Rights Act of 1991) along with additional state laws.[5]

In the employment setting, the employer can help manage the risks of using social media in a discriminatory fashion by having someone in the human resources (HR) department do the online screening who is not part of the hiring process. The HR screener can report whether the review came back clean or report on particular red flags without discussing the race, disabilities, or other types of information that might lead to a discriminatory adverse decision.

Prospective employees must be very mindful that employers are looking for these red flags when choosing among candidates. No one wants to hire employees who speak poorly of their current employers. Nor will employers be keen to select candidates who are not careful about photographs featuring alcohol or drug usage. Employers also want to avoid controversy and conflict in their workforce. Racist, sexist, homophobic, or inflammatory language will suggest that the prospective employee will not be conducive to a collegial work environment.

Although the antidiscrimination laws apply to private employers, the First Amendment's right of free speech does not. Employers have very wide latitude to decide whether or not to hire someone. Even if the employer is a governmental entity, there is little case law to suggest that the government is prohibited from using a candidate's social media as a factor in deciding not to employ the individual. Public employees do have the right to speak as private citizens on matters of public concern, so hiring procedures should respect this basic right. The HR departments of public employers will tend to view such right much as they do the other protections of antidiscrimination laws.[6]

2. Colleges and Universities

The laws regulating university admissions are somewhat less restrictive than for those of hiring. In addition to reviewing a college applicant's grades and standardized test scores, college admissions offices review personal statements, references, applications, and backgrounds in order to distinguish students who stand out from students who are less exceptional. Schools may look at criteria such as maturity, personality, and community engagement to help them shape the class. Other schools will emphasize a student's history in overcoming adversity as an additional criterion.

Selective colleges often use race and gender criteria to ensure that the admissions profile of the entering class reflects the diversity sought by the institution in its student body. Diversity, unlike discrimination, remains legal. "The Supreme Court has held that attaining student body diversity may be a compelling interest."[7] The Supreme Court has sided with public and private universities as they build admissions profiles that reflect the importance of racial diversity in "promoting cross-racial understanding, breaking down racial stereotypes, fostering a robust exchange of ideas, cultivating 'a set of leaders with legitimacy in the eyes of the citizenry,' exposing them to different cultures, and preparing them for the challenges of an increasingly diverse workforce."[8] The rules set out by the Supreme Court require that race cannot be used alone or applied in a mechanical manner that guarantees or bars applicants based on race. Instead, the requirements must be narrowly tailored to the clear and concrete goals of the institution's admissions policies.

As a result, selective colleges are keenly interested in the race of their applicants, as well as other indicators of diversity used to create a well-balanced entering class. Colleges routinely use social media as a tool to explore these issues and ensure that the candidates who are applying match the application submitted. The 2019 admissions scandal involving a conspiracy among rich parents to buy seats for their children has only increased the diligence of college admissions offices to be sure that external admissions coaches are not trying to create false profiles for the applicants.[9]

Colleges, of course, cannot discriminate against particular students based on their race, gender, nationality, religion, sexual identity, disability, marital status, or military status.[10] As such, like employers, they need to take care that their use of social media content does not lead to allegations that they have used the social media profiles to eliminate applicants from consideration based on these factors.

For public universities, there is an unanswered question whether the use of a student's social media posts to rescind an offer of admission violates the student's First Amendment rights. Public universities recognize that their students have free speech rights. To be fully compliant with the First Amendment, public universities must tailor their codes of conduct to punish only narrowly defined forms of offensive speech, which amounts to fighting words, true threats, and incitement to violence. They can also penalize speech if it creates a hostile educational environment, meaning that penalty is for speech and conduct that is severe, persistent, or pervasive enough to create a hostile environment.

Finally, public universities can ensure that the conduct in the classroom is appropriate for the educational objectives of instruction. The university has much more authority to punish offensive speech or behavior that occurs in the classroom than when the statements are off campus or online. Despite these three spheres of authority, many policies go further. When it comes to public universities, there is continuing doubt whether these more intrusive policies are constitutional.

The same concerns are equally true of the actions to rescind applications based on precollegiate social media posts. Professor Clay Calvert, however, suggests that the First Amendment rights of the university and its constitutional right to control admissions provides a countervailing interest that allows public universities to rescind admissions based on the public social media of the candidates.[11] He notes that the Supreme Court has recognized the First Amendment rights of the academic institutions, as well as the constitutionally recognized academic freedom to control the university's faculty hiring and student admissions policies.[12] Undoubtedly, this is an area where public universities will find themselves tested in the courts if the use of social media continues to be the source of admissions rescissions in years to come.

3. Limits on Social Media Review

While there is no limit to the social media review for content that the candidate has made publicly available, some employers have gone further. Some employers and even some colleges have sought to review the private accounts of their candidates. In response, twenty-six states have barred employers from requesting access to employees' or potential employees' social media accounts. Sixteen states have enacted similar laws to protect college applicants. There is no federal law prohibiting the practices, but the pressure from the states may have stopped most employers from using the technique. Since most colleges recruit from multiple states, the variety of state laws has essentially ended the practice. In addition to the state law protections, the sharing of the password is a violation of the terms of service agreement with most social media companies. The request, therefore, also might violate the Federal Trade Commission Act as an unfair or deceptive trade practice. Applicants who are asked to provide private passwords should report the school to the social media company and to the FTC.

Only slightly less intrusive than asking for an applicant's password, some prospective employers and colleges would ask the candidate to sign into their account so that the interviewer could "look over their shoulder" and take a peek at the private content on the social media sites. This practice, known as shoulder surfing, is also prohibited by some of the states that protect employee privacy, but there are fewer legal protections against the practice. Nonetheless, it remains an invasion of privacy, raising concerns related to discriminatory hiring or unfair trade practices.

Prospective employers and universities will also use friend requests to connect and learn more about candidates. Some of the states that prohibit employer or university access to social media accounts also prohibit the employers or universities from requiring that the company be added to the list of friends or contacts. Most states, however, do not bar this type of request and none of the states prohibit the candidate from voluntarily agreeing to friending the prospective employer or university.

To the contrary, many job opportunities arise through the social media network of job seekers. Few job candidates would refuse to friend someone at the company where they are hoping to work. Nonetheless, this can create yet another point of access for the prospective employer or university to gain access to posts that were not intended to be shared publicly.

Employers also have the right to whatever information they can acquire elsewhere. For example, many employers will use credit checks and criminal background checks as part of the employment process. While there are regulations specifying that the job applicant must be notified of these inquiries and detailing how the search information may be used, both credit and criminal checks are available to employers. Fortunately, universities do not use these tools for their admissions practices.

Finally, both employers and universities will use information provided to them by third parties. It does not matter if the candidate had never intended for the message to go public. This means that if a candidate sends a private message to a friend or posts an Instagram "view once" message that the recipient captures, then that recipient can forward it. Most of the publicly announced rescissions of college acceptance letters were triggered by public outrage at the students' posts. Members of the public sent the offending messages to the universities, putting pressure on the universities to respond publicly.

D. WHAT TO BUILD

For the candidate who wants to create a great impression, there are a number of steps that can help create a positive online presence. The best set of online tools will depend on the nature of the candidate's interest and focus. A college athlete's profile will look very different from that of an art student who wishes to feature a digital portfolio.

For students competing to get into selective universities or competing for jobs, the candidate needs a resume. Unfortunately, resumes are not universal.

A candidate needs to specify a resume for a particular job. The focus needed in a job resume will not present the candidate well as part of a college application. To help manage the use of different resumes, the candidate should use different social media tools to present different resumes.

1. Professional Social Media

The first stop for a professional online presence is LinkedIn. LinkedIn is the world's largest professional social media site. The very size makes it somewhat unwieldy, yet it remains a very helpful first step in building a professional presence. The content is mostly professional in nature, which means that unlike Facebook, Instagram, or Tumblr, there are no significant concerns when employers and employees are connected on the site. The same is true of students and teachers.

There are alternatives to LinkedIn, but for most users, these should be used as complements rather than replacements. Xing is much like LinkedIn and more popular outside the U.S. Sumry might be helpful to search for employment and learn an industry. Networking for Professionals provides the service listed in its name. Many other sites are more explicitly about employment, including Jobs.com, Monster, Beyond, Opportunity, and many others.

Students can use the general social media sites to pursue their broad educational interest, while using the job boards and industry-specific sites to search for particular employment opportunities. The key in all social media is to keep it current and fresh. This means that the profiles should be updated regularly. Professional networking sites do not put a premium on posting actively, so there is no pressure to post something to each story daily. But they provide an excellent way to learn more about candidates' areas of interest and connect with leaders in students' areas of interest.

2. Online Portfolios

Students who have a body of work to present can do so by building an online portfolio. These are not for everybody, because the candidate will be judged by the quality and the curation of the work they present. Students can post content to a free website on Google Sites, Wix, Webs, or other hosting services. Building online portfolios requires the student design compelling websites and provide equally compelling content. A strong portfolio usually includes some very striking images, a small amount of text to introduce the student, and visual collection of images, infographics, and short explanatory text that emphasizes the unique and compelling story about the student.

The online portfolio is not a resume. It typically features one thematic aspect of the student's personality, which means that it may leave out other significant aspects about the student. Since every student is unique and each student has a story to tell, the online portfolio can help students let their individual stories emerge.

3. Personal Social Media

Being a candidate for a job or college does not require that one removes all social media presence. Instead, the social media presence should be understood to be used, at least in part, to present the candidate to the public.

Most social media platforms have tools to control whether content is made public or kept restricted to a designated circle of friends or contacts. None of the posted content is truly private in the legal sense. Social media companies share content with advertisers and other third parties, as listed in each company's privacy policy. Posted content can be obtained by subpoena in a lawsuit or obtained by law enforcement with a court order. The user can keep some content nonpublic, but the user cannot truly make the content private.

Knowing their public social media presence may be scrutinized, adolescents should pay close attention to the privacy settings on each gaming and social media account. Content posted using the public setting should be content similar to the candidate's resume or portfolio. Teens should limit their posts to content that presents the student in the best possible light. Photos from participation in charitable or public service events are excellent to highlight the candidate's civic engagement. Other social events are less relevant to the general public. Linking and reposting stories that are positive, uplifting, and tied to the student's area of interest reinforce the commitment of the candidate. Other content, even if interesting, will tend to distract from that message and should be restricted to nonpublic channels. The point is not to censor the student. Instead, the goal is to choose between the public and nonpublic posts to emphasize the personality and positive attributes.

4. Finding Fit—Using Search and Social Media for Colleges and Employers

Virtually all colleges use social media to create a sense of community for their students, alumni, and prospective students. It is unlikely that selective colleges will use their own social media sites as a filter to identify exceptional candidates, though on rare occasion such a student will catch the attention of an admissions staff person. Nonetheless, participating in the online social media of a college candidate's prospective schools is very helpful for the student. After all, the college choice is a two-way negotiation. The universities are selecting among their choice of qualified candidates, but the candidates are also choosing among their prospective schools. The right choice in a future university is the school with the best fit rather than the best rankings. Fit often comes down to campus culture, and a college's culture will come through in its social media presence. Students should use this tool to help them decide which of their choices is the best school to attend.

The same advice applies to job applications. Job satisfaction is also about fit, respect, and autonomy more than salary and title. If an applicant has the opportunity to choose among job offers, then getting to know a company by following its social media is an excellent tool to understand the institutional culture and values.

Social media is just one online tool. Candidates should also conduct their own online searches about the colleges or potential employers. These searches will reveal what current students and employees think about the institution. The searches should reveal any newsworthy history about the health of the institution, the leadership, and the kind of experience the candidate is likely to have at the institution.

E. WHAT TO AVOID

Schools and employers use social media as a tool to help understand the true nature of the candidate. All candidates should be honest and accurate when presenting themselves to the prospective employers or colleges. Candidates should avoid any online posts that are false or misleading regarding the candidate's background or accomplishments. While puffing up one's social media presence is not as bad as falsifying credentials on a resume, it still raises a red flag for the potential employer or university regarding the trustworthiness of the candidate.

Candidates should always be very careful never to disclose nonpublic information on social media. If a candidate for a new job has inside information about their current employer, the disclosure of that information could greatly harm the employer. The failure to protect that confidential information would be a red flag for other potential employers regarding the candidate's ethics and trustworthiness.

Schools and employers are also very concerned about candidates who would publicly badmouth their existing employers or institutions. Even if a candidate hates flipping burgers after high school, the candidate should avoid complaining online. Future employers will read those posts as an indication that they may someday be subject to the same treatment. The same advice applies to students complaining about teachers. Negative comments are not received positively in the admissions office.

Candidates should also consider the false, double standard that employers and colleges use when looking at online profiles. Hiring committees and admissions offices want to see an idealized version of the applicant. Sexualized photos and photos of drinking are likely to harm the candidacy even though such conduct is legal for adults over eighteen or twenty-one, respectively. Photographs featuring drug use will have an even more harmful effect.

Employers and universities are also very focused on maintaining a climate of civility and inclusiveness. This translates into a very low tolerance for speech that can be understood as racist, sexist, misogynistic, homophobic, or otherwise intolerant. The concern goes beyond the posts and videos created by the student to include the likes, retweets, and shares that a student might make that are pointed.

Some students deal with the double standard regarding their social media profiles by creating separate "Grandma-Facing" Facebook pages in order to have very innocent social media available for potential employers, colleges, as well as for certain relatives. These students then use pseudonyms for their actual social media accounts. This technique will make it easier for the student to present a positive public persona without needing to scrub the candidate's active social media. However, if the other social media becomes linked to the candidate, then the technique will backfire. Employers and colleges will likely see the intentional manipulation of the social media as both an indication of the candidate's lack of candor and the candidate's ongoing efforts to post questionable content.

Well before a student begins to apply for jobs or college, the student should scrutinize all the content posted to social media. Candidates should run Google, Bing, and social media searches to see how they appear online. Parents should help with this process, but before doing so, they should let their children know they will be looking. Neither the parents nor the children will benefit from surprise revelations that come from conducting the online search.

Students should remove any content that might be considered offensive or embarrassing. While some candidates will feel that their public presence is more important than the job or university offer, they should understand that if they have posted highly problematic content, they are making a conscious choice to pass over the opportunity. Free speech guarantees the right to say what one wants, not to be free from the consequences of one's speech.

Even if a candidate takes down potentially harmful content, it might be too late. Candidates' content may have been publicly shared by others on social media. Candidates might also be tagged in offensive content posted by classmates and others. Candidates should take steps to remove their own offensive content, close accounts where needed, and do what they can to have offensive content posted by friends and classmates taken down as well.

The best practice is never to participate in the creation of harmful or offensive content. The second-best practice is never to post such content. When both of those have failed, the candidate can at least remove the content and hope that the Internet has moved on.

There are also services that promise to help remove offensive content for a fee. Generally, these companies should be avoided. There is little evidence that these services can remove content. In contrast, there are reports that suggest that such services may collaborate with slander sites to perpetuate the content in an effort to extort money from individuals victimized by harmful, online content.[13]

Chapter 8

Copyright, Creativity, and the Teen Artist

A. INTRODUCTION

As noted in chapter 7, participation in the creative ecology of the Internet has many positive benefits. Teens become connected with peers, earn positive reinforcement for their work, and engage in productive, creative activities. The benefits, however, go well beyond these positive attributes. Empirical research by the Brookings Institution demonstrated significant benefit to school systems that provide arts education, such as a reduction in disciplinary infractions, increase in writing proficiency, and increases in measures on compassion.[1] The Brookings Institution goes further, explaining that studies show "arts participation is related to behaviors that contribute to the health of civil society, such as increased civic engagement, greater social tolerance, and reductions in other-regarding behavior" for adults.[2]

Some researchers emphasize the importance of creativity as part of the development of individual talents, fostering economic opportunities, practicing problem-solving skills, and more generally expanding the participant learning and problem-solving skills.[3] For others, creative works are important because they create beauty, help explore the artist's and audience's emotional experiences, and build a shared culture.

For parents seeking to foster independent, engaged, and resilient young adults, the Internet provides a wide range of opportunities for their teens to learn about the arts and become involved in positive, expressive activities. Whether art is valuable for art's sake or valuable for the developmental experience it provides to the artist, there is no doubt that art and creativity are essential to personal growth and learning. Digital technology has made the ability to create, curate, and share art easier than ever. Parents should take advantage of these resources and celebrate these creative opportunities with their children.

The digital technology revolution has made it easier than ever for a person to explore their creative side as authors, artists, singers, musicians, filmmakers, game designers, and much more. With access to maker spaces, creators can move beyond just digital creations to produce clothing, products, and works of art without needing to personally own expensive production equipment or rely on large corporate backing. Using video-sharing platforms such as YouTube, Vimeo, Facebook Watch, Twitch, and DailyMotion, creators can create and upload videos. For visual artists, DeviantArt is the largest sharing platform, followed by CGSociety, Pinterest, Behance, Instagram, and Tumblr.

For musicians, Spotify allows artists to have home pages on which they can add their music to the streaming service. Pandora, SoundCloud, MySpace, MixCloud, and other platforms host music by artists, and some also enable the artist to sell merchandise. Creative writers can use platforms such as Wattpad, FanFiction.net, Figment, Smashwords, and Goodreads. All creators can also share their content on Facebook, Twitter, and Instagram, so most creators use a combination of these various platforms and services to promote their works and get feedback from others.

Each platform has its own terms of service (TOS) agreement or end user license agreement (EULA). Although these agreements vary from one to another, they all typically require that the creator abide by copyright and other intellectual property laws; only post content that the creator owns or has permission to upload; and not upload information that is harmful to other parties, such as by invading the other party's right to privacy or defaming the other party. By uploading to the service, the creator gives the platform the right to redistribute the creator's content. Some platforms condition the use on the ability to attach advertising to the content, while others do not put advertising directly on the user-generated content. The agreements will allow the company to suspend or cancel accounts for those creators who violate the terms of the agreement.

B. COPYRIGHT

Most creative works are protected by some form of intellectual property. Copyright protects expressive and literary works such as books, poems, music, choreography, and videos. Patents protect new inventions. Trademarks protect words and symbols when they are used in commerce to represent the source of goods and services. Publicity rights protect a person's name and likeness from being used in commerce without the permission of the person. Finally, trade secrets protect confidential information that has economic value.

Each of the hosting platforms requires that the party uploading content is the copyright holder for the content or has the right to upload the content, so it is very important for online creators to have a basic understanding of copyright.

1. Copyright Coverage

Copyright protects original works of authorship fixed in a tangible form of expression. Copyright protection begins as soon as the work is fixed. Although there are benefits to registering a work with the U.S. Copyright Office, protection begins at fixation not registration.

The Copyright Act provides the following categories of protected works:

- Literary works;
- Musical works, including any accompanying words;
- Dramatic works, including any accompanying music;
- Pantomimes and choreographic works;
- Pictorial, graphic, and sculptural works;
- Motion pictures and other audiovisual works;
- Sound recordings; and
- Architectural works.[4]

A computer program is considered a literary work, while a videogame would be an audiovisual work.

Copyright law also specifically excludes certain types of works, designed to protect the expression an author creates but not the underlying facts or ideas that go into a work. The excluded items include the following:

- Ideas, procedures, methods, systems, processes, concepts, principles, discoveries, or devices;
- Titles, names, short phrases, and slogans; mere listings of ingredients or contents;
- Works that are not fixed in a tangible form of expression, such as an improvised speech or performance that is not written down or otherwise recorded;
- Works consisting entirely of information that is commonly available and contains no originality; and
- Works by the U.S. government, court opinions, and the laws published by states.[5]

In a cookbook, for example, the list of ingredients and directions on how to make the recipe would not be protected under copyright, but the background information, the history of the recipe, and any other exposition added to the recipe would be protected. In addition, while the individual recipe would not be protected by copyright, the cookbook author would have copyright protection in the order, selection, and arrangement of the recipes in the book. As a result, another cookbook publisher could copy the individual recipe's ingredient list and cooking instructions, but that publisher could not copy the cookbook as a whole without violating the copyright owned by the cookbook author.

In general, because of these limitations on copyright, a story's abstract plot is not protected by copyright, but the detailed story structure will receive copyright protection. The story of boy meets girl—or boy meets boy—will not be protected by copyright. But when the story involves specific characters, events, and sequences, those elements will combine to move the plot from an abstract idea to a protected story structure.

2. Copyright Term

For an individual author, the length of copyright is seventy years following the death of the author. In the case of a joint work prepared by two or more authors, the term of copyright lasts for seventy years after the last surviving author's death. If the work is copyrighted by a corporation or otherwise made as a work for hire, the duration of copyright will be 95 years from publication or 120 years from creation (whichever is shorter). An author makes a work as a work for hire when either the person makes the copyrighted work in the ordinary course of the author's employment, or in certain cases, if the work was specially commissioned as a work for hire. In all other situations, the work vests in the author at the time the work is created and fixed on paper, on a computer's memory, or in any other permanent medium.

3. The Public Domain and the Creative Commons License

Once the term of copyright has expired, the work falls into the public domain, meaning that the work is free for anyone to use in any manner they wish. The same is true of works created before the existence of copyright (or the United States). The works of William Shakespeare, Mary Shelley, Leonardo Da Vinci, Antonio Vivaldi, and others never received copyright protection and remained at all times in the public domain. The F. Scott Fitzgerald novel *The Great Gatsby* was published in 1925 and entered the public domain in 2021.

For modern works, all works published in the United States more than ninety-five years ago are in the public domain. As of 2021, this means that works published in 1925 are in the public domain. In the case of music, however, it is important to distinguish between the composition and the sound recording. The sound recording of a nineteenth-century composition might have been recorded recently and that recording is still protected by copyright even though the composition is in the public domain.

For works created between 1923 and 1964, a work received the full length of copyright protection only if it was renewed in the twenty-eighth year of the copyright. For many works, the copyright owner never renewed the copyright, meaning that the work has also fallen into the public domain. Unfortunately, it is not easy to be sure there is no continuing copyright protection for works that were not renewed. A consortium led by the New York Public Library and Internet Archive have published a directory that should be very helpful. A study by the New York Public Library suggests that only one-quarter of works published were later renewed, meaning that there is a large trove of works not covered by copyright. For works published after 1964, there was no obligation to register a renewal of the work to maintain copyright protection, and for modern works there is not even an obligation to register the work at all.

For many creators, however, there is little interest in enforcing copyright restrictions. Instead, many authors want their works to be freely shared. The easiest way to find content intended to be shared is to look for a Creative Commons license, designated by the initials "CC." The Creative Commons organization touts more than 1.6 billion works that have been created and made available for free with only modest copyright restrictions. Creators use the Creative Commons license with six different features. The basic license "allows reusers to distribute, remix, adapt, and build upon the material in any medium or format, so long as attribution is given to the creator. The license allows for commercial use."[6] This license, however, does require that the original creator be identified and given credit. Another license requires that the user agrees that any works created or remixed also include the same Creative Commons license. Other licenses restrict the redistribution or reuse to noncommercial purposes. There is also a designation provided by Creative Commons to allow an author to dedicate the work to the public domain and remove all possible restrictions.

The Creative Commons licenses are extremely helpful to promote research and share creative works. The Creative Commons license expands upon the public domain, making it simple for nonprofessional bloggers and website designers to find high-quality images to include in their sites, incorporate music and sound effects, and expand on their own creative work through the benefit of others.

Students—and their parents—should look to the public domain works and works with the Creative Commons license as the best material to use when seeking to adapt materials for school projects or other creative works. By using public domain and Creative Commons materials, students are assured that the new works they create will not trigger claims of copyright infringement by content owners.

The lesson of the Creative Commons licensing scheme also emphasizes the importance of attribution. Although millions of Creative Commons participants have been willing to give away their creative works, the majority insisted on having credit or attribution for their work. The Creative Commons organization adjusted its early licensing scheme to reflect the importance of attribution to creators of their works. Unfortunately, copyright law has not made this same adjustment. Under U.S. copyright law, there is only a small right for credit for an author or creator. Instead, credit is usually provided as a function of contract with a publisher or distributor. Despite the cultural and social importance of credit and attribution, the law has yet to catch up with the credit. Still, for online creators, it is important to include credit wherever possible.

4. Copyright Licenses and Terms of Service Agreements

Most copyrighted works are shared under a license granted by the copyright owner. An exclusive license means that all the rights being assigned by the copyright owner are being granted to the licensee. If, instead, a license is nonexclusive, the copyright owner can also license the same work to multiple licensees. To be a valid exclusive license, the agreement must be in writing and signed by the copyright owner licensing the works.

Every social media platform, as well as most online gaming and other services, uses a TOS or EULA that sets out the terms and conditions of service. One of the key provisions in the TOS is the nonexclusive copyright assignment provision. As a condition of using apps and online platforms, the service providers generally require a nonexclusive copyright license that gives the company the right to use the copyrighted works uploaded by the user or created on the site. By clicking "I Agree" on the TOS, the user is signing the license agreement and granting permission to let the platform use the user's copyrighted material. If a user is uploading someone else's copyrighted work without permission, then the user may be both violating the copyright of that third party and breaching the user agreement.

While some licenses limit this right to only allow the posts to be used by the social media site as instructed by the user, other licenses give the social media company the right to use the pictures, videos, and text for any purpose the social media platform chooses. This means that student artists may find that they have given permission for their creative works to be used by the social platform for purposes well beyond hosting the content on the student's website or in the student's social media feed. If a student is a serious artist, the family should review the terms of service carefully before granting rights to the social media company.

In addition to express licenses, copyright law also recognizes implied licenses that are based on the conduct of the parties and the normal course of dealing. For example, copyright law specifically authorizes users to make a single backup of any software purchased. Section 117 of the Copyright Act allows for a single archival copy of computer programs. Section 117 does not extend to the other content on a computer, and it does not cover the use of multiple backups to protect against data corruption. Instead, however, given the industry practice to use multiple copies and to mirror entire drives, the right to do so is most likely granted by the copyright owner as an implied license. Few, if any, computer companies or media companies have complained about this practice, and many recommend that these safety procedures are followed.

C. FAIR USE AND FAN FICTION

As a limit on the legal protections for copyrighted works, copyright law also provides that some uses of copyrighted works can be made without permission under the fair use doctrine. Fair use is an essential defense to claims of copyright infringement to help ensure that the values of free speech are not diminished by copyright ownership.

At its simplest, fair use ensures that copyright is not violated every time an email is forwarded, a sentence from a book is quoted, or a picture is shown on the news. Fair use promotes comment, criticism, news reporting, teaching, scholarship, and research.[7] Fair use is broader in educational settings than in commercial settings, but is available for both noncommercial and commercial uses.

1. Fair Use Test

The test for fair use has been largely the same since 1841, but the modern copyright law codified the test in Section 107 of the Copyright Act:

[T]he fair use of a copyrighted work, including such use by reproduction in copies or phonorecords or by any other means specified by that section, for purposes such as criticism, comment, news reporting, teaching (including multiple copies for classroom use), scholarship, or research, is not an infringement of copyright.

In determining whether the use made of a work in any particular case is a fair use the factors to be considered shall include—

(1) the purpose and character of the use, including whether such use is of a commercial nature or is for nonprofit educational purposes;

(2) the nature of the copyrighted work;

(3) the amount and substantiality of the portion used in relation to the copyrighted work as a whole; and

(4) the effect of the use upon the potential market for or value of the copyrighted work.

The fact that a work is unpublished shall not itself bar a finding of fair use if such finding is made upon consideration of all the above factors.[8]

In applying the test to each question, the courts will generally start with the introductory paragraph to assess whether the alleged fair use falls into one of the uses described in the introduction and will then proceed to analyze each of the four factors listed. Through court interpretation, the first factor has taken on a second meaning, which is the extent to which the work is "transformative." As the Copyright Office explains, "transformative uses are those that add something new, with a further purpose or different character, and do not substitute for the original use of the work."[9] A highly transformed work is also unlikely to compete with the original work in the marketplace. As a result, under the first and fourth factor of the fair use test, when a new work is sufficiently transformative, it will generally not be found to infringe the original work.

The second factor, the nature of the work, reflects the copyright goal of protecting creative expression. Creative, fictional works will receive broader copyright protection than technical, academic, or news items.

The third factor, the amount and substantiality of the work taken, will balance the amount of a work that has been copied. Reproducing three paragraphs of a book is far less of an infringement than copying three paragraphs of a five-paragraph essay. This factor is qualitative as well as quantitative, meaning that if the "heart of a work" has been taken, the amount copied can be much less substantial. For example, there are no preset minimum amounts that may be copied. There is no three-note, three-bar, or thirty-second rule for music. The amount copied is just one of the four factors.

The last factor, the effect on the potential market for the copyrighted work, looks at the market harms created by the alleged infringement. Courts look at the extent to which the new work will serve as a market substitute for the copied work. A movie review does not substitute for seeing the movie, so it does not have a potential to replace it in the marketplace. In contrast, an unauthorized version of a song recording may compete directly with the original song for streams, downloads, and sales.

Once the court has assessed each of the four factors, it makes a determination based on the totality of the factors and any other considerations that might be important in a particular case.

For the online creator, the fair use test is very frustrating. It does not provide enough predictability in advance. Worse, if the creator gets into a legal dispute with a copyright owner, the dispute will be expensive, time-consuming, and distracting.

2. Fan Fiction and Safe Harbors

For most works, the creator can gauge the extent to which a particular creation is fair use depending on the copyright owner's response to similar uses by other parties. For example, some copyright owners are far more aggressive in policing their works than are other owners. Similarly, some types of use are much more likely to be considered unobjectionable than others.

In the world of fan fiction, for example, there are millions of short stories, pictures, and other works that have been created without permission of the copyright owners, and they likely do not meet the standards of fair use, but they are still permitted to flourish. Instead, the media companies that own the copyrights have acquiesced to their fans' engagement with the content.

The Organization for Transformative Works supports the Archive of Our Own (AO3) and other fan fiction sites. AO3 boasts "more than 40,670 fandoms, 3,102,000 users, [and] 6,933,000 works." Other sites include Fanfiction.net, Commaful, Wattpad, and DeviantArt.

In the video realm, fan fiction is a bit more complicated. The projects can range from simple compilation videos to professionally created feature-length films. Following a legal victory by Paramount regarding *Axanar*, a $1 million crowdfunded feature film, Paramount and CBS published fan fiction guidelines that guarantee fans will not be sued if they stay within the published rules. (The prequel, *"Prelude to Axanar,"* remains one of the better Star Trek episodes produced in the past ten years.)

The guidelines are a form of safe harbor, meaning that the people following the guidelines are not saying the rules permit more than would be permitted under fair use or less than would generally be permitted under fair use. Instead, the safe harbor guidelines mean that the copyright owners will not object to any projects that follow these rules.

Parents should encourage their children to respect copyright, which comes closer than any other system for establishing the normative, ethical values for the Internet. At the same time, parents can rest assured that in areas such as fan fiction, participating in the reading, viewing, and creating of this content remains a positive and largely sanctioned activity. Creating fan fiction may be considered excellent practice at developing an author's or artist's expressive skills inside the fictional world created by film, television, and literature.

D. CONTENT MANAGEMENT BY THE ISPS

In the online environment, the concern that an individual's post will trigger a copyright lawsuit simply does not fit with the reality that billions of posts, searches, and files are being uploaded and downloaded daily. It could happen, but so could a lightning strike on a sunny day or an alligator attack in Iowa. Individuals are occasionally sued for copyright infringement, but these cases are extremely rare and usually occur only after letters demanding an end to the alleged copyright infringement have gone ignored.

To discourage litigation and promote the Internet and digital technology, Congress enacted two statutes designed to protect the ISPs that host user content and reduce the likelihood of litigation. One provision deals with copyrighted works and the other deals with other litigation involving online posts.

1. Copyright Notice and Takedown Rules under Section 512

When Congress amended the copyright law in 1998, it added protections for ISPs from copyright infringement claims made because the users or subscribers of the Internet service were uploading pirated works or other works that were being shared without the copyright owner's permission. In the absence of the amendment, these companies could be liable merely for storing the unauthorized works, even if the ISPs were unaware of the claims of copyright infringement.

The law that governs the rules regarding online copyrighted works is Section 512 of the Copyright Act, passed as part of the Digital Millennium Copyright Act (DMCA). Under §512, when a copyright owner identifies a work that it owns as having been posted without authorization, the copyright owner can send a notice to the ISP. If the ISP follows the law, it cannot be sued for copyright infringement by the copyright owner.

To receive protection under the law, the ISP must meet certain minimums:

- The ISP must have a registered a copyright agent with the U.S. Copyright Office and posted information to its website on how copyright owners can file a takedown notice.
- The ISP must have an operating notice and takedown procedure that complies with the statute.
- The ISP must not ignore red flags that infringing activity is occurring on its site.
- The ISP cannot receive any direct financial benefit from the infringing material on its site.[10]

Under the law, the copyright owner must send a notice regarding the copyrighted work to the ISP with identification of the work that the owner claims has been infringed and identification of the work that the copyright owner claims is infringing and its location, as well as the contact information of the copyright owner, and a signed statement that the copyright owner "has a good faith belief that use of the material in the manner complained of is not authorized by the copyright owner, its agent, or the law." The requirement for the signed statement has been understood to mean that the copyright owner does not believe the use is being made would qualify as fair use.

Once the ISP receives the notice, it must act reasonably to remove the identified material and to let the subscriber who posted the material know that it has been removed. The subscriber can object to the removal. If the subscriber objects, the ISP has the option—but not the obligation—to repost the content. At that point, any potential legal action by the copyright holder can only be against the subscriber who posted the work, not the ISP.

Although §512 seems simple in theory, there are many objections in practice. The process for DMCA takedowns created by Congress contemplated a manual process where a person would send a letter with the correct information to a staff person at the ISP. That staff person would look up the information, and then respond to the letter. The scale of the ISPs makes such a model impossible. YouTube, for example, receives 500 hours of video to be posted each minute. Other major social media platforms also host far more content than they could review manually.

Instead, YouTube, for example, uses its Content Verification and Content ID systems to allow the exclusive owners of copyrighted libraries of works to be part of a digital directory of copyrighted content. Under the Content ID system, whenever a subscriber uploads a file, it is automatically scanned to see what content, if any, is matched by the Content ID system. If the content is matched as being flagged under the Content ID system, the software will either block the video, track the video's viewership statistics, or monetize the video for the benefit of the copyright owner. The copyright owner can choose how aggressively it wishes to control the enforcement of the copyright. Other companies have their own automation tools and monetization strategies.

The problem with §512 is that while it promotes the protection of some copyrighted works, it is far too inefficient to stop copyright pirates who aggressively post and repost new and original works. Feature films can be found online days after they first appear in movie theaters. Books might show up online even before they are available in bookstores. Section 512 does little to stop the harm caused by this type of piracy.

On the other hand, §512 does not require the ISPs to respect free speech and fair use. The ISPs can choose whether or not to host any particular video or post, and if they choose not to repost a work, it is within the right of the ISP to do so, even if the amount of copyrighted work in the post would fall squarely within the fair use protection. Algorithms are particularly weak at identifying comment or criticism. The law does not encourage the ISPs to protect fair use, and the automation often ignores the public's interest in comment, criticism, and research entirely.

Congress and the Copyright Office are exploring ways to update and modify §512; however, it is hard to imagine any system that can protect both fair use and the copyright owner's interests. One option is to expand the use of safe harbor rules and create a system for protecting clips under 30 seconds or other simple rules to expand fair use with some bright-line tests. While these would help, they do not fit well with fair use as it has been understood for over 150 years.

2. ISP Immunity from Online Posts under Section 230 and the Challenges for Victims of Harassment

In addition to the ISP immunity from copyright actions for service providers, Congress adopted another, even more sweeping law to provide the ISPs with immunity from liability for the content posted by their users. Under section 230 of the Communications Decency Act, "[n]o provider or user of an interactive computer service shall be treated as the publisher or speaker of any information provided by another information content provider."[11] At its heart, this provision means that when a subscriber or user of an ISP posts content on the site, the ISP will be immune from lawsuits based on defamation, trademark infringement, or any other claim that the ISP was the party making the defamatory statement.

This protection for the ISPs is very different from the laws that govern book and other print publishers. If a publisher reproduces a defamatory statement in print, the law holds that publisher responsible for the harm in the same manner as the party who published the harmful content.

Free speech advocates are highly supportive of §230. The Electronic Frontier Foundation (EFF), for example, describes §230 as "the most important law protecting Internet speech" and "one of the most valuable tools for protecting freedom of expression and innovation on the Internet."[12]

Critics of §230 focus on the extremely broad scope given to the rule by the courts. Although Congress wrote the law to protect the ISPs from being treated as speakers or publishers, courts interpreting the law extended the liability protection for being distributors and resellers of content. A bookstore or newsstand, for example, will be held accountable for selling defamatory content once the seller has actual knowledge that the material the bookseller is offering for sale has defamatory content. In contrast, an ISP can have actual knowledge of the defamatory content on its site and is immune from lawsuits to remove the content.[13]

In the late 1990s, the courts were very concerned about the risk that a multitude of defamation cases against the ISPs would hobble the start-up Internet companies. Although the nature of the Internet has changed dramatically since that time, only Congress can revise the understanding of the law.

Section 230 also provides the ISPs the ability to remove content the ISP deems as harmful or in violation of its community standards. Congress specifically protected the ISPs from editing or removing content, including "any action voluntarily taken in good faith to restrict access to or availability of material that the provider or user considers to be obscene, lewd, lascivious, filthy, excessively violent, harassing, or otherwise objectionable, whether or not such material is constitutionally protected."[14] This broad provision goes much further than the contractual rights in the TOS agreement, allowing the ISPs to protect themselves and their users from unwanted content.

Under this provision of §230, many sites remove hate speech and violent content from their sites, though critics note that often this is done only slowly and sporadically. There is no obligation that the content be removed. The broad sweep of §230 means that social media platforms cannot be held legally responsible for being inconsistent in how they remove the content.

Despite the broad immunity from lawsuits, many social media platforms have privacy policies, TOS agreements, or community guidelines that prohibit harmful content of various types. Some provide simple forms that can be submitted to object to offensive content. Facebook, for example, has a form to help users remove content they believe is defamatory or otherwise violates the person's legal rights. Even so, Facebook's introduction to the form recommends that the victim seek guidance from an attorney.

For victims of online harassment through defamation, cyberbullying, invasion of privacy, revenge porn, or other actions, there is no automatic notice and takedown procedure similar to that for copyright infringement. These issues and the strategies parents and adolescents can use to address them are discussed in chapters 9–13. If the harassment involves the use of photographs, victims will sometimes seek to use copyright claims to remove the content, but this does not work unless the victim can lawfully obtain ownership of the copyrighted works.

In many situations, victims need to engage attorneys and begin an arduous process to send demand letters to the content host, while at the same time seeking the identities of the actual individuals involved in the harassment. Often, the ISPs will not divulge the identities of the harassers without a court order. Because of the free speech concerns involved, courts will not issue those orders to disclose the identities of the harassing parties without substantial evidence that the unidentified individuals have published content that is defamatory or is otherwise not protected by the First Amendment.

Even if a court does issue a subpoena requiring the disclosure of the identities of the harassers, the information is only helpful if the ISP involved has true information regarding the identity of its users. Most social media sites allow users who have not verified their identity. As a result, the process to remove offensive content is difficult, expensive, and time consuming. Since the damage done by online harassment is immediate and long-lasting, the current regulation of the Internet simply does not provide helpful recourse for victims of online harassment.

The most important step a person can take to defend against harassment is to minimize the ability of harassers to be effective.

- Avoid engaging with trolls and other online provocateurs. Trolls are not seeking to have thoughtful, engaged, civil debate designed to further the thinking of the participants in the conversation. They are trying to anger and offend. Those who respond are the most likely to become the target for repeated attacks. Their content spreads virally, so that it can only be effective if people respond to it. Never answer a troll.
- Avoid publishing personal contact information online. The less personal information is available to harassers, the fewer vectors they have to interfere with a person's private life. Unfortunately, most real estate records are public, but telephone numbers and online names do not need to be.
- Avoid creating sexually explicit images and videos. While some sexually explicit content is created by perpetrators without the knowledge of their sexual partners, a great deal of sexually explicit content is created consensually. The content is later weaponized after the relationship goes sour. If the photo isn't taken, it cannot be shared.
- Act quickly to remove any highly offensive content. Once content has been shared online, it is very difficult to have it removed. But the situation becomes much worse once the content has been shared on multiple sites. At that point, the content is likely to be reposted by third parties entirely unknown to the victim as well as by parties who are careful to remain anonymous. Once harmful content has moved to multiple sites, the difficulty will grow.
- Take advantage of the various tools on each social media platform. Each site will use its own forms and protocols to request the elimination of harmful content.
- Check with the legal authorities in the state. State laws vary considerably regarding the privacy rights of the residents and the protection from unauthorized sexually explicit content. The federal government does not have significant protections, but the state may be able to help.

None of these steps can eliminate the risks, but they can lower the risks somewhat.

Section 230 worked very effectively to eliminate the many claims that people would have brought against social media companies and other ISPs for having their feelings hurt online. As a result of the law, nearly all of these lawsuits are dismissed without ever being heard. At the same time, however, the Internet has become a platform for a small, but highly vocal element to use social media platforms to radicalize information, to harass and bully those with whom they disagree, and to publish content that would have been deemed too offensive to ever be broadcast by mass media. These harms are not insubstantial. But they remain only a very small part of the overall Internet and digital media experience.

Chapter 9

Mature and Explicit Content

This chapter and the chapters which follow focus on the concerns parents often have regarding the nature of some of the content found online in websites, apps, and social media. Offensive content means very different things to different families. Nonetheless, there are some general guidelines regarding the maturity level needed for children to engage in certain content and extreme examples of graphic and obscene content that most parents wish to keep away from their children.

This chapter addresses the complex relationship between sexual information, sexually explicit content, and other forms of content that are often deemed inappropriate. The following four chapters address particular types of content that are constitutionally protected but often harmful to adolescents.

A. INTRODUCTION

The Internet is often closely associated with pornography and adult content. The Internet, much like the video cassette recorder, achieved its early economic growth as a result of the sale of pornographic content. Of course, not all content about or involving sex is pornographic. Statistical information suggests that many adolescents and young adults turn to the Internet for education, information, and entertainment involving sexual identity and sexual activity.

For some parents and households, this is a particularly fraught topic. For some, any discussion of sexual activity, sexual education, gender identity, or premarital sex are topics to be understood only through religious traditions. Parents need to establish their own standards and expectations regarding sex and sexually explicit content. This chapter, however, provides additional background so that families can make these decisions in the context of the modern cultural data and with distinctions made among the wide variety of content that ranges from uniformly useful medical information all the way to illegal obscenity.

Adolescents of all ages are curious about these topics. By understanding the research and distinguishing the scare tactics from the realistic issues, parents may be better able to have a positive influence on their children's maturation and development regarding sexual identity and development. The Internet provides instant, unfiltered access to nudity, sexually explicit content, pornography, and more. As a result, parents must recognize that they will likely need to address these topics with more candor than was required in prior generations. This chapter helps provide context for those struggling with the prevalence of sexual content in digital media, and the strategies available for parents who wish to address these concerns.

B. SEX EDUCATION

Talking about sex is often embarrassing. Because of the secrecy surrounding topics involving sex, people sometimes feel very uncomfortable discussing topics even though the issues are very common. Where health care issues are involved, this can lead to people ignoring health concerns until they become much more serious. For adolescents, often both health concerns and sex are difficult subjects to address, making the combination even more problematic.

Sex education is mandated in most public school systems, with almost every state participating in federal programs that provide sex education. Since the 1990s, however, the official strategy for pregnancy control is abstinence-only education (AOE).[1] Some of the components of this education are healthy for adolescents, such as the "holistic individual and societal benefits associated with personal responsibility, self-regulation, goal setting, healthy decision-making, and a focus on the future"; "the foundational components of healthy relationships"; and "how to resist and avoid, and receive help regarding, sexual coercion and dating violence."[2] Although the federal program operates with the stated goal of promoting abstinence, the law also provides that "any information provided on contraception is medically accurate and complete and ensures that students understand that contraception offers physical risk reduction, but not risk elimination."[3]

Nonetheless, a significant body of research demonstrates that abstinence education does little or nothing to change adolescents' sexual activity.[4] Instead, the majority of teens have become sexually active before they reach eighteen. For women, the median age for engaging in sex is 17.4 years of age, while for men, the median age for engaging in sex is slightly older at 17.7

years of age.[5] Since many teens engage in behaviors that are sexual but do not result in intercourse, the age at which they begin to expose themselves to sexually transmitted diseases (STDs) is even younger.

The Centers for Disease Control and Prevention (CDC) provides its own sixteen-point guidance on sex education.[6] Instead of abstinence only, the CDC sexual health education (SHE) approach emphasizes the importance of addressing "the health needs of all students, including the needs of lesbian, gay, bisexual, transgender, and questioning youth," as well as connecting "students to sexual health and other health services at school or in the community."[7] Despite these mandates, many schools fail to meet their requirements to teach prevention of STDs, reduce teen pregnancy rates, or help students address the related emotional and behavioral health issues associated with sexual growth.

Unsurprisingly, parents and teens have turned to the Internet for resources. Dozens of apps and sites have been published to provide some of the guidance missing from the public school sex education programs. From a student's perspective, the teens are also able to participate privately, in their own home. Planned Parenthood, for example, has a wide range of information, including a series of videos on consent and learning how to understand when a potential partner wants sex. Sex Positive Families, Amaze, Young Men's Health, Center for Young Women's Health, and KidsHealth are other examples of resources that have a wide range of content and age-appropriate tools for families and their children to address the topics in a constructive, non-embarrassing manner.

Recognizing that the majority of teens are sexually active before graduating high school can help parents recognize the need children have for information regarding safe sex, STDs, healthy relationships, and birth control. By participating in their children's sex education, parents can help ensure that their children are receiving accurate and complete guidance relevant to their child's maturity level, sexual identity, and peer environment. Parents who ignore their children's sexual development do not slow it down, they simply leave all influence to their children's peers and social media feeds.

C. SEXUALIZATION AND BODY SHAMING ACROSS MEDIA

In addition to the basic need of children to receive support and guidance from their parents while navigating puberty and sexual development, adolescents also need help to fend off the inappropriate sexualization and stereotyping rampant on social media and other media services. The issue has existed throughout Western history. Mattel's Barbie was designed as a modified version of Lilli, a German novelty doll marketed to men. Barbie's popularity soared at first, but by 1968 there were social protests over Barbie and the objectification of women at the Miss America pageant. Nonetheless, although sexualization and objectification are not new, the intimacy of social media exacerbates the problem for teens and young adults.

Sexual objectification occurs for all sexual identities, but it is primarily focused on young women.[8] According to the American Psychological Association (APA), sexual objectification occurs when any or all of these four factors are present:

- A person's value comes only from his or her sexual appeal or behavior, to the exclusion of other characteristics;
- A person is held to a standard that equates physical attractiveness (narrowly defined) with being sexy;
- A person is sexually objectified—that is, made into a thing for others' sexual use, rather than seen as a person with the capacity for independent action and decision-making; and/or
- Sexuality is inappropriately imposed upon a person.[9]

As the APA report points out, "[v]irtually every media form studied provides ample evidence of the sexualization of women, including television, music videos, music lyrics, movies, magazines, sports media, videogames, the Internet, and advertising."[10] These themes that a women's worth is defined by her attractiveness and sexuality are reinforced on social media as well as by all forms of traditional media. "Sexuality discourses on social media are shaping women's experience with technology, their perceptions of themselves, and ultimately, their educational and career choices and goals."[11]

Within the constraints of the household's values, adolescents should be able to make decisions about how they present themselves. Adolescents need autonomy and a sense of control over their dress and the manner of their looks. At the same time, however, there is tremendous social pressure for young women to meet a fictionalized ideal of thin, busty, and ornamental. For many teens, the inability to conform to this false model of body shape, sexual readiness, and objectified role leaves them with stress, anxiety, and doubts over their self-worth.

Cultural cues further reinforce these media tropes. When friends and family members describe young girls, there is a tendency to use compliments like cute and pretty, reinforcing the importance of looks over achievements. The girls' male siblings are never called pretty and even cute is dropped well before boys enter puberty. The Girl Scouts has also written about this problem: "the sad truth is that more than half of girls in first through third grades think their 'ideal weight' is less than their actual weight. Six-year-old girls aren't just aware of their weight; they think there's something wrong with it."[12] Children and teens are particularly sensitive to the feedback and criticism they receive.

Adolescents cannot live up to the fictional ideal of the size 2 (or smaller) model featured in clothing ads. When they receive comments about their weight or their looks from friends, family, and strangers on social media, the combination often leads to low self-esteem and much worse. It can also lead to depression, social isolation, eating disorders, and body dysmorphic disorders—obsessions a person can have regarding the flaws in their appearance.

Industry is not motivated to pull back on its body shaming messaging. The U.S. cosmetic industry is estimated to amount to about $49.2 billion in 2019. That does not come close to the weight loss industry, which was worth an estimated $71 billion in 2020. Against this onslaught, the best that parents and educators can do is point out the hypocrisy of these industries and empower teens to be proud of who they are and how they look.

Parents and educators need to be mindful of their own, critical role in promoting healthy attitudes toward one's looks. Loving supportive comments are essential for a healthy household, but those comments can emphasize skills and attitude rather than the child's looks. If children ask about their weight or looks, parents need to be supportive of their children's needs without being critical of their weight or looks. Parents must also recognize that body shaming comments are a particularly invidious and effective form of bullying. Social media comments and posts designed to shame a person should be reported rather than ignored. The adolescents in the household should be reminded about the importance of respecting themselves and others. It provides another perfect illustration of the Golden Rule and the importance of treating all people with respect.

D. SEXUAL ORIENTATION AND GENDER IDENTITY

Another challenging aspect of adolescence is the development of a person's sexual identity. For adolescents who are coming out to their friends and family or are questioning their sexual identity, there are also helpful resources designed specifically for those challenges.

About 3.5% Americans identify themselves as lesbian, gay, or bisexual while 0.3% identify themselves as transgender. The LGBT (lesbian, gay, bisexual, and transgender) community belongs to almost every race, ethnicity, religion, age, and socioeconomic group.[13]

Other reports suggest the LGBTQ population is twice the amount quoted, hovering at around 7 percent. These resources are particularly important

because there are additional public health risks for adolescents who are coming out.

In some of the studies reported, LGBTQ teens were reported to have five
times as many reports of suicidal ideation. These teens are "are prone to be
isolated and disconnected from the social networks" which may further the
risk of depression.[14] STDs, including HIV, tend to run twice as high as in
teens who are heterosexual.

> LGBT youth are at a higher risk for substance use, sexually transmitted diseases
> (STDs), cancers, cardiovascular diseases, obesity, bullying, isolation, rejection,
> anxiety, depression, and suicide as compared to the general population. LGBT
> youth receive poor quality of care due to stigma, lack of healthcare providers'
> awareness, and insensitivity to the unique needs of this community.[15]

The risks of STDs and high-risk sexual behavior are also related to the
high degree of victimization and family rejection that occurs to LGBTQ
adolescents.

> Peer victimization is one of the leading causes of high-risk sexual behaviors in
> middle and high school students. LGBT youth are frequently bullied at schools.
> They frequently get into fights, engage in truancy, and struggle with emotional
> distress and conduct problems . . . Early victimization and emotional distress
> explained about 50% of disparities between LGBT and heterosexual youth in
> emotional distress in both boys and girls.[16]

Many of the negative consequences for LGBTQ health and well-being start
with rejection by one or more family members. Those adolescents who do not
experience rejection by one or more of their parents are much more likely to
avoid the negative consequences of the stigma, isolation, and negative health
consequences than those who are rejected or even made homeless as a result
of coming out. LGBTQ adolescents are reported to make up 40 percent of the
population of homeless youth, five times the number that would be predicted
based on population size.

Studies since the 1990s indicate that children first start identifying their
sexual identity with "their first 'crush' or attraction for another person, on
average, at around age 10."[17] As noted in the research, younger children need
additional family support to address their sexual and gender identity, making
a positive family involvement even more essential to their overall well-being.
The Child Welfare Information Gateway provides a list of resources on how
to help families support their LGBTQ children.[18]

Online resources available to parents and adolescents can play an extremely
important role in helping families build a healthy relationship and maintain a

supportive environment that will avoid the negative consequences of family rejection. Parents who want to protect their children from the negative health and social consequences can use the resources to help them support their LGBTQ children and teens, assuring that the adolescents remain in a healthy, supportive environment and avoid many of the high-risk health consequences facing LGBTQ adolescents.

The Trevor Project publishes "Coming Out: A Handbook for LGBTQ Young People." The CDC has its own LGBTQ Youth Resources with a long list of guides, lists, and discussion tools,[19] as does the Matthew Shepard Foundation. Johns Hopkins University publishes Tips for Parents of LGBTQ Youth,[20] which provides a very helpful outline and advice for parents. The Gay-Straight Alliance (GSA) is an organization active in many school systems that can provide additional resources. PFLAG has strong family resources for making family support successful, and there are many others. There are also many publications specifically designed to help families with strong religious beliefs that make coming out more challenging.

By taking advantage of these resources, parents can educate themselves regarding the challenges their children and teens are facing when coming out and dealing with potential peer isolation and other negative pressures associated with coming out. When the parents take their own action to educate themselves and support their children, it removes the burden from the adolescents, so that the children do not have to teach their parents how to parent.

The online support communities are important both for the teens coming out to their parents, and in many cases, for the parents as well. Some parents are not prepared to provide their children the support they need, but parenting organizations and other resources are available to help the parents understand what their children are going through and how best to support them. As noted earlier, many children become homeless as a result of their coming out. To avoid such an outcome, parents must be loving and supportive to help their children deal with the difficulties teens often face from their peers when coming out. Some parents might struggle with the sexual identity of their teens. If the parent themselves need support, they should seek it out from peer group organizations and professional assistance while remaining supportive of their children.

E. NUDITY, SEXUALLY EXPLICIT CONTENT, AND OBSCENITY

Adolescents are very curious about sex, and the Internet has a tremendous amount of information, misinformation, and imagery to offer. The Internet has made access to pornography and nudity difficult to avoid, so it is certainly available upon demand to adolescents. Parents need to recognize how much content is freely available to their children, and be prepared to address the moral and ethical issues surrounding nudity and pornography with them in a constructive and candid manner.

To some critics, the Internet is little more than an open marketplace for pornography. Some estimates suggest that as much as 30 percent of Internet search traffic involves pornography, but this number is largely based on the early days of the Internet, when most users were young men, and the commercial pornography industry was ecstatic to find a way to deliver content directly to customers free from high distribution costs and threats of police intervention.

More recent studies suggest that pornography accounts for somewhere between 4 percent to 15 percent of Internet traffic.[21] Web search traffic for pornography is estimated to be approximately 13 percent of the search traffic.[22] In comparison, in 1989, protestors campaigned against the Metropolitan Museum. The group Guerilla Girls purchased billboards asking "[d]o women have to be naked to get into the Met Museum?"[23] The ads noted that "less than 4% of artists in the modern art section of the museum were by women, but 76% of the nudes were female."[24]

There is an important distinction between nudity and pornography, but that distinction is sometimes highly subjective and contextual. The National Coalition Against Censorship acknowledges that there is no legal definition for pornography, but suggests the following distinction—"the sole purpose of pornography is to create sexual arousal and that art (even as it might arouse some viewers) has multiple layers of meaning and creates multiple effects."[25] This distinction does not begin to address whether sexually explicit works can sometimes still be considered artistic or whether a piece that moves from merely risqué to explicit loses its artistic merit.

Pornography not only stirs our bodies, it stirs our ethical and political selves. Pornography draws out our beliefs about gender and sexuality, race and class, power and self-hood. Pornography is about much more than just sex. Whatever you think of pornography, whether you consume it or abhor it, or both, it is now a highly visible part of our world and one we all need to discuss and deal with.[26]

Whatever the definition, the Internet serves as a shockingly easy tool to access nude, erotic, and sexually explicit content. Images, stories, video, games, and explicit music are readily available to children and adults alike. A study by Relationships in America posits that "43% of men and 9% of women report watching pornography in the past week. On the flip side, far more women than men have not used pornography recently: 34% of men and 72% of women report not viewing pornography in at least a year, if at all."[27]

Other studies suggest that approximately one-third of minors report unwanted exposure to online pornography.[28]

The government has largely been unable to regulate the distribution of sexually explicit content other than child pornography (which is covered in the next section). Congress passed the Communications Decency Act in 1995 to criminalize the transmission of obscene or indecent materials, but that law was struck down as unconstitutional by the Supreme Court in 1997.[29] Congress responded with the Child Online Protection Act in 1998, but this law was also found unconstitutional.[30] Neither law was able to distinguish distributing content to minors from the more general distribution of sexually explicit materials.

The government is unable to restrict sexually explicit content because it remains protected by the First Amendment's guarantee of free speech unless it is found to be obscene. Terms including pornographic, indecent, and sexually explicit have no clear definitions and do not exempt the content from First Amendment protection. The only works that can be legally banned or criminalized based on their sexual content are works that are obscene, which requires a three-part test as defined by the Supreme Court in *Miller v. California* (1973). The *Miller* test for obscenity requires a work to meet these three criteria:

1. Whether the average person, applying contemporary adult community standards, finds that the matter, taken as a whole, appeals to prurient interests (i.e., an erotic, lascivious, abnormal, unhealthy, degrading, shameful, or morbid interest in nudity, sex, or excretion);
2. Whether the average person, applying contemporary adult community standards, finds that the matter depicts or describes sexual conduct in a patently offensive way (i.e., ultimate sexual acts, normal or perverted, actual or simulated, masturbation, excretory functions, lewd exhibition of the genitals, or sado-masochistic sexual abuse); and
3. Whether a reasonable person finds that the matter, taken as a whole, lacks serious literary, artistic, political, or scientific value.[31]

The sale or intent to sell or distribute obscene content is a federal crime as well as a crime in many states. Possession is itself not illegal, but federal law prohibits the receiving of obscene content through the U.S. mails, common carriers, or computer networks, such as the Internet. Despite the wide-ranging power to criminalize the distribution and sale of obscenity, it is very difficult for prosecutors to establish the facts necessary to prove that content is obscene rather than being merely offensive. As a result, almost all legal actions have been focused on protecting minors rather than trying to regulate obscenity more generally.

Despite the failure of the government to stop the production or distribution of pornography, the widespread fears that the Internet has made us a nation of pornographers is somewhat overstated. Researchers have used data from the General Social Survey (GSS) to assess how young adults' and more mature adults' attitudes and uses of pornography have changed as technology has improved access.[32] During the period studied from 1981 through 2012, the number of male adults ages 18–26 who viewed an X-rated movie in the past year increased from 44.9 percent (1981–1989) to 61.5 percent (2008–2012). Women saw a smaller increase, from 28 percent (1981–1989) to 35.7 percent (2008–2012). Viewership declines for both men and women for older participants in the study.

For adults in their fifties, however, the consumption of pornography drops in half, while the attitude that pornography should be illegal nearly doubles.[33] The longitudinal data highlights that this is a change in behavior of the population as it matures. As such, it suggests two helpful observations for parents and families. First, the parents' attitude toward pornography is likely to be much more negative than the attitude of the older teens and young adults in the family. Second, the attitudes of the young adults are going to become less accepting of pornography as they mature.

Given these two observations, parents should likely emphasize that filming and distributing any sexually explicit content by the family's young-adult children will likely result in their children regretting it as they get older. Minors, as discussed in the next section, should never be filmed engaged in sexually explicit content, under any circumstances. But college-aged young adults who knowingly and voluntarily participate in filming online sexual content are likely to regret their participation as they get older.

Parents are unlikely to be able to stop access to sexually explicit content by their teens. For younger children, parents can use Internet filters and access-controlled web browsers to limit the access by their children. None of these tools, however, will stop a student from using equipment outside the home that is not similarly restricted. Most do not provide sufficient lock-outs to stop zealous teens from circumventing the technology by adding unrestricted browsers, virtual private network (VPN) access, or other tools. Instead, parents should be prepared to talk candidly with the adolescents about the content they find online to help the children separate out the fantasy content being sold from a healthy understanding of nudity, sexuality, and morality. Each family will bring its own ethics and traditions to that conversation.

F. PROHIBITED CONTENT: CHILD PORNOGRAPHY

Although the public's understanding of pornography is highly nuanced and conflicted, there is nearly universal condemnation of child pornography and sexually explicit content involving minors. As the Supreme Court explained, "[t]he prevention of sexual exploitation and abuse of children constitutes a government objective of surpassing importance."[34]

For purposes of the law, a minor is a person under the age of eighteen. Once a person has reached adulthood, the person is fully protected by the protections of the First Amendment. Under eighteen, however, Congress and the courts are willing to enforce much more stringent laws to protect the minors. This is particularly true regarding the participation of minors in the creation of sexually explicit materials. As a result of this distinction, the Supreme Court has upheld laws that criminalize and prohibit the distribution of all child pornography, whether or not that pornography would be considered legally obscene. Unlike the obscenity laws, the Supreme Court has also upheld laws that criminalize the possession of child pornography.

The legal theories behind the prohibitions against child pornography focus on the individual and societal harms triggered by the creation of child pornography. Depictions of children engaged in sexual activity are legally understood to be a form of child abuse.

The U.S. Department of Justice treats child pornography as contraband. The federal criminal code and most state criminal laws define child pornography as any visual depiction of sexually explicit conduct involving a minor.[35] Photographs, videos, and other works that appear to depict an identifiable, actual minor are all covered by the law.

Prosecutorial Remedies and Tools Against the Exploitation of Children Today Act of 2003 ("PROTECT Act") updated the laws on child pornography, as well as introducing the federal Amber Alert system and providing additional protections for crimes against minors.[36] As construed by the Supreme Court, the PROTECT Act prohibits the knowing distribution of material that either contains "(i) an obscene visual depiction of a minor engaging in sexually explicit conduct"; or "(ii) a visual depiction of an actual minor engaging in sexually explicit conduct."[37] The distinction between the two types of works eliminates the definition of child pornography for sexually explicit content depicting a minor made using computer graphics or animation techniques. Manga art, for example, is often quite sexually explicit, but to obtain a conviction for possession of such works under the PROTECT Act, the prosecutors would also have to establish that the works met the test for obscenity. When the work was made using an actual minor, however, the prosecution does not need to prove the work was obscene.

In the HBO film *The Tale*, for example, a movie depicting the real-life sexual abuse of the film's director was made to graphically simulate sex between the thirteen-year-old star and her thirty-five-year-old co-star. Unable to find a suitable adult for the role, the production shot the sex scenes without the two stars together. The production used a vertical bed, meaning that the young actress was never lying in a bed at all, but instead standing in front of one. While working on the scenes, the actress' mother, a psychiatrist, her studio teacher, and a SAG-AFTRA union representative were all present. In those situations where the directors needed to have the two actors together, an adult body-double was used instead of the thirteen-year-old star. These steps illustrate how the illusion of sexually explicit conduct can be simulated, and they stand in stark contrast to the sexual abuse perpetrated to create child pornography.[38]

To help prosecute child pornography and sex abuse cases, the FBI operates the Child Exploitation, Internet Crimes Against Children, and Human Trafficking Task Forces. These task forces coordinate with other federal, state, and local law enforcement agencies and other divisions within the Department of Justice to prosecute cases and protect children being harmed by child pornography.

One of the most effective national resources to protect against child abuse and child pornography is the National Center for Missing & Exploited Children (NCMEC). In its brochure on reporting child sexual exploitation, NCMEC provides this advice:

> If you or your child are exposed to CSAM [Child Sexual Abuse Material] online immediately report this to the National Center for Missing & Exploited Children (NCMEC) at www.cybertipline.org. Reports may be made 24 hours a day, 7 days a week. Reporting these incidents to NCMEC is the first step in addressing the situation. Your report will allow law enforcement to start an investigation, help keep other children safe, and start the recovery process for you and your child.[39]

Other resources include the FBI, the National Childhood Traumatic Stress Network,[40] and the National Sexual Assault Hotline (1-800-656-HOPE (4673)).[41]

NCMEC creates a digital fingerprint of the images of child pornography shared on the Internet, which it uses to help law enforcement search and track the illegal content. More importantly, when NCMEC identifies a work not in its database, it alerts federal authorities to help track down the origins of that image or video in the attempt to protect the children involved in the production of the child pornography and bring quick prosecution against the people involved in making child pornography.

Parents should understand that the laws against child pornography are very strict and aggressively enforced. Even sexually active teens can be charged with child pornography for creating images or videos of themselves involved in sexually explicit conduct. While these prosecutions are rare and inconsistent with the intent behind the child pornography laws, the risk of an overzealous prosecutor should not be ignored.

As noted elsewhere, the laws involving depictions of minors and nudity have become much more explicit and aggressive as Congress and state legislatures attempt to deal with content considered objectionable on the Internet. As a result, bathtub pictures and videos that might have been considered harmless in the 1960s might be characterized as sexually explicit content in today's environment. Parents should be careful to avoid creating any content that could potentially be construed as even coming close to falling into this category and ensure that none of their other children or family members make a similar error. While this has a chilling effect on speech, when it comes to the depiction of sexually explicit material involving minors, it is much better to be safe than to face decades of time in state or federal prison.

G. VIOLENT CONTENT AND MATURE GAMES

Parents are often concerned about the wide range of violent videogames on the market. In some adolescents, the continued exposure to violent videogames has been associated with an increase in the player's level of aggression. A significant body of research has attempted to answer this question. In 2018, the Proceedings of the National Academy of Sciences (PNAS) published a review of more than 17,000 studies and surveys to help address the sharp debate among researchers whether this effect was real, or a bias built into the research because researchers were trying to find a relationship.[42]

The PNAS study concurred with the majority of earlier studies that violent videogames are associated with increases in aggression in the players of those games. The analysis concluded that "playing violent videogames is associated with greater levels of overt physical aggression over time, after accounting for prior aggression. These findings support the general claim that violent videogame play is associated with increases in physical aggression over time."[43] In affirming the large body of literature finding the link between violent videogames and aggression, the report also supported the related concern that violent videogames are associated with a loss or lack of empathy for victims of violence.

There remain a number of studies that continue to disagree with the assessment that violent videogames have an impact on the player's behavior.[44] More importantly, there is very little science that equates the violent videogames to a change in violence more generally. An earlier article in the Harvard Mental Health Letter adds these additional notes:

- Much of the research on violent videogame use relies on measures to assess aggression that don't correlate with real-world violence. Some studies are observational and don't prove cause and effect.

- Federal crime statistics suggest that serious violent crimes among youths have decreased since 1996, even as videogame sales have soared.
- Parents can protect children from potential harm by limiting use of videogames and taking other common-sense precautions.[45]

Nonetheless, despite the caveats regarding the research, the majority of health organizations, including the American Academy of Pediatrics and the American Academy of Child & Adolescent Psychiatry take the position that exposure to violent games can contribute to violent behavior or other harmful consequences for children.

While these findings are evidence of a persistent correlation between the violent content and the twin harms of increased aggression and decreased empathy, the research does not provide sufficient evidence to reverse the longstanding Supreme Court view of violent content that it remains fully protected speech under the First Amendment. Although states have tried to find a way to redefine the most extremely violent content as "obscene," in order to remove it from constitutional protection, none of these efforts have withstood Supreme Court review. In *Brown v. Entertainment Merchants Association*,[46] the Supreme Court made absolutely clear that there can be no expansion of the definition of obscenity to take harmful violent content into account. As a result, there is very little regulatory assistance that municipalities or states can use to restrict violent content.

Parents, however, are often quite concerned about the violent nature of the content in videogames. To address these concerns, the videogame industry, like the motion picture and television industries, has tried to use a voluntary rating system as a way to keep mature content out of the hands of minors.

According to the ESRB, "nearly nine out of 10 parents who purchase physical videogames for their kids are aware of the ESRB ratings, and three out of four regularly check the ratings to decide what's appropriate for their kids."[47] The ESRB further claims that 83 percent of parents require their children to get permission before playing games.[48]

The ESRB is most effective at enforcing its rules against large retailers. The ESRB has a sophisticated rating and enforcement system. The ESRB uses secret shoppers to help ensure that retailers are following the ratings guidelines and works closely with large online stores including Walmart.com, Target.com, BestBuy.com, Amazon.com and GameStop.com among others.

At the same time, however, access to videogames is easier than ever. A survey by PC Gamer reports that 90 percent of PC gamers have pirated a game rather than purchasing it legally.[49] The survey suggests that 35 percent of players actively use pirated content rather than purchased content to acquire their games.[50] Teens also exchange games, subscribe to gaming services, and use other methods to access games. Since teens often have easy access to games outside of retail purchases, reliance on the ratings systems is only the first step to address the issues of game content.

For parents, the most important question is the extent to which there is an impact on attitude and behavior for the adolescents in the household. The data strongly suggest that there is strong negative impact on some players while there is little or no negative impact for other players. If a person in the household exhibits aggressive or antisocial behavior or a loss of empathy as a result of using violent games, then the negative behavior should be identified, and the amount of time spent in that activity should be reduced or eliminated.

Parents might also feel it is important to restrict access to violent, antisocial content because of its message and content. Parents should also discuss this issue with their children. For most families, graphic, realistic violence against women will likely be far more offensive than similar violence against zombies or alien monsters.

For some gamers, parents might be more concerned about the amount of time spent gaming rather than the nature of the content in any particular game. For others, there may be certain games that drive more aggressive responses. Parents should understand their teen's interests and behaviors. If the teen's behavior changes as a result of spending too much time playing videogames, then like any online activity, the parents should discuss the issue with the teen and manage the time spent. If the parent does not approve of particular content, then the parent can set those limits. Enforcement of those limits must come from an understanding between the parent and child, since neither rating systems nor technological strategies will stop the determined teen.

Parents should also watch the games being played by their children. This will give the parents a better understanding of what really happens within the game play. The data suggest that parents should be mindful of the content in the videogames, but ultimately, the experience affects each player differently. By discussing the games and observing the conduct, parents can make informed decisions on how best to manage violent games within their households.

Chapter 10

Cyberstalking and Online Harassment

A. INTRODUCTION—THE HARMS
OF ONLINE HARASSMENT

Although parents and teachers are likely aware of the persistent risk of online harassment, the depth and breadth of the problem may not be obvious. Even though digital media has become an essential part of everyday life for most Americans, the experience is not always a rosy one. It is not uncommon for writers to receive death threats for unpopular posts or for athletes to receive hate-filled posts because of errors on the field or comments off the field. High school athletes have received attacks regarding their choice of where to play in college.

For professional athletes, actors, and media personalities, hurtful and despicable online comments may be part of the cost of celebrity, but the public should not simply accept this as the new normal. Worse, these attacks are not limited to professionals. High school athletes, cheerleaders, and other school celebrities are often the focus of shameful attacks. For other students, the bullying, harassment, and stalking come from within the school, using the power of digital media to magnify and exacerbate bullying behavior. The real harm of online harassment cannot be overstated. This example is reprinted from the 2016 U.S. Attorneys' Bulletin:

On a series of handwritten flashcards, Amanda Todd detailed the torment she had dealt with for over four years and posted it to the Internet via a YouTube video:

Hello. I've decided to tell you about my never ending story. In 7th grade I would go with friends on webcam, meet and talk to new people. Then got called stunning, beautiful, perfect etc. They wanted me to flash. So I did. . . .

one year later . . . I got a msg on facebook. From him . . . Don't know how he knew me . . . It said . . . if you don't put on a show for me I send ur boobs. He knew my adress, school, relatives, friends family names.

Christmas break . . . Knock at my door at 4 It was the police . . . my photo was sent to everyone. I then got really sick and got . . . Anxiety major depression panic disorder. . . .

A year past and the guy came back with my new list of friends and school. But made a facebook page. My boobs were a profile pic. . . .

Cried every night, lost all my friends and respect people had from me . . . Then nobody liked me name calling, judged . . . I can never get that Photo back . . . I started cutting . . . Didn't have any friends and I sat at lunch alone So I moved Schools again.

After a month later I started talking to an old guy friend We back and fourth texted and he started to say he . . . Liked me . . . Led me on He had a girlfriend . . . I thought he like me . . . 1 week later I get a text get out of your school. His girlfriend and 15 others came including hiself. . . .

The girls and 2 others just said look around nobody likes you Infront of my new School (50) people . . . A guy than yelled just punch her already So she did... she threw me to the ground a punched me several times Kids filmed it. I was all alone and left on the ground. Teachers ran over but I just went and layed in a ditch and my dad found me. I wanted to die so bad . . . when he brought me home I drank bleach . . . It killed me inside and I thought I was gonna actully die. Ambulence came and brought me to the hospital and flushed me. After I got home all I saw was on facebook—She deserved it, did you wash the mud out of your hair?—I hope shes dead. nobody cared . . . I moved away to another city to my moms. another school. . . .

I didn't wanna press charges because I wanted to move on 6 months has gone by . . . people are posting pics of bleach clorex and ditches. tagging me . . . I was doing alot better too. They said . . . She should try a different bleach. I hope she dies this time and isn't so stupid.

Why do I get this? I messed up but why follow me. They said I hope she sees this and kills herself . . . Why do I get this? I messed up but why follow me. I left your guys city . . . Im constanty crying now . . . Im stuck . . . whats left of me now . . . nothing stops I have nobody. . . .

I need someone :(my name is Amanda Todd.

A few months later, at age fifteen, Amanda killed herself at her home in British Columbia.[1]

Although national statistics suggest that approximately 1.4 percent of adults suffer from online cyberstalking in any given year, this number goes up substantially for women and increases to 3.4 percent for individuals who were divorced or separated.

In contrast, for students, the numbers are substantially worse. According to a Pew Research Survey, 59 percent of teens 13–17 have been victims of cyberbullying of some kind. The most common version of the online abuse is name-calling, with 42 percent of students having been called names.[2] A quarter of all students report receiving explicit images they did not request and 7 percent of students have had their explicit images shared without their consent.[3] More than a fifth of students (21 percent) have been stalked by others using digital media, and nearly a third (32 percent) have been the victims of false rumor campaigns.[4] Girls are more likely to be the targets of false rumors and of sexually explicit content than boys, but both groups are victimized substantially. Girls, however, are much more likely to be the targets of four or more different forms of online harassment than boys. Fifteen percent of girls report the high levels of targeted abuse, compared to only 4 percent of boys.

The teens in the survey universally agreed that cyberbullying and online harassment are a problem, with 63 percent describing it as a major problem. The survey found that the teens do not believe that schools, social media platforms, or politicians are helping solve the problems. The only good news is that the teens surveyed found that parents were more effective than the other groups in addressing these concerns.[5]

As defined by the Department of Justice, "The term 'stalking' means engaging in a course of conduct directed at a specific person that would cause a reasonable person to fear for his or her safety or the safety of others or suffer substantial emotional distress."[6] Cyberstalking emphasizes the use of online and digital media to conduct the stalking behavior. Aggressors use email, chat, blogs, text messaging, social media, and anywhere that the victim might come into contact with the harassment. Cyberstalking typically manifests through one or more of these activities:

- Repeated, unwanted, intrusive, and frightening communications from the perpetrator by phone, mail, and/or email
- Repeatedly leaving or sending the victim unwanted items, presents, or flowers
- Following or lying-in-wait for the victim at places such as home, school, work, or place of recreation
- Making direct or indirect threats to harm the victim, the victim's children, relatives, friends, or pets
- Damaging or threatening to damage the victim's property
- Harassing the victim through the Internet
- Posting information or spreading rumors about the victim on the Internet, in a public place, or by word of mouth
- Obtaining personal information about the victim by accessing public records, using Internet search services, hiring private investigators, searching through

the victim's garbage, following the victim, and contacting the victim's friends, family, coworkers, or neighbors, and so on.[7]

There are laws criminalizing stalking and cyberstalking in all states as well as federal anti-stalking laws. The laws generally distinguish cyberstalking from cyberharassment. In cyberharassment statutes, the laws are focused on speech that is general in nature, whereas cyberstalking laws are focused on narrow conduct.

The federal website stopbullying.gov provides a brief checklist for the steps to take when stalking, cyberbullying, or online harassment starts. The following is a summary:

- **Call 911**—if there has been a crime or someone is at immediate risk of harm.
- **Contact the National Suicide Prevention Lifeline** online or at 1-800-273-TALK (8255)—if someone is feeling hopeless, helpless, thinking of suicide.
- **Find a local counselor or other mental health services**—if someone is acting differently than normal, such as always seeming sad or anxious, struggling to complete tasks, or not being able to care for themselves.
- **To address bullying**—contact the teacher, school counselor, school principal, school superintendent, or the State Department of Education.
- **To address an inadequate response to bullying based on race, color, national origin, sex, disability, or religion**—contact the school superintendent, State Department of Education, U.S. Department of Education, Office for Civil Rights, or the U.S. Department of Justice, Civil Rights Division.[8]

For parents and teachers, the most important step is to intervene early to break the cycle of harassment and address the anxiety and depression which are commonly associated with such attacks. Victims of these attacks need help to feel safe and secure. If the conduct involves another student, parents should immediately involve the school, but they should be prepared to move beyond the teachers, counselors, and principals if the response is not sufficient or the behavior continues. Law enforcement is limited in its options regarding cyberbullying because of the limits on law enforcement required under the First Amendment. Schools have more latitude to enforce their codes of conduct, so the school should be the institution that responds most effectively, though unfortunately, that is often not the case.

B. HARASSMENT VERSUS PROTECTED SPEECH

Despite the intentional, harmful nature of cyberbullying, many courts addressing cyberbullying legislation have found the state statutes to be overbroad or otherwise inconsistent with the First Amendment. The First Amendment protects most speech, unless it falls into a very narrow category of unprotected speech, including defamatory speech, obscenity, child pornography, incitement, fighting words, and true threats, as well as fraud and other speech integral to criminal conduct. Importantly, courts continue to recognize that the intent to commit harm to another person's mental, physical, or emotional condition is criminal conduct, and therefore can be treated as speech outside of First Amendment protection.

Most cyberstalking and online harassment can be criminalized only if it meets the test for intentional harm or true threats. True threats only occur when the person becomes an aggressor and "means to communicate a serious expression of an intent to commit an act of unlawful violence to a particular individual or group of individuals . . . Intimidation in the constitutionally proscribable sense of the word is a type of true threat, where a speaker directs a threat to a person or group of persons with the intent of placing the victim in fear of bodily harm or death."[9] Fighting words are somewhat different, meaning those "likely to provoke the average person to retaliation, and thereby cause a breach of the peace."[10] In practice, fighting words are restricted primarily to face-to-face confrontations that are highly likely to escalate into blows.

Federal law provides a stalking statute, as do most states. The federal law penalizes whoever,

> with the intent to kill, injure, harass, intimidate, or place under surveillance with intent to kill, injure, harass, or intimidate another person, uses the mail, any interactive computer service or electronic communication service or electronic communication system of interstate commerce, or any other facility of interstate or foreign commerce to engage in a course of conduct that (A) places that person in reasonable fear of the death of or serious bodily injury to [the] person or a [family member]; or (B) causes, attempts to cause, or would be reasonably expected to cause substantial emotional distress to [the] person [or a family member].[11]

The federal law limits the law to intentional crimes. Although this makes the law harder to apply, it helps ensure that the law is consistent with the First Amendment. State laws often try to be more inclusive, but the result is that those laws are often declared unconstitutional.[12] There are many other examples of criminal conduct conducted through speech, such as criminal conspiracies, fraud, and blackmail. As such, the criminalization of intentional abuse will sometimes be understood as falling within the criminal speech categories of exceptions to the First Amendment.

When a particular aggressor singles out a target for ongoing abuse, the cyberstalking and online harassment laws might provide a solution. In many other situations, however, the harassment comes from casual interactions with many of the victim's classmates and with total strangers who enjoy participating in the trolling culture online.

C. OBLIGATIONS OF THE SCHOOL

Although the federal government has many mandates regarding K-12 education, there are no federal programs, curricula, or staff training mandates regarding bullying for the schools. Federal resources do not reflect the number of students who report being bullied or harassed while in school. All states have tried to address these concerns with state-based programs, but these programs vary widely in their scope and effectiveness.

Data from the Centers for Disease Control and Prevention suggest that school bullying is twice as frequent during middle school years than in other grades. At the school district level, this creates a clear focus for anti-bullying efforts and educational programs aimed at stamping out the harmful behavior. These data also highlight that school and parental intervention are more likely to be useful than criminal laws.

For parents, dealing with cyberbullying and harassment is a difficult challenge. Many of the reported incidents occur in schools, where the overall attitude toward bullying is one of resignation. Teachers want the bullying to stop but feel powerless to stop it. If the teachers do not feel supported in their efforts to stop racist, sexist, or homophobic slurs in the halls, they will do little to help the targeted victims of the antisocial behavior. The culture feeds on itself. In such an environment, other students will not report such behaviors, fearing retaliation for standing up to harassment as well.

For parents trying to reverse a culture of intolerance in a school, the first step is to speak with the student's teachers, counselors, and principals. Parents should also focus on those attributes of the harassment that might trigger federal obligations on the part of the school district. When the bullying involves race, national origin, color, sex, age, disability, or religion, schools receiving federal funds must report and resolve the situation. In those cases, both the U.S. Department of Education's Office for Civil Rights and the U.S. Department of Justice's Civil Rights Division have a responsibility to investigate.

1. State Laws

Among the fifty states and District of Columbia, every jurisdiction has some legislation addressing cyberbullying, although these vary greatly. More than forty of the jurisdictions supplement the state criminal laws with policies that require the school districts to investigate and address bullying. In Ohio, for example, the state passed the Jessica Logan Act, named after a teen who sent nude photographs of herself to her boyfriend. The pictures were shared with other students, leading to a campaign of harassment against her. Jessica struggled with isolation, anxiety, and depression, leading to her suicide shortly after graduation.[13] The definition of the prohibited conduct is carefully defined:

(a) Any intentional written, verbal, electronic, or physical act that a student has exhibited toward another particular student more than once and the behavior both:
  (i) Causes mental or physical harm to the other student; (ii) Is sufficiently severe, persistent, or pervasive that it creates an intimidating, threatening, or abusive educational environment for the other student.
(b) Violence within a dating relationship.[14]

The law is severely limited, however, because it does not include civil or criminal penalties. Instead, it merely requires that the school systems provide disciplinary policies to address the harassment. Even if the policies are inadequate, the law does not provide the victim or the victim's parents additional remedies against the school or the perpetrators. Many of the actions taken by a student to harass another student will constitute criminal actions under other state laws and give rise to civil liability, but the failure to incorporate direct consequences directly into the cyberbullying laws severely limit the impact of these laws.

Understandably, criminal charges are a last resort to address cyberbullying, but the ability to use the court system provides schools powerful authority to stop aggressive behavior. Despite this, few states are willing to provide additional authority. Instead, the problems of cyberbullying continue to grow.

2. Legal Authority of the Schools to Police

States are somewhat reluctant to take more authoritative steps to manage conflict among students that evolves into bullying because of the complex constitutional protections for student speech that influence these laws.

The constitutional standard for regulation of student speech was set in *Tinker v. Des Moines Independent Community School District* (1969).[15] *Tinker* involved five students who chose to wear small black armbands to school to protest the Vietnam War. After the students were punished for their behavior, the dispute was heard by the Supreme Court. The Supreme Court began by noting that students do not "shed their constitutional rights to freedom of speech or expression at the schoolhouse gate," but went on to recognize "the special characteristics of the school environment."

The court established that to take action to limit the speech of the students, the school district would need to show that the speech "would materially and substantially interfere with the requirements of appropriate discipline in the operation of the school."[16] The Supreme Court expanded upon *Tinker* with *Bethel School District v. Fraser* (1986). In *Bethel*, the court made clear that *Tinker* did not limit the schools' power to police vulgar and offensive content.

> Surely it is a highly appropriate function of public school education to prohibit the use of vulgar and offensive terms in public discourse. Indeed, the "funda-mental values necessary to the maintenance of a democratic political system" disfavor the use of terms of debate highly offensive or highly threatening to others. Nothing in the Constitution prohibits the states from insisting that certain modes of expression are inappropriate and subject to sanctions. The inculcation of these values is truly the "work of the schools."[17]

In addition to the right to protect the schools from speech that would mate-rially and substantially interfere with the appropriate discipline in the opera-tion of the school, the court recognized that schools could prohibit sexual innuendo, vulgar, or similar speech. This rule was extended further in *Morse v. Frederick* (2007),[18] where the court allowed a school to take action against a student for displaying a banner, "BONG HiTS 4 JESUS," at the 2002 Olympic Torch Relay as it passed through Juneau, Alaska.[19] Students were released from school to attend the relay, transforming it into a school-sanc-tioned event, and thus avoiding the question regarding off-campus speech in that case. The Supreme Court found that the school had the authority to order the removal of the banner and to punish the student who refused to do so, but did not go so far as to allow schools to prohibit all offensive speech. Instead, the court held that the banner could be removed because it could reasonably be viewed as promoting illegal drug use.

The fourth of the Supreme Court cases on student speech involved the ability of a school to control and censor the contents of a school-run student newspaper. In *Hazelwood School District v. Kuhlmeier* (1988),[20] the Supreme Court addressed the extent to which the First Amendment protected the free speech rights of the students working on a high school newspaper produced as part of the school's Journalism II course. The Supreme Court found that *Tinker* did not apply to the paper since it was produced as part of a course's curriculum. In a broad endorsement of the school's authority, the Supreme Court held that "educators do not offend the First Amendment by exercis-ing editorial control over the style and content of student speech in school-sponsored expressive activities so long as their actions are reasonably related to legitimate pedagogical concerns."[21]

In each of the four cases, the Supreme Court has been careful to establish that the authority of the school district has been to manage and censor on-campus speech or speech that was part of the school's off-campus school-sanctioned activities. In 2021, the Supreme Court took a cautious step to address the issue of student speech that occurs on social media.

In *Mahanoy Area Sch. Dist. v. B. L. by and through Levy*,[22] the Supreme Court took up a student's challenge to her suspension from junior varsity cheerleading squad based on the cheerleader posting a Snapchat message to her friends in which she held up her middle finger to the camera with the words "f*** school f*** softball f*** cheer f*** everything" superimposed on the image. "The student's speech took place outside of school hours and away from the school's campus."[23] The student, B.L., was upset because she was not elevated to the varsity cheerleading team. B.L. did not send her Snap beyond her 250 friends. Although her friends included other members of the cheerleading teams, it did not include any of the coaches or school administrators. The court held that while the school may have a valid inter-est to control student speech off campus, the school district violated B.L's First Amendment rights in reprimanding her for her post, which is protected speech.

The lower courts had struggled to develop a standard that reflects the case-law of *Tinker*, *Fraser*, *Frederick*, and *Kuhlmeier*. The Supreme Court used the framework of these four cases to provide some limited guidance for the courts and for the school districts when regulating online speech.

> We have made clear that students do not "shed their constitutional rights to free-dom of speech or expression," even "at the school house gate." But we have also made clear that courts must apply the First Amendment "in light of the special characteristics of the school environment." One such characteristic, which we have stressed, is the fact that schools at times stand in loco parentis, i.e., in the place of parents.[24]
>
> This Court has previously outlined three specific categories of student speech that schools may regulate in certain circumstances: (1) "indecent," "lewd," or "vulgar" speech uttered during a school assembly on school grounds; (2) speech, uttered during a class trip, that promotes "illegal drug use"; and (3) speech that others may reasonably perceive as "bear[ing] the imprimatur of the school," such as that appearing in a school-sponsored newspaper.[25]

The long tradition of this framework is helpful in the context of online student speech, but the divergent approaches taken by courts to apply these rules in the online and off-campus settings have not been particularly helpful. The Supreme Court acknowledged this, noting the many areas where schools and parents have an expectation of supervision and assistance by school districts. The examples in the opinion included "serious or severe bullying or harassment targeting particular individuals; threats aimed at teachers or other students; the failure to follow rules concerning lessons, the writing of papers, the use of computers, or participation in other online school activities; and breaches of school security devices, including material maintained within school computers."[26]

The Supreme Court did not directly address these examples. By listing them, however, it encouraged lower courts to continue to use the prior opinions to reach problematic behavior in these situations. To help the lower courts, the Supreme Court instead provided three guidelines to help shape future decisions by schools and courts:

> First, a school, in relation to off-campus speech, will rarely stand in loco parentis. The doctrine of in loco parentis treats school administrators as standing in the place of students' parents under circumstances where the children's actual parents cannot protect, guide, and discipline them. Geographically speaking, off-campus speech will normally fall within the zone of parental, rather than school-related, responsibility.
>
> Second, from the student speaker's perspective, regulations of off-campus speech, when coupled with regulations of on-campus speech, include all the speech a student utters during the full 24-hour day. That means courts must be more skeptical of a school's efforts to regulate off-campus speech, for doing so may mean the student cannot engage in that kind of speech at all. When it comes to political or religious speech that occurs outside school or a school program or activity, the school will have a heavy burden to justify intervention.
>
> Third, the school itself has an interest in protecting a student's unpopular expression, especially when the expression takes place off campus. America's public schools are the nurseries of democracy. Our representative democracy only works if we protect the "marketplace of ideas." his free exchange facilitates an informed public opinion, which, when transmitted to lawmakers, helps produce laws that reflect the People's will. That protection must include the protection of unpopular ideas, for popular ideas have less need for protection. Thus, schools have a strong interest in ensuring that future generations understand the workings in practice of the well-known aphorism, "I disapprove of what you say, but I will defend to the death your right to say it."[27]

3. Extension of Civil Rights Protections to Gender Identity

The Supreme Court has also been active on the issue of civil rights laws involving sexual orientation and gender identity. At issue has been the statutory meaning of the word "sex." In *Bostock v. Clayton County, Georgia*

(2020),[28] the Supreme Court determined that under Title VII the phrase "because of . . . sex" included sexual orientation and gender identity.[29] Title VII applies only in the context of employment discrimination, but many of the civil rights laws use the same terms and definitions. As a result, this decision will likely be extended in the education arena.

Although school districts have sometimes argued that homophobic attacks are outside the U.S. civil rights laws, the *Bostock* decision will likely extend beyond Title VII's employment discrimination context to the rights under Title IX and Title IV governing schools and colleges, further extending the protections already afforded by those laws. For parents and adolescents dealing with cyberbullying, it is quite common that some of the attacks will violate the student's federal and state civil rights and the obligations of the school under these laws and the laws of the ADA and Section 504 of the Rehabilitation Act.

4. How to Work with the School

Parents should document the harassment to the greatest extent possible, and report the information to the school through the teacher, principal, and counselor as soon as they have the information in hand. Documentation includes screenshots of messages, complete email threads including the IP addresses of the senders, recordings of harassing calls, and the date and time of the harassing content as it is created.

Parents should also document all communications with the school and with law enforcement. If the school responds quickly and positively, the parents should ask for the responses to be summarized or provided in writing so there is a contemporaneous record of the school's efforts.

If the school is nonresponsive, then the record of the parents' efforts will help establish a timeline and document the failure of the school to meet its state and federal obligations under the law. That documentation will be very helpful to provide evidence to the school district and to the civil rights investigators, if the situation is permitted to continue to fester. These are the steps that a school should take to address the complaint regarding harassment:

- The school should begin an immediate investigation into the incident. The inquiry "must be prompt, thorough, and impartial." It should be documented throughout each step and the written record should be available to the victim and the parents. However, the school may redact the names of students in the report provided to the complainant's parents.[30]
- The school's process should include interviews with the "targeted students, offending students, and witnesses."[31]

- The school "should communicate with targeted students regarding steps taken to end harassment [and] check in with targeted students to ensure that harassment has ceased."[32]
- Finally, "when an investigation reveals that harassment has occurred, a school should take steps reasonably calculated to end the harassment, eliminate any hostile environment, prevent harassment from recurring, and prevent retaliation against the targeted student(s) or complainant(s)."[33]

At the same time these steps are being taken, it is important to address the impact on the student. The student's mental health and well-being should be at the forefront of any strategy to address the issue. This includes helping the student with appropriate counseling and support, as well as involving the student in the strategy to address the bullying. In many cases, the student will understand the context and ramifications of the proposed resolution better than the parents or school officials. This perspective should be given great weight in deciding how best to proceed.

Chapter 11

Digital Self-Harm, Sexploitation, and Online Sexual Predators

A. INTRODUCTION

In addition to harassment and cyberbullying, social media and online engagement open the door to a myriad of other risks. In some cases, the risk is created by the technology, but in most cases, social media and online communications serve to reduce the transaction costs or social friction to risky behaviors that exist in person as well as online. A wide range of global research projects identify that approximately 13–18 percent of adolescents "engage in self-injurious behaviors during their lifetime and that this behavior has been on the rise over the last two decades."[1] The rates of self-harm vary considerably depending on the nature of the behavior. "Typical conceptualizations include cutting, scratching, biting, or hitting (oneself); abusing pills; eating disorders; and/or reckless or bone breaking behaviors." It should not be surprising then, that a percentage of adolescents use the Internet and social media to engage in high-risk behaviors or behaviors that could be understood as including a self-harm component.

Three particular concerns stand out. In areas such as digital self-harm, sexploitation, and interactions with sexual predators who lurk online, the victims of these attacks sometimes become vulnerable because of their battles with anxiety, prior situations of abuse, or misplaced trust in those who will later do the victims harm. "An adolescent's decision to self-harm may not be as much a call for help as a demonstration of felt pain and distress."[2]

In each of these examples, the best strategies for reducing the risks are to create healthier environments for the adolescents to reduce the underlying causes that trigger inappropriate conduct. Many of these risks are triggered by harassment, isolation, or other social situations. These threats have the

155

potential to revictimize children who have already suffered from harassment or from other situations that exacerbate anxiety and isolation.

B. DIGITAL SELF-HARM

Digital self-harm has only recently been identified as a distinct form of self-harm in the scientific literature, beginning with an early blog post in 2010. The research has coalesced around the definition of digital self-harm as the "anonymous online posting, sending, or otherwise sharing of hurtful content about oneself."[3] Digital self-harm does not stand alone. Studies have shown that "digital self-harm was positively associated with physical self-harm, school bullying victimization and cyberbullying victimization, deviance, drug use, and depressive symptoms. Male and non-heterosexual youth were also more likely to report having engaged in digital self-harm."[4]

A recent study based on the 2019 Florida Youth Substance Abuse Survey provided a data set from 10,424 Florida middle school and high school students. Among this survey set, "6% of participants reported having engaged in any amount of digital self-harm within the past 30 days, and 10% reported having done so at least once within the prior 12 months."[5] The percentage of middle and high school students who reported digital self-harm in this 2019 assessment is higher than in prior studies. An earlier report identified 9 percent of college freshman as having engaged in digital self-harm when they had been in high school, suggesting that the number may be increasing.[6] Alternatively, it may be that the number is higher among middle school students than high school students, which is true of bullying incidents as well.

Digital self-harm is not widely recognized among researchers, and it is an important predictor of risk for the students who are engaging in this form of self-harm. "Much attention in clinical, school, and community settings has been given to traditional forms of self-injury among teens (e.g., cutting and burning), not only because of the damage that is physically done and the internal turmoil it betrays, but also because self-harm has been linked to suicide."[7]

Unlike cutting or similar behaviors, the network effects of social media may result in a student's digital online bullying leading to aggression and bullying by others, expanding the scope of the harm and unintentionally triggering escalation of the abuse.

The phenomenon that is now recognized as digital self-harm was originally documented by danah boyd, Partner Researcher at Microsoft Research and the founder/president of Data & Society. She explained that the social media site Formspring[8] was unable to block bullying posts because the posts were coming from the victim's own account.[9] "As [Formspring] started looking into specific cases of teens answering 'anonymous' harassing questions, they started realizing that a number of vicious questions were posted by the Formspring account owners themselves."

For parents, all signs indicating self-harm are warning signs. Recognizing that a child's online posts might be the source of both bullying and self-harm will also help address the right steps to intervene. Changing schools is often essential to end bullying by changing the environment in which the harm occurs. But if the cyberbullying has self-harm at its root, then the change in school and the other school-based interventions will be ineffective.

Parents dealing with serious situations involving self-harm may need to take more intrusive actions to help them properly diagnose the situation. This is one situation where parents may wish to temporarily utilize keystroke loggers to help identify whether the student has become the author of the anonymous, harassing posts. In most cases, such an intrusion into the privacy of the student is unwarranted and unwise, but in certain cases that risk might be warranted, such as if there is a risk of suicide or if the family is preparing to take drastic actions to curb the abuse, which it believes is coming from peers at school.

Given the size of the problem reported from the 2019 data, digital self-harm is a larger and much more serious situation than has previously been recognized. As such, parents need to be aware and ready to intervene.

C. SEXPLOITATION AND REVENGE PORN

In many of the cyberbullying cases, the attackers used sexually explicit materials. In 2010, college freshman Tyler Clementi jumped off the George Washington Bridge to his death after learning that his roommate secretly live streamed Tyler having sex in his dorm room with another male student.[10] Jessica Logan and Amanda Todd, both suicide victims mentioned earlier, had their cyberstalking and bullying begin with the distribution of nude photographs.

The nonconsensual production or distribution of nude and sexually exploitative imagery is a direct, harmful invasion of privacy. The highly personal nature of the invasion often leads to severe anxiety and depression. When the distribution is started by someone with whom the victim has had an intimate relationship, the sense of betrayal is magnified. For adolescents, the problem may be further exacerbated because it may out the person regarding their sexual identity or their sexual activity to parents, family, and classmates.

Victims are often blackmailed by the holders of the explicit images for money or for creating even more pictures and videos. The attackers can use the vulnerability and isolation of being the victim of sexploitation to further harm the victim. In addition, the willingness to provide nude photographs and sexually explicit videos, may, in some cases, be a form of self-harm.

Terms such as revenge porn and sexploitation have been used to capture the sense of betrayal often associated with nonconsensual publication of nude and sexually explicit content. As noted in chapter 9, the distribution of images for minors will often be treated as violating child pornography laws.

Beginning in 2012, Dr. Holly Jacobs began the End Revenge Porn campaign to raise awareness to this form of stalking and invasion of privacy. Her efforts led to the development of the Cyber Civil Rights Initiative (CCRI).[11] In less than a decade, more than forty-six states plus the District of Columbia have enacted statutes designed to stop the practice of revenge porn and sexploitation.[12]

CCRI provides a crisis helpline—844-878-CCRI (2274)—and guidance on how to remove offensive content from online platforms. The guidance provides steps on how to request removal of the content for many of the most popular platforms.

Many of the popular social media platforms, including Facebook, Instagram, Twitter, and Tumblr, have policies that restrict or prohibit nudity and pornography. All sites have policies that prohibit the photographs and videos of minors. By documenting the nature of the image, its location, and the age of the victim (for minors), sites will typically remove the content quite expeditiously. If Google, Bing, and Yahoo are contacted to remove search results, their assistance will not remove the content from the page where the images were found. Unfortunately, much of this content is further uploaded to pornography sites that do not have meaningful content restrictions or operational takedown policies. Many of these sites are hosted outside the United States in jurisdictions that have little or no interest in enforcing takedown requests or actions under U.S. law.

The FTC encourages victims of revenge porn and sexploitative content to contact it if the social media platform or hosting company is nonresponsive. The FTC points to its success in shuttering MyEx.com as an example of the FTC's ability to intervene successfully in stopping online predators from taking advantage of the victims a second time.[13]

In addition to revenge porn and sexploitative content, there are also numerous instances of grooming behavior, communication with a minor that becomes increasingly sexual in order to entice the child into later sexual behavior. Grooming communications intended to entice minors into the creation of sexually explicit images or videos fall within the definition of solicitation of child pornography, which the Supreme Court has found is outside the First Amendment and may be properly prosecuted.[14] As the court explained, "offers to provide or requests to obtain unlawful material, whether as part of a commercial exchange or not, are similarly undeserving of First Amendment protection."[15]

State laws that criminalize grooming behavior may further narrow their laws to protect younger children in ways similar to statutory rape laws. These statutes vary considerably. In general, they try to protect children while recognizing that minors who are sixteen or seventeen years of age may be sexually active with partners who are young adults, though often only a year or two older.

D. ONLINE SEXUAL PREDATORS— DIGITAL STRANGER DANGER

The data collected regarding statutory rape and sexual assaults on minors paint a compelling picture that the risks are far more likely to come from someone who knows the victim than from an Internet stranger. According to a 2000 report from the U.S. Department of Justice Bureau of Justice Statistics, among adolescents 12–17, less than 10 percent of the attackers were strangers. A quarter of the perpetrators were family members, and two-thirds were characterized as acquaintances.[16]

A recent Canadian study highlighted the difficulty of analyzing the data. "We do know that roughly 55 percent of all victims of sexual assault are under the age of eighteen (although youth under eighteen make up only 20 percent of the population) and that over 80 percent of these complainants are female."[17] The report was written in response to an increase in the minimum age of consent in Canada from fourteen to sixteen years old. The report was written to highlight that the increase in legal protection for adolescents would not criminalize consensual sex among teens, but help address abusive behavior foisted on teens by older adults.

The findings highlight that the risks of sexual assault are much more commonly found at home than online.

Existing data indicate that the complainant's relationship to the perpetrator of the sexual assault shifts as girls move into adolescence. As the age of the complainant increases, the percentage of sexual assaults that take place in the home decreases. A majority of sexual offences against children are committed by family members, whereas for adolescent girls between the ages of fourteen and seventeen, as many as 72 percent of offences are committed by someone outside of the family. Most of these men, however, are not strangers; most adolescent complainants know their perpetrator. When the perpetrator is a family member, he is most likely to be the complainant's father, brother, or other male relative. Canadian data suggest that, for youth between the ages of twelve and fifteen, only approximately 13 percent of reported sexual assaults are committed by strangers.[18]

For some adults, the thought of young children using the Internet harkens their worst fears of stranger danger. There are certainly predators using the Internet to find victims, and social media tools create powerful opportunities for pedophiles and others to troll for victims. At the same time, however, the data suggest that these events are far less frequent than might be suggested in the popular press.

Although incidents of online harassment have continued to increase, unwanted sexual solicitations have declined on the Internet. "Unwanted sexual solicitations declined from 19% in 2000 to 13% in 2005 and 9% in 2010."[19] Undoubtedly, these numbers translate into hundreds of thousands of unwanted encounters. At the same time, however, they are significantly different from the data suggesting that 50 percent or more of adolescents are being accosted sexually online.

One reason for the discrepancy is that some sources conflate the threat of a sexual solicitation with the presence of pornography or sexual content online. These are very different experiences that pose substantially different risks and should not be combined. "The reality about Internet-initiated sex crimes— those in which sex offenders meet juvenile victims online—is different, more complex, and serious but less archetypically frightening than the publicity about these crimes suggests."[20] The online child molester spends time with their intended victims online prior to their initial meeting "to establish trust and confidence in their victims . . . Often they introduce talk of sex and then arrange to meet the adolescents in person for sexual encounters. In 89% of cases with face-to-face meetings, offenders had [some form of] sexual inter-course . . . with victims."[21]

The nature of the stranger danger scenario is that the online child molester is not really a stranger, using personally identifiable information to steal the child in the dark. The child molester is almost always a middle-aged adult male who connects with the adolescent online and begins a conversation designed to entice the minor into a sexual relationship. In only 5 percent of the cases did the molester first falsely identify himself as a teenager.[22]

Adolescents can reduce these risks greatly by avoiding online relation-ships with adults they do not know. Many of the victims to these predators have problem relationships with their parents and so they may be seeking out other adults to fill that gap. Data suggest that these struggling teens may also be turning to alcohol and drugs or to increased sexual activity. The behavior associated with connecting with a stranger online and agreeing to meet that stranger is part of a larger pattern of increasingly self-destructive behavior. These are behaviors symptomatic of stress, depression, anxiety, or abuse, and the focus on interdiction should be aimed at these underlying issues.

While managing the online connections can help reduce the potential for a predator to make a connection with a vulnerable teen, the teen needs help to address the underlying issues that make the teens vulnerable to an adult solicitation for grooming and statutory rape. Individual counseling, school support, and family counseling might all be helpful to address these broader issues to help decrease the likelihood that an adolescent would be open to the predator's grooming activity.

If a teen reports the grooming behavior of the predator, it is essential that the parents, teachers, or other adults who learn of the behavior take the situation seriously and report the behavior immediately to law enforcement. Reporting the grooming behavior is even more important if the parents find out from a source other than the teen. The data suggest that refusing the invitation of such a predator will stop the person from bothering the adolescent. But that predator will simply move on to another teen he can meet online elsewhere. By contacting law enforcement, state or federal authorities can begin the process to identify the perpetrator and eliminate the risk to the general public.

E. WORKING WITH LAW ENFORCEMENT

If an adolescent is the victim of a serious stalking or cyberbullying situation, it is appropriate to involve law enforcement. Although most school bullying laws do not include criminal provisions, many of the examples of cyberbullying involve a multitude of violations of state or federal laws. Having filed a police report also will be helpful in later obtaining a civil restraining order.

Parents, however, should be mindful that the criminal justice system does not represent the victim in its operation. For example, although anti-child pornography laws might be violated when a nude photo of a student is distributed throughout the school, those laws do not provide a very good strategy to stop the harassment triggered by the distribution of the photos. Child pornography is a sex crime and those convicted of possessing child pornography will be required to register as sex offenders for the rest of their lives. The victim of the harassment, subject of the photo, and classmate of those students may not want that outcome and the continuing stigma for all the students involved. But law enforcement is not obligated to listen to the wishes of the victim.

Each state has its own set of applicable laws, and cyberbullying and school harassment may involve the application of laws not commonly enforced by local law enforcement. Given the constant change in technology, the accusations may also involve apps and platforms that are unfamiliar to the investigating officers. Before speaking to the police, parents will find it helpful to do research on their own state laws.[23] Parents should document as much as they can about the harassment and discuss the decision to go to the police with the victim before approaching the police.

In providing advice to journalists, Pen America notes that there are times when it is important to take the next step and go to the police. These same guidelines can help parents and their teens decide whether to involve the police:

- You've received or been named in direct threats of violence (i.e., threats that suggest a time, place, or location are more likely to be taken seriously by law enforcement).
- An online abuser has published nonconsensual, sexually explicit images of you.
- You've been stalked via electronic communication.
- You know your online harasser and wish to seek a restraining order.[24]

These types of incidents are all very serious and reflect a concern that the abuse will continue to escalate. Police intervention may discourage some of a victim's attackers from continuing to escalate the situation.

Parents also should consider requesting a restraining order whenever the identity of the attacker is known. In Florida, for example, the state can issue the Stalking Violence Injunction, one of the five types of restraining orders available to protect victims from violence and intimidation. Most states will have some form of restraining order available for victims of stalking and online harassment. Once a restraining order is issued, the person protected by the order should inform the school as well as any other relevant institutions. Police must respond immediately to the violation of the restraining order.

When dealing with both the school and law enforcement, parents may want to have the help of an attorney experienced in this type of law. The emotional toll from harassment extends well beyond the adolescent to impact the entire family. Having an attorney to provide assistance allows the family to address the emotional turmoil and let the professional navigate the technical aspects of the complaint procedure.

Chapter 12

Radicalization

A. CONTEXTUALIZING RADICAL EXTREMISM

Like the Internet risks discussed in the previous chapter, the number of individuals who fall prey to these threats are a tiny fraction of the adolescents who use the Internet. At the same time, however, the threat of radicalization carries both the risk to the teen involved and to the larger community. Parents must be engaged with their teen's online activities and political engagement to help reduce the risk that strongly held beliefs do not veer into violent extremism.

Talking to adolescents about extremism is often a daunting task. Many point out that America's founding fathers embraced radical, antigovernmental rhetoric that led to violence and revolution. Five years after the American revolution, however, George Washington and other revolutionary war leaders supported the use of military force against the Shay Rebellion and rebels challenging the democratically elected leaders of the states.

The United States and the world's democracies operate under the rule of law, reserving to legal and political processes the authority to the three branches of government rather than the power of violence. The U.S. Constitution protects the right to protest, but never to use violence as part of the constitutional process to petition the government for redress of grievances.

It is within this framework that parents are called upon to support an adolescent's political awareness, while ensuring that a teen's exploration of political, religious, and ideological thought can be developed without resort to violence or radical extremism.

The FBI offers this distinction: violent extremism is the "encouraging, condoning, justifying, or supporting the commission of a violent act to achieve political, ideological, religious, social, or economic goals."[1] USAID provides a similar approach, defining violent extremist activities as the "advocating, engaging in, preparing, or otherwise supporting ideologically motivated or justified violence to further social, economic or political objectives."[2]

The story of Zachary Chesser provides an example of the potential for an adolescent to become obsessed with radical ideology and violence.

Zachary Chesser was an average high school student in northern Virginia. He participated in his high school's Gifted and Talented program, joined his high school break-dancing team, and worked part-time at a video rental store.

In the summer of 2008, 18-year-old Chesser converted to Islam and quickly became radicalized, solely on the Internet. He began posting views that supported Islamist terrorist groups, watching sermons by Anwar al Awlaki, and exchanging emails with the cleric about joining Al Shabab. Within weeks, he had quit his job because he "objected to working at a place that rented videos featuring naked women" and became increasingly hostile to his parents.

In 2010, he uploaded a YouTube video in which he threatened the creators of the television show South Park after an episode depicted the Prophet Muhammad dressed in a bear costume. In July 2010 . . . Chesser was arrested for attempting to provide material support to a terrorist organization. He pled guilty in October 2010 to three federal felony charges—communicating threats, soliciting violent jihadists to desensitize law enforcement, and attempting to provide material support to a designated foreign terrorist organization—and was sentenced in 2011 to 25 years in federal prison.[3]

Like the other societal risks discussed throughout the book, radicalization is not unique to Internet interactions. Neither the 1995 Oklahoma City bombing of the Murrah Federal Building by domestic, right-wing terrorists nor the al-Qaeda terrorist attacks on 9/11 were rooted in an Internet-focused radicalization.

In the United States, the history of radical extremism involving violence is most frequently associated with right-wing hate groups. In a list of the ten attacks with the greatest fatalities by U.S. domestic extremists (and thus excluding the attack of 9/11), five of the ten attacks were perpetrated by right-wing groups, three were perpetrated by Islamist extremists, and two in 1972 involved left-wing attacks.[4] Although there had been radical leftist extremism in the 1960s and early 1970s, in the current century, the vast majority of all attacks and all deaths have been caused by right-wing domestic terrorism, far more than any other source.

The Internet has not been involved in all these incidents. Nonetheless, the Internet provides a unique opportunity to create an environment conducive to radicalization. "Right-wing terror incidents occur consistently because the movements from which they emanate are mature extremist movements with deep-seated roots. The Internet has made it easier for extremists to meet each other (and thus engage in plots), as well as to self-radicalize and become lone wolf offenders."[5]

In the UK, the Rand Corporation created a small study of fifteen incidents involving British domestic terrorism. In that report, Rand identified five potential roles the Internet can play in promoting radicalization:

1. The Internet creates more opportunities to become radicalized.
2. The Internet acts as an "echo chamber": a place where individuals find their ideas supported and echoed by other like-minded individuals.
3. The Internet accelerates the process of radicalization.
4. The Internet allows radicalization to occur without physical contact.
5. The Internet increases opportunities for self-radicalization.[6]

The data from the study are largely anecdotal, given its small size and the wide range of experiences that can lead a person to become radicalized. Nonetheless, the study found that many of these concerns were supported by the evidence in the study.

> For all 15 individuals that we researched, the internet had been a key source of information, communication and of propaganda for their extremist beliefs. Secondly, our research supports the suggestion that the internet may act as an "echo chamber" for extremist beliefs; in other words, the internet may provide a greater opportunity than offline interactions to confirm existing beliefs.[7]

The data could not differentiate the role of the Internet in facilitating the radicalization process rather than accelerating the radicalization process. The study also distinguished between self-radicalization, meaning a person becomes radical entirely on the person's own, rather than using the Internet to join a community of radical extremists, which is likely to be the greater threat.

The Department of Homeland Security recognizes that the problem of radical extremism is a grave national threat. "Arguably, the use of the Internet to radicalize and recruit homegrown terrorists is the single-most important and dangerous innovation since the terrorist attacks of September 11, 2001."[8]

Speaking generally about those who are more likely to fall into radicalization, the FBI identifies social alienation, anxiety, frustration, and painful experiences as conditions that could potentially give rise to the use of radical extremism as an outlet.[9] This rather unhelpful list describes the high school experience for many, if not most, teens, and yet only a tiny few would find radical extremism as a way to gain "power," "achievement," "affiliation," "importance," "purpose," "morality," and "excitement,"[10] the list of personal needs associated with radical extremism. These lists suggest that radical extremism is an alternative to the socially positive coping mechanisms chosen by the vast majority of frustrated, alienated teens.

A European study of radicalized European adolescents suggests that teens differ from adults who have joined radical extremist groups or espouse such ideology. These research studies emphasize that there is no particular predictor regarding whether an individual will gravitate toward violence and extremism. At the same time, when groups of minors who espoused radical affiliation were compared to young adults with similar affiliation, the number of incidents of self-harm and histories of abuse tended to be higher for the minors.[11] This suggests that for teens, the affiliation with radical extremism may be more about getting out of their present situation of alienation than the importance of the ideals they espouse.

B. DEEPFAKES AND DISINFORMATION

The echo chamber effect of the Internet has the potential to reinforce radical content, presenting it as mainstream information, and through that process, reeducating the individuals who learn their facts and information from that isolated perspective. The echo chamber effect is often made worse through the use of disinformation. Sometimes referred to as "alternate facts" or "fake news," many of the radical sources of information are comprised of falsified information, partial truths, and extreme interpretations of sources. To a casual online reader, this disinformation will create what seems to be credible sources for the extremist positions being espoused.

Increasingly, however, the problem of isolation triggered by the echo chamber has been matched with an even more dangerous phenomenon described as deepfakes, where the documentary photographic and video evidence has been altered in a manner that is very difficult to detect for the casual observer.

As computer software has become faster, the ability to distinguish real content from doctored content has become much harder. Improved editing tools have extended the most sophisticated Hollywood special effects to home software. One particularly pernicious version of this phenomenon goes by the name of deepfakes, which increasingly has become a generic term for high-quality falsified video and audio images. Deepfakes are videos using artificial intelligence software to easily edit aspects of a video to create the illusion that people in the videos are making statements they never made.

Deepfakes and similar techniques are frequently used to impose celebrities' faces onto pornographic videos, but they have also been used to create false video imagery. For example, such doctored footage has been used to prove—falsely—that U.S. troops committed atrocities abroad and that politicians have made speeches far different than the ones they actually presented. In one instance, cleric Anwar al-Awlaki, an operative for al-Qaeda, created hundreds of videos designed to radicalize followers and spur them to violence. In 2009, Arid Uka of Frankfurt, Germany, viewed these videos, including "a fabricated Jihadi propaganda video depicting the rape of an Iraqi girl by U.S soldiers. The video production posted on social media had actually utilised footage from Brian de Palma's fictional production, *Redacted*."[12] Motivated to avenge the atrocities, Uka shot U.S. servicemen stationed in Frankfurt, Germany and was sentenced to life in prison.

C. INTERVENTION STRATEGIES

Particularly among teens, the early stages of radicalization are not dissimilar from early stages of becoming a hacker or putting oneself into environments that would create risks of engaging with child molesters and other abusers. These teens are often struggling with anxiety, feelings of helplessness, isolation, and alienation. Whether the individual finds radical religious or political philosophy a way out or turns to hacking, drugs, or other antisocial behaviors, the need for nonpunitive intervention remains the same.

In Europe, there has been an effort to create a European Community-wide Radicalization Awareness Network (RAN), developed to provide strategies for intervention and support of students who are showing predisposition toward violent radicalization.

Members of the RAN network "pool knowledge, exchange experiences, develop new initiatives and especially highlight best practices to prevent radicalization."[13] Based on the experiences of the RAN members, these teams suggest

- training support for practitioners who are dealing with people at risk for radicalization;
- exit strategies for those who have already radicalized and even committed violent acts;
- community work;
- education for youth;
- family support;
- alternative narratives to counter recruitment strategies;
- multiagency approaches involving a great variety of social actors; and
- prison and probation measures.[14]

The intervention strategy to stop a teen from becoming radicalized likely takes two somewhat independent sets of strategies. From the perspective of the teen's vulnerability, parents, schools, psychologists, and social workers need to address the underlying issues exacerbating the anxiety, isolation, and alienation being felt by the student. By engaging the student in positive experiences, helping build a peer network, and treating the underlying issues, the student will have less need to seek radical ideologies or to be willing to take violent action.

The second aspect of the intervention should focus on reversing the false narrative that extremism and violence are the appropriate solution for the social situation. Teens "should be educated on citizenship, political, religious and ethnic tolerance, non-prejudiced thinking, extremism, democratic values, cultural diversity, and the historical consequences of ethnically and politically motivated violence."[15] The civic education and engagement will likely be much more effective if the underlying emotional and cognitive issues are addressed. By treating both the cause and the manifestation of the antisocial behavior, students are much more likely to abandon radicalization and return to a more balanced lifestyle.

D. SCHOOL SHOOTINGS

Loosely related to the concern about adolescents becoming radicalized is the concern about adolescents who manifest their anger and disillusionment on their schools and classmates. "There have been 64 shootings since 2018. The COVID-19 pandemic appears to have interrupted the trend line. The 2020 figure, with 10 shootings, was significantly lower than 2019, with 25 shootings and 2018 with 24."[16] These figures do not include shootings in 2021 and beyond.

The teens who might gravitate to such actions fit a profile similar to those who are prone to radicalization. "Almost every school shooter, no matter what their socioeconomic status might be; all have some very specific characteristics that seem to be universal between them: depression, anger and rage towards others."[17] Such a description may be accurate, but it does not create a sufficiently narrow or defined group to establish a profile for law enforcement.

Adolescents involved in school shootings, however, rarely act without telegraphing their intentions. The former student who murdered seventeen former classmates at Marjory Stoneman Douglas High School in Florida had been expelled from the school. News reports discuss "how he was fascinated by talk of guns and preoccupied with wars and terrorists; how he posted photos of weapons on social media."[18] Given slightly different triggers, such an individual could have become radicalized toward a political or religious clause, seeking out a different target than the person's former school.

School shooters differ from the radicalized students in one important aspect—only a small subset of the adolescents who join radical groups are prepared to actually commit violence, even if the group itself espouses an ideology of violence. Adolescents who are depressed, angry, and struggling with rage may become that much worse and commit acts of violence, but most do not. Most of the students who fit the overgeneralized profile for the potential violence retain the impulse control and ethical decision-making to resist such horrific, antisocial behavior. Adolescents with these severe anger and depression issues need significant medical and social assistance, but unlike radicalized adolescents, there is no external group suggesting that their behavior is part of a larger political or social agenda. They just need help before they act out.

Parents must carefully balance the privacy rights of their children with the needs of safety for the public and the mental health of their children. If parents or teachers are told about musings of suicide, murder, or terrorist activities from social media acquaintances of the adolescents, they need to treat these concerns very seriously. Although overreacting may create some embarrassment and difficulty for the teens concerned, the consequences of ignoring the activities are much greater. At the same time, parents and teachers must understand that modern literature is replete with these themes. A student writing fan fiction in the world of *The Hunger Games* or drawing characters preparing for battle in *Halo* is engaging in an activity quite different than one creating a hit list of classmates for elimination, harming animals, or trying to acquire illegal weapons online. Through communication with the teen, the parents and teachers can assess the reasons behind the teen's conduct and differentiate creative engagement with modern culture from suicidal and homicidal inclinations. When in doubt, the parents should seek out guidance from qualified mental health professionals. If a threat is imminent, parents should call the police.

Chapter 13

The Dark Web

A. THE REST OF THE INTERNET

The Internet is not merely a communications platform. The technologies provide a range of services to promote commerce and trade in every imaginable type of good and service, including those that are legal and those that are not. For parents to understand how some of these transactions occur, it is helpful to look at the actual structure of the Internet and the web. The Internet is the connection of interconnected computer networks that share a common protocol and operating language. The interconnections allow the data on each networked device to be accessed and shared on the network by every other machine.

The World Wide Web or web, in contrast, is one of the technologies that operate on the Internet. Web pages all use standardized coding to enable any web browser to render the page and ensure that the user experience is nearly identical from device to device and from browser to browser. The Internet, rather than the web, powers the connections for apps, smart speakers, and other remote devices.

Packets of Internet data are transmitted around the globe through a network of intercontinental fiberoptic networks, national transmission lines, and lines using phone lines, coaxial cable, satellites, or fiberoptic cable in each region, city, and town. The system for transmitting data packets is also supplemented with additional wireless technologies. Both Wi-Fi and Bluetooth use radio frequencies to transmit data. Wi-Fi uses lower frequencies and much greater power to send the data packets, making it the primary tool for wireless home and commercial networking. Bluetooth devices use higher frequencies and work at a much closer range. Bluetooth is much more limited in the number of megabits per second that can be transmitted than Wi-Fi.

The Internet, then, is essentially made up of the devices that allow the transfer of digital data on any interconnected networks and the data that is stored and available on those networks. A small part of that data is made up of web pages, but there is much more content than just websites.

When most people search the Internet, they use search engines such as Google, Bing, Duck Duck Go, or others to review indexes of the web. Search engines primarily read and index the content on the web pages that are open to the public. Many organizations also create web pages for internal use that are flagged or programmed to tell the search engines not to index those pages. Additional web pages are posted to intranet systems that are protected by passwords and firewalls from access outside their institutional networks. As a result, not even the entire web is indexed and available to Google or Bing. Estimates suggest that the indexable and accessible portion of the Internet is 5 percent of the total content hosted using Internet protocols. The other 95 percent is sometimes called the deep web.

B. THE DEEP WEB

The deep web is a term used to refer to the content that is on the Internet but either not publicly available or not publicly addressable. Most of the deep web content is made up of private databases such as those used by private corporations and agencies that store documents for internal use only. Examples include customer information at banks and health care organizations, documents stored at private enterprises, and faculty and student content at universities. The deep web represents a massive amount of content, but the content is unremarkable. It is the digital filing system of nearly every office in the world. Most of an Internet user's personal files and records accessed at their banks, credit card companies, employers, or school are stored without being available to the search engines, making all this content part of the deep web.

There are also many websites and online content that are not connected to the indexed web due to broken links or because the content is retained as archival copies. For example, when a corporate website is updated, the old website often is not erased. Instead, the Internet addresses are merely pointed to the new sites. If the company needs to retrieve information from the old site, the pages continue to be available to those with the actual address and appropriate access. There are often news reports about the deep web and the hidden secrets that adolescents might find. If the story is about the deep web, the authors are trying to scare their readers. The deep web simply reflects the public nature of the content and the portion designed to be published publicly.

C. THE DARK WEB

The dark web refers to a small subset of the deep web that is specifically designed to provide anonymity. Sites on the dark web can only be accessed with specialized software designed to ensure that the IP address and the location of the user are not made public or stored. Using these tools, an anonymous user can access content and conduct business that the user does not want anyone to find, particularly governments and law enforcement agencies.

Anonymity, in and of itself, is not illegal. Governments need anonymity to conduct their own operations to surveil other governments and those suspected of illegal behavior. Journalists and researchers often need anonymity to protect themselves from censorship or from governmental or private attacks on investigative journalism. Because there is often a legitimate need for anonymity, there are many privacy advocates who strongly support the continued availability of tools to surf and use the Internet anonymously.

The most common of these tools is The Onion Router (TOR) Browser. The TOR Browser relies on a distributed network. When a user clicks on a hyperlink in the TOR Browser, the request is sent to a TOR node, which sends it through two other nodes before resolving at the requested page. In this way, no one monitoring the computer can read the information on the computer or on the page to connect the user and the site. Work on the TOR Browser was first started at the U.S. Naval Academy. It later received funding from the Electronic Frontier Foundation and became its own nonprofit company in 2006.

In addition to providing anonymous search tools for indexed websites, there are also websites that can only be accessed by the TOR Browser. These use the ".onion" extension. These sites are not indexed by search engines and do not open in other browsers. A 2018 study estimated approximately 65,000 .onion sites.[1]

TOR, however, does not stop all monitoring of Internet traffic. In 2013, for example, the FBI successfully injected tracking software into TOR nodes which is used to break up a massive child pornography ring.[2] TOR also does not stop a .onion website from using software to provide tracing of users.

A virtual private network (VPN) provides more security than a TOR Browser, and it is the method preferred by security advocates to ensure privacy and data security. A VPN masks the IP address of the user and uses encryption of the data being transmitted to protect from being observed. A VPN works with all web browsers, so that it provides an excellent form of privacy and security when working online. But a VPN does not have the software needed to unlock the secure markets on the dark web.

The true dark web is a very small part of the deep web, but it relies on the TOR Browser and other tools to let buyers and sellers of illegal drugs, weapons, and content engage in transactions. While a small amount of content available through the .onion TOR system is for political speech and whistleblower content, a much larger portion is dedicated to child pornography, sale of drugs, transactions in digital currencies, and other unregulated or illegal transactions.

The markets for these services were made famous by The Silk Road, a widely known marketplace for all things illegal. The FBI shut down the site in 2013, extraditing its operator from Thailand. In a press release regarding the conviction of its founder, the FBI explained that "Silk Road was used by thousands of drug dealers and other unlawful vendors to distribute illegal drugs and other illicit goods and services to more than 100,000 buyers, and to launder hundreds of millions of dollars derived from those unlawful transactions."[3]

Despite the seizure of The Silk Road, many other markets continue to operate. In addition to drugs, guns, and pornography, the markets have increasingly become the home for transactions to buy and sell malware, hacking tools, and stolen identities. In 2019, a partnership of Interpol and the European Union was able "to make arrests and shut down 50 illicit dark-websites, including Wall Street Market and Valhalla, two of the largest drug markets."[4]

D. TORRENTING AND ILLEGAL FILE SHARING

The other common illegal practice on the Internet is the unauthorized sharing of copyright-protected commercial movies, TV episodes, books, games, and music. While perhaps it is a slight overstatement, it seems that every work created in the twenty-first century has been pirated. Many of these can be found through a Google search on public websites. But the vast majority of infringing works are available using BitTorrent software off the BitTorrent network.

Torrenting has become the most popular form of peer-to-peer (P2P) file sharing. File sharing using a P2P network is not illegal. There are some technological reasons to use file-sharing technology to collaborate with others on large files and data sets. The vast majority of use of P2P file sharing, however, is to download files that have been stored and made available without the permission of the copyright owner.

P2P file sharing avoids the evidentiary traps that allowed companies to be sued for gathering and storing massive amounts of unauthorized copyrighted works. Instead, the files reside on the various users of the network. Each member of the network allows software to index the user's files. When someone requests a movie or song, the software sifts through the index and then downloads small parts of the file from multiple sources. The coordination allows for very fast download speeds and reduces the likelihood that the Internet traffic will be noticed for any particular user.

In numerous cases, the Supreme Court has found that services which provide free downloads to the public have infringed the rights of the copyright owners[5] by facilitating the copyright infringement by the consumers who have downloaded the files.[6] Downloading from an unauthorized site is rarely fair use. In limited instances, the access of an otherwise unavailable copy of a work through a BitTorrent network will be fair use, but only if the downloading was part of a person's activities that otherwise qualify as fair use.

While torrenting the occasional file will go unnoticed or unflagged by a consumer's ISPs, active torrenting will quickly attract the attention of many Internet service providers. Many ISPs will send warning letters to households where there is a strong likelihood of illegal downloading, and some ISPs will bar the customer from their services. Parents may be very surprised to receive such a letter, particularly if they are unaware of the BitTorrent traffic and the volume of downloads being accessed by their children.

Since most of the files available on BitTorrent sites are illegal copies, there is no quality control for the files. BitTorrent downloads are an excellent method for hackers to distribute malware and ransomware. While only a fraction of the files available have malware installed, much of the malware distributed comes through these files.

BitTorrent downloads are also a great way for adolescents to circumvent the age restrictions on content. Mature games, pornography, and even child pornography are readily available for anyone with a BitTorrent account.

To avoid detection, most torrenters will use a VPN to ensure that the torrenter's Internet address is hidden and the data stream is encrypted. The use of the VPN will help protect a torrenter from the ISP's knowledge of the unauthorized downloads, but it will not protect from malware being installed during the networking sessions.

For parents, the use of BitTorrent creates a substantial risk to the data security protections of the computer, tablet, or phone. It is never wise to allow BitTorrent software to reside on a device that is also used for confidential information, such as to do work from home or to access banking and healthcare records. Therefore, adolescents should not be given permission to install any BitTorrent software on shared home computers.

Parents are best advised to prohibit the use of BitTorrent completely. The risks are substantial, and the use will likely be to download illegal content. Most parents hold this line, although many other teens get permission to use BitTorrent software or manage to install it without the knowledge of their parents. Parents will sometimes rationalize the use as a small infraction of the copyright laws, or limit the use to the very occasional movie or music album.

Given the vast amount of content uploaded to sites like YouTube, it is hard to defend the position that the unauthorized content on BitTorrent sites is worse, since it is only a matter of degree. Still, copyright should be respected. If not, streaming services—and their investment in new content—would collapse without the respect for copyright that keeps most people from stealing the material rather than paying for it.

Parents should remember that teens who have installed BitTorrent may not realize the importance of only using the software with a VPN. This creates an added layer of vulnerability to the use of the equipment. Parents may find themselves in a very awkward position if their home Internet service is disrupted because of improper use of content by the children in the household.

Finally, parents should remain diligent about what is installed on their computers. Ideally, the parents should operate administrator accounts to control the installation of software and limit the risks of malware being installed. BitTorrent is just one of many programs that children and teens might install on their own. By using an administrator account, parents can maintain the safety of their equipment and ensure that software programs are properly vetted before being installed.

Chapter 14

My Child the Hacker

A. HACKING EXPLAINED

Hacking is a widely used and poorly defined term for a wide range of activities designed to infiltrate networked equipment and the computers, tablets, mobile phones, and smart devices that run on those networks. Hacking can be as simple as guessing another person's password, or as complex as the ultra-sophisticated 2020 hack on the tech firm SolarWinds that Russia used to steal nuclear, military, and intelligence, secrets along with business information from thousands of U.S. companies.

Hacking covers a wide range of malicious attacks on computer networks. In the early days of computing, hacking was largely romanticized by computer coders who could use their superior computer programming skills to find back doors into software. Today, however, cybercrime has become a global business enterprise run by organized crime and often supported by belligerent foreign nations who use online disruptions as part of an ongoing digital Cold War. Cybersecurity Ventures pegs the global cost of cybercrime at $6 trillion, with an expected 15 percent growth each year.[1]

Despite the large-scale nature of many cyberattacks conducted by governments or by organized crime, there is still ample opportunity for other types of hackers. Some hacks are perpetrated by groups using cyberattacks as a form of social protest. Perhaps the most famous of these groups was Anonymous, a loose collective of "hacktivists" dedicated to social protests and disruptions, often targeting government agencies, but also attacking banks and some religious organizations. In a comprehensive study of 67,000 respondents, 5.4 percent of adolescents self-identify as using a computer to hack in the past twelve months.[2]

At the same time, anyone can become a hacker, and many hackers first dabble with cybercrime while in high school.

> Many think that "hacker" refers to some self-taught whiz kid or rogue program-mer skilled at modifying computer hardware or software so it can be used in ways outside the original developers' intent. . . . Hacking has evolved from teenage mischief into a billion-dollar growth business, whose adherents have established a criminal infrastructure that develops and sells turnkey hacking tools to would-be crooks with less sophisticated technical skills (known as "script kiddies").[3]

There are no studies to predict the likelihood that a teen will turn to hack-ing as a hobby or to begin a life of crime. Only a tiny fraction of adolescents will devote themselves to building their computer and technology skills to become a criminal hacker. Nonetheless, at 5.4 percent of teens reporting they have hacked a computer system in the past year, the potential for hacking to become a problem is real. If nothing else, the hackers that support the current global enterprise often started as adolescents.

News reporting regarding hacking often uses the terms "black hat" hackers to differentiate between those hackers who undertake criminal activity from "white hat" hackers who provide security companies, software developers, and law enforcement the insights needed to improve security. These same reports will paint "grey hat" hackers as those who straddle the lines.

In reality, these labels suggest much stronger distinctions than really exist. Many large companies, for example, offer "bug bounty programs," which are incentive programs that pay hackers and computer coders to inform the com-pany if any vulnerabilities exist in their cybersecurity procedures, programs, or security. The bug bounty programs typically emphasize that the volunteer white hat hackers must be very careful to not breach the terms of the program or violate federal criminal laws protecting computer systems. At Intel, for example, the bug bounty program includes this warning:

> If you follow the program terms, we will not initiate a lawsuit or law enforce-ment investigation against you in response to your report . . . Never attempt to access anyone else's data or personal information including by exploiting a vulnerability. Such activity is unauthorized. If during your testing you interacted with or obtained access to data or personal information of others, you must:
>
> - Stop your testing immediately and cease any activity that involves the data or personal information or the vulnerability.
> - Do not save, copy, store, transfer, disclose, or otherwise retain the data or personal information.
> - Alert Intel immediately and support our investigation and mitigation efforts.

Failure to comply with any of the above will immediately disqualify any report from bounty award eligibility.[4]

Any person who fails to follow the bug bounty procedures risks violating the Computer Fraud and Abuse Act (CFAA), a federal law which criminalizes the unauthorized intrusion into computer systems as well as other state and federal laws. The skills and strategies to participate in the bug bounty programs and the skills needed to hack illegally into computer networks are the same. The difference is the intent of the hacker, the data accessed by the hack, and the use of the information learned. If the hacker breaks into a computer system to report the vulnerability, the hacker is a white hat security researcher. If the hacker copies the data, redistributes the information, or blackmails the company for the return of the data, the hacker is a black hat criminal.

There is an important distinction between becoming an ethical hacker and a malicious hacker. Parents of technologically interested teens are often encouraged to get their children into computers and robotics. Hacking programs that emphasize ethical hacking will train participants in the very same skills being sought by malicious hackers. The difference is the purpose to which the online activity is put. The EC-Council has an example of a Code of Ethics that can serve as a roadmap to help parents discuss the importance of ethical hacking with their teens.[5] There are also free, online courses for students to learn these skills and participate along with other peers who share this interest.

B. SIGNS OF A MALICIOUS ADOLESCENT HACKER

The goal for parents is to ensure that any computer activities conducted by their teens are productive and legal. Parents sometimes have a difficult time addressing concerns about their teens' computer programming activities. Like most tools, the tools commonly used for computer hacking all have perfectly benign and wholly appropriate uses. In addition, the development of a teen's computer programming skills is very valuable and important. Society needs the skills from the next generation of computer experts. Teens interested in computer programming will find themselves with many opportunities for high-quality employment and professional development.

At the same time, adolescents do not assess risk in the same manner as adults. What the government will treat as a serious criminal act, teens might consider to be only a joke. School computer systems and state standardized testing systems, for example, are often the target for computer malware.

Students may consider changing grades or posting grades to be something of a prank, but these are all felonies.

Security expert and InfoWorld columnist Roger Grimes has written an excellent, first-person account of his battle to stop his stepson from his burgeoning life as a hacker.[6] Grimes was able to step in and stop his stepson, but the young man's classmates were later arrested for "hacking the school's computers, changing grades, and . . . posting nude photos of one of their girlfriends to a public website—the latter of which resulted in multiple felonies."[7] Grimes lists eleven signs that a teen has become a hacker:

1. They flat out tell you (or brag about how easy it is to hack)
2. They seem to know a little too much about you
3. Their (technical) secrecy is off the charts
4. They have multiple accounts you can't access
5. You find hacking tools on their computer
6. You overhear them using hacking terms
7. Your Internet provider tells you to stop hacking
8. Their close (computer) friends have been investigated
9. They consistently switch to "boss screens" when you walk into the room
10. Your monitoring tools never show any activity
11. Failing grades suddenly improve to top scores[8]

Grimes' list provides an excellent risk map to help understand when a teen's curiosity transforms into harmful, antisocial behavior. Most students do not become malicious hackers, and most teens are very protective of their online footprint. Parents must look at the totality of the activities before jumping to conclusions. At the same time, parents must not willfully blind themselves to the behavior of their children.

There is also a growing body of psychological research regarding adolescent hacking. Not surprisingly, the research suggests that teens involved in cybercrimes are very much like teens involved in noncomputer crime. "Many of the social and behavioral factors associated with traditional acts of crime and delinquency are also evident in predicting cybercrimes. For instance, there is a significant relationship observed between low self-control and participation in simple forms of hacking, such as password guessing and manipulation of data."[9]

Hackers do not start off with great technical skills. Instead, they start off with the same types of low self-control that get the adolescents into trouble more generally. And they are encouraged by peers they find online and in their social circles to join in the activities. "Deviant peer associations influence the likelihood of hacking generally . . . Peer associations also play a critical role in learning methods and justifications to hack."[10]

1. Look Ma, I'm a Hacker

Parents should be observant about any changes in behavior that suggest their children are involved with peers involved with vandalism or criminal activity. Hacking and illegal file sharing are really just two more behaviors that fall into the range of criminal activities frequented by disaffected teens with low self-control.[11]

For some teens, however, there is less social stigma about hacking than there might be for shoplifting or vandalism. This means that they are more likely to talk about it at home. In many cases, the early hacking efforts are pranks that the teen treats as funny, not serious, malicious, or criminal. If a teen brags about hacking to the teen's parents, siblings, or friends, parents need to take the statements very seriously.

Parents may tend to dismiss these statements, since the teen who brags about hacking is likely inexperienced at it. The teens will grow to realize the risks as they get deeper into the hacking culture and become much more secretive later. Many hacks and exploits, however, are easily found online. Far more are sold on the dark web. These exploits do not take serious programming skills, so they are available for even casual computer users. Parents should not assume their children cannot be hackers because they do not have computer skills. Many will start by finding the hacks. Some will study these exploits to gain deeper programming skills, pulling themselves deeper into the hacking activity.

Even if the teens have not pointed out their own work as hackers, they often highlight their hacking by pointing out the hacks, using the language of hacking, using terms like "fuzzing," "doxing," "lulz," "pwned," "swatting," or "warez." Briefly, fuzzing means adding false data to a computer system. Doxing is the practice of publicly releasing the private documents or files of an individual to embarrass or out the person or the person's private conduct. Lulz is a hacker variation on the text message "lol" meaning "for laughs." Pwned means to get the better of an adversary or opponent. Swatting is the false reporting of an emergency to the police to trigger an armed emergency response. Warez is the term used for pirated software or the file-trading community that used the term. There are more terms of art used by hackers to show off their participation.

If the teen has not disclosed the teen's hacker activities, the family's Internet Service Provider or neighbors may have done. ISPs routinely send letters to stop illegal downloading and access to known hacking resources. If an ISP sends a letter or makes a telephone call, investigate immediately rather than simply accusing the ISP of getting it wrong. While the ISPs certainly can get these warning signs wrong, they may also be providing parents notice that there is something going on in the house.

The same is true if there are reports at the student's school, local law enforcement, or parents of the teen's peer group. Hacking is a very social activity. Teens often turn to hacking to be part of a community. For many, they find that community online. But some will find that community at school.

Finally, Grimes also points out that adolescent hackers might show off by hinting at private information the household hacker has learned about their parents or siblings. "It's not uncommon for hacking kids to monitor their parents' online activities, usually in hopes of capturing admin passwords or to learn how to turn off any anti-hacking devices, such as firewalls and parental controls."[12] Once the teens have access to their parents' accounts, however, "curiosity gets the best of them and they end up reading their parents' emails or social media chats."[13]

2. The Tools of the Hacker

In February 2020, a group associated with the UK's National Crime Agency (NCA) published a poster listing six computer technologies that the poster suggested was evidence that the child had become a hacker. The poster gained notoriety for providing a rather hysterical approach to tools that have used both by legitimate computer users and by malicious hackers. The NCA tweeted its distance from the poster, explaining that "the NCA was not involved in the production or release of this poster. There are many tools which tech-savvy children use, some of which can be used for both legal & illegal purposes, so it is vital that parents & children know how these tools can be used safely."[14]

The poster included Discord, a very popular communications platform used extensively for online gaming and other social media. The poster also included Kali Linux, an open-source penetration testing platform; Metasploit, a network testing tool; and the TOR browser. The only item on the poster that a teen should never own is a Wi-Fi Pineapple, a device that allows someone to spoof a public Wi-Fi signal. The other tools are all perfectly legal and used frequently to improve data security.

The question for parents, however, is not whether these are "good" or "bad" tools. The question is whether the adolescent in the household is using these tools for their intended purpose or using them to execute malicious hacks. In addition to these tools, a VPN will also hide the teen's activities from the ISP and from the parent's network security protocols. If a teen has reconfigured a computer to run Linux, operate using a VPN, and surf on a TOR browser, it is reasonable to ask questions about the nature of the activity. It is more likely the teen is illegally downloading software and media than that the teen has started hacking, but the setup works equally well for both, and both are illegal. The empirical research notes "that youth who engaged in digital piracy were significantly more likely to also hack, consistent with prior research examining patterns of engagement in cyberdeviance broadly."[15]

Very few, if any, adolescents participate in bug bounty programs or work in cybersecurity research. Adolescents who design their computers to feature the tools of hacking are more likely to be hacking than conducting approved security work. Parents should take these technologies seriously, while recognizing that merely accessing the free tools is not the same as committing illegal acts.

While it should be acknowledged that there is also a correlation between heavy online gaming and hacking, this correlation, without much more, really does not serve as a red flag. Computer gaming is ubiquitous, so that while the small percentage of hackers are also gamers, the relationship tells us very little. The research suggests a correlation between hacking and car ownership as well. Many correlations have little causal or predictive value.

3. Hiding in Plain Sight

The third set of warning signs is even harder to differentiate from normal teen behavior, because this tends to focus on the level of security that the teen has adopted to protect the teen's privacy. Most teens are protective of their online activities, and in fact, most online users are increasingly protective of their privacy. It is not uncommon for computer users to have boss screens that can quickly be triggered to hide the personal content on a computer. Many computer games have been shipped with boss keys, and the NCAA included a boss key in its 2014 website for March Madness.

An adolescent's desire for privacy will only become a red flag regarding antisocial behavior if it becomes extreme. If teens refuse to be parted from their laptops, ask to install additional cybersecurity equipment in the home, or respond inappropriately and extremely to requests by parents to check in on their online activity, then parents should take these demands as warning signals that their children may be involved in hacking or other forms of inappropriate behavior. If parents have established their respect for their children's privacy and also been clear about the limits of their children's privacy, then only sudden or extreme changes in the teen's response to those house rules would signal a potential issue.

C. STEPS TO STOP HACKING FROM HOME

Parents should make every effort to stop malicious hacking and other antisocial behaviors as soon as they become aware of these activities. For parents of teens who are truly interested in the technology and skills involved, rather than the antisocial harms, the parents should emphasize the importance and obligations for their child to meet the goals of the ethical hacking community. For most families, the onset of a teen's hacking will grow gradually over time. The earlier the parents intervene, the less parents will face opposition and significant planning.

From a technological standpoint, the battle to stop hacking from the home can be thought of as a technological battle over control of the home computer network and its devices. This is actually quite similar to the cybersecurity strategies employed in corporate settings. Many of the cybersecurity breaches that occur in industry are triggered by disgruntled employees and employees who have financial motives for harming their employer, including those employees who are about to leave. Companies focus many of their cybersecurity efforts at eliminating access to corporate systems to employees who do not have a business need for those systems.

Parents should treat the home computer network in much the same way. It should be designed to provide access only to the responsible adult or adults in the family who are responsible for cybersecurity. This also has the benefit of stopping neighbors, occasional visitors, or vendors from breaching the system.

The adults in the household should also take steps to provide a mechanism for them to gain access to each other's account in the event of death or an incapacitating accident or illness. Chapter 18 provides an introduction on how every household should prepare the digital estate. A good plan to lock down the household will have the unintended consequence of locking out the surviving spouse, so additional planning is needed to be sure this does not happen.

1. Password Management

Control of the home system begins with good password security. Every adult in the family should use a password management tool and be sure to use strong passwords that are authenticated. This also means using strong passwords on mobile phones and other devices that could be used to reset passwords. The mobile devices should time out after five minutes or less so that a teen cannot pick up a phone that was recently used and quickly use it to authenticate the teen's reset of a password.

Unless the passwords are secure, none of the other steps to protect the home system will work. If the parents have a printout of all the household passwords in a drawer, then the children in the house will also have access to the list, unless the list is kept in a safe deposit box.

PC Magazine lists Keeper Password Manager & Digital Vault, LastPass, Dashlane, and Bitwarden Premium as their top four programs for 2021.[16] Most web browsers have password management built into their systems. These generally work well, though most security advocates suggest using a stronger, third-party program. The non-browser-based products will also work across platforms, synching the Chrome browser passwords on a computer with the Safari browser passwords stored in an iPhone. They also have features to share passwords for certain shared apps and programs, such as Netflix or Disney+ passwords that are regularly shared with the teens in the house.

2. Control the Network

To fully protect the home computer system from hacking, it is important for the adult family member managing the system to install a router with strong security and enable it properly. The equipment provided by the major ISPs all provide high-quality tools with basic, built-in security. But the security provided by the ISPs must be turned on and implemented properly.

To protect from outside attacks, the first step is to name the Wi-Fi network by changing the Service Set Identifier (SSID). Avoid giving identifying information about the address or the equipment brand. Instead, choose a favorite sports team, vacation location, or something that the family will recognize easily but an outsider would not connect to the home.

Even more importantly, once the network is renamed, it must have a new user name and password. The default user names and passwords are publicly available. This means that anyone can drive up to the house and gain control of the network. The password for the router is not entered very often, so it should be a very strong password to protect from outside attacks.

While these steps work well for attacks by outsiders, they do not work nearly as well to manage the entrepreneurial adolescent in the home. The teen can reset the router and return it to its default setting by simply holding down the reset button for ten seconds and powering the system off and back on. The parental network manager must be sure that the system has not had its password changed by periodically checking on the system.

The router also should be set to turn on the encryption that is standard on modern routers. The router also will provide a list of connected devices. It may take some time to decipher, but it will show all the computers, mobile phones, smart TVs, streaming devices, and Internet-connected bulbs and plugs used in the house. This also will provide a tool to see if any adolescent members of the family are introducing new devices they hope are beyond parental control.

3. Control the Devices

When setting up the household's computers, parents can gain control of the system by setting up any new devices and establishing that the parents have the administrator control of each computer and laptop. If only the parents have administrator privileges, then they can control whether additional software is added to the system. Both Windows and Mac systems have administrator and parental controls to help ensure that unauthorized software is not included on the device.

In Windows, for example, the account used to set up the account for the first time is assigned administrator privileges. These top-level controls enable the administrator to add new users, install software, and make other changes. When a new device is configured for the first time, the parent in charge of the network should create an administrator account that will be used only for managing the device. Needless to say, it should have a very strong password. The administrative log in should only be used when the family's administrator is making changes to the system. Macs also enable the parental controls to be managed remotely over the network.

Each member of the family authorized to use that device should then be added as new users. This includes the family member who set up the computer. This way, if the family's administrator is logged in but away from the computer, the entrepreneurial adolescent will not be able to pop onto the computer and load unauthorized software. By having all members of the family use the computer in standard mode rather than administrator mode, the chances of unauthorized software will go down considerably.

Windows 10 also has parental controls that help monitor the accounts of the children and that can be used to block access to apps or websites. There are also many third-party software programs that can review and monitor the systems for attempts at adding new programs or monitor the network traffic. While these strategies will stop a lot of entrepreneurial adolescents from getting unauthorized software onto the systems, the companies do not make them unbreakable. Customers often lose their user names and passwords. Without the ability to work around these systems, customers would lose a tremendous amount of data. As a result, there are techniques suggested on the Internet that provide ways to create alternative administrator access to these devices.

4. Monitor the System

Since the steps to lock down the devices and the network are not fool-proof, the most important step is to pay attention to the network and the activity on it. As noted earlier, the amount of monitoring needed is directly related to the number and severity of the warning signs that a member of the household has started to download illegal software, torrent media files and software, or install suites of hacking tools. If there are no suggestions that these activities are of concern, then only casual attention need be paid to the computer use of the teens.

If the teens, however, are beginning to stray into these behaviors, then it is important to take steps to monitor the network and the devices more actively. By installing an administrator account on each computer in the household, the parents have the ability to monitor what is happening with those machines. If the situation is more severe, then the parents can opt to install additional surveillance tools to monitor the behavior on the computers and mobile phones in the household.

Monitoring can be a double-edged sword. There is a certain amount of network and device safety that the parents should undertake to keep the household network free from malware and third-party problems. The parental administrator should be making sure that each computer's security updates are installing regularly and that the devices have regular hygiene. This entails a small amount of interaction with the teens' computers.

If the teens have demonstrated that there are problems with their online behavior, then it might be appropriate to increase the monitoring and be more explicit that the monitoring is designed to control the behavior inside the household. If the household includes one of the 5.4 percent of teens with "low self-control" and an interest in hacking, then the parents may wish to provide clear statements that they are intervening to stop the behavior. For example, if the parents have put the teen on notice that monitoring software is being used as a consequence of the teen's prior misconduct, then there can be a negotiation regarding the amount of privacy that will be afforded to the teen and the level of monitoring that will be required by the parent. Using monitoring tools and "stalking" a teen without a candid discussion will invariably worsen the relationship between the parent and the teen. Monitoring teens in secret demonstrates the very invasions of privacy that the anti-hacking laws are designed to prohibit. While the parent generally will not run afoul of federal law, secret spying rarely will create the desired outcome.

The parents' choice to police the network and devices can be analogized to the enforcement of speed laws. The jurisdiction puts up signs to inform the public about the authorized speed. The jurisdiction often installs warning devices to remind drivers as well. Where jurisdictions use speed traps to make money, they are no longer seeking public safety. Instead, they are after punishment and revenue. For parents, the effective monitoring approach should include the road signs and warning devices. Hidden speed traps only lead to anger and resentment, both on the road and in the home.

Chapter 15

Everyday Safety Online

Safe Shopping, Consumer Privacy, and Government's Rights to Search

A. INTRODUCTION

One of the issues that receives the most attention in the online economy is consumer privacy. There are only three ways to make money on the Internet. A business can use the technology to sell goods and services; a business can sell advertising space; and/or a business can sell information to those who wish to sell advertising or goods and services. Most of the Internet economy is fueled by the sales of products and services. But some of the largest Internet companies such as Google and Facebook earn hundreds of billions of dollars selling space to advertisers based on detailed, intimate tracking of their customers. In addition, a small number of very influential companies have also made a business out of selling analytical information about the billions of people who use the Internet and other technologies in their daily lives.

The easiest way to make money on the Internet is by selling something. Today an untold number of vendors sell new and used products, computer software, mobile device apps, and every type of service through online stores. Fueled by the pandemic lockdown, online sales grew at the fastest pace in history. "Consumers spent $861.12 billion online with U.S. merchants in 2020, up an incredible 44.0% year over year, according to Digital Commerce 360 estimates. That's the highest annual U.S. ecommerce growth in at least two decades. It's also nearly triple the 15.1% jump in 2019."[1] While it is likely these changes will permanently increase the scope of online retail, the extent to which these changes will permanently change in-store retail remains to be seen.

Despite the tremendous growth of online shopping, the consumer experience has yet to be perfected. Most websites use the metaphor of a shopping cart for customers to use to identify which items they are thinking about

189

buying. Most consumers, however, only purchase about one-fifth of the items placed in carts.

For many customers, the shipping and tax charges are disclosed only at the end of the shopping experience, and these costs can often discourage purchases. Shipping costs, in particular, are a significant issue for customers and retailers. Retailers use free-shipping incentives to get customers to buy more by setting price minimums for free shipping. Amazon sells a premium service, Amazon Prime, for customers willing to pay for free shipping. To compete, Walmart, the largest U.S. retailer, has moved aggressively into the online marketplace by offering free shipping without a subscription fee.

B. ECOMMERCE AND SAFE SHOPPING

Just as online shopping has seen explosive growth, so have the opportunities for online criminals to take advantage of shoppers through slick, fake websites and false offers. The Better Business Bureau (BBB) reported that "[o]nline purchase scams ranked among the top three riskiest scams for the last three years."[2] According to the BBB, the most frequent website sales scam was offering a very low price in the web page but then changing the price in the shopping cart or adding additional costs. "Scammers offered high demand products at a significantly reduced dollar amount, which then increased the desire to purchase the item."[3]

The consumer protection advice from USA.gov provides these guidelines when conducting online shopping:

- Use websites that you know or trust.
- Compare prices and deals, including free shipping, and extended service contracts.
- Use promo codes from sellers, to get discounts or free shipping.
- Get a complete description of the item and parts included.
- Find out about the delivery timeline, warranties, and the return policy.
- Verify the full price of the item, including extra fees.
- Read product and seller reviews from past customers and independent experts.
- Pay with a credit card. Federal laws protect you if you need to dispute charges. You don't have that same protection with other methods of payment.
- Use a secure browser. Look for a URL that starts with "https" rather than "http." Also look for a closed padlock icon, usually in the web address bar.
- Avoid making online purchases on public Wi-Fi hotspots. These may not be secure, and someone may steal your payment information over the network.
- Save your purchase order with details of the product and your confirmation number.[4]

Many of these suggestions are designed to protect the consumer from being defrauded by a disreputable online vendor. Although most online retailers are reputable, those conducting commercial fraud can easily set up websites that promise deals too good to be true. By using a credit card and sticking with known companies, a consumer can avoid being scammed.

Consumers should also avoid public Wi-Fi hotspots and unsecured web browsers to be sure that the payment information is not stolen by criminals monitoring the Internet traffic. When shopping outside the home, the consumer can avoid some of these risks by turning off their Wi-Fi and relying on the mobile phone's cellular service for connections to the retail sites.

Consumer scams are also more likely when shopping through social media rather than through well-established retailers. "Consumers who lost money to online purchase scams reported the following platforms as the place where they saw the product: Facebook, Google, a direct merchant website, Instagram, or pop up ads on social media when they were actively shopping."[5] The fear of fraud discourages shoppers from trying out smaller local shops, which need to attract business to compete with larger retailers, but at the same time, it is much easier for fraud to occur when shopping at stores that do not have a well-known track record. Particularly when shopping at untried online stores, consumers should be very careful to recheck prices, taxes, shipping costs, and any other service charges before completing the transaction.

C. ADVERTISING AND PROMOTION

One of the earliest commercial uses of the Internet was to advertise. Advertisers buy placement on blogs, search results, social media feeds, and YouTube videos. Many videogames also use advertising to generate revenue rather than selling the game. Online advertising has significantly displaced the use of print, radio, and even television as the primary advertising medium. Online advertising has become a dominant part of the economy. "[S]ocial media advertising revenues reached $41.5 billion in 2020. That 16.3% year-over-year growth attributes social media with nearly 30% of all internet advertising revenue (29.6%)."[6]

YouTube and other digital media platforms have also taken a significant part of the online ad revenue. "Digital video experienced the greatest increase (20.6% year-over-year) in advertising revenue growth, generating $26.2 billion in 2020. Digital video increased its share of total internet ad revenue by 1.3% year-over-year, reaching 18.7%."[7]

Advertisers use a real-time auction system to determine which advertiser will acquire each ad on a particular web page, video, game, or social media feed. Advertisers set a budget for the amount of money they are willing to spend on various search phrases or placements on various sites, and the automated advertising software conducts an auction to place the ad for the highest bidder.

Online advertising began with only contextual advertising. Contextual advertising matched the content of the ad with the content from the placement of the ad. Much like a television or magazine ad, contextual advertising assumes only very general attributes about the customer. If a website has a story about off-road trailbikes, the advertisers can make strong assumptions that the readers are interested in trailbikes, and more general assumptions that such readers might also be beer drinkers or interested in camouflage clothing. These assumptions are little more than stereotypes, but over time, the effectiveness of contextual ads improves as the advertiser builds up known associations between content and audiences on particular services.

Through the use of customer tracking, however, Internet advertisers were able to learn a great deal more about the consumers. Each visitor of a website is tracked using small text files known as "cookies." By downloading a cookie into a browser, the software is able to track the interactions between that browser and the web pages the browser visits. Unless the cookies are deleted, this tracking will accumulate from session to session, building up information about all the activities of the browser. The persistent cookies that stay on the computer help both website operators and advertisers develop a very clear picture of the interests and preferences of the user or users of a browser. In some cases, this information will be matched with identifying information from the customer's online purchases, email address, or from data available through credit cards and other financial transactions. Even if there is no personal information used to learn the name of the specific individual, the advertising software has learned a great deal regarding the preferences of the person or persons using that particular device.

Using the cookies and online activities to direct the advertising is known as behavioral advertising. Behavioral advertising is heavily used and generally does not violate state or federal privacy law. California law requires companies to provide a "do not track" option to reduce the cookies and tracking devices. While other laws have attempted to limit cookies, in practice, those policies merely require companies to remind visitors that the site is using cookies. For those consumers who would prefer to avoid behavioral advertising, they can delete the cookies manually or use blocking software to reduce the number of cookies being used.

For many services, such as Google, a person is likely to have the same account open on multiple devices, such as a computer, a mobile phone, and a tablet. Through the phone, Google is able to integrate the information from the cookies with the GPS tracking of movements, and the use of search terms. Through this network of data points, Google can identify the shops and restaurants of most interest to the customer. Google uses this information to sell advertising to its customers—the advertisers—and increase the value of the ads. An ad for a restaurant, for example, is much more valuable to the advertiser if it only is distributed within the range of that restaurant's delivery service, than if the ad were promoted to people living in distant towns or states.

To the public, behavioral advertising is something of a double-edged sword. Customers appreciate the intelligence of the map programs. For a consumer who is traveling, Google's recommended restaurants are very helpful, even though Google was able to identify the restaurants based on the profile of the restaurants that the consumer had previously visited.

At the same time, consumers do not like to be stalked by their devices or have their options dictated by the advertisers. When a person looks up a product that is out of their normal behavior pattern, the appearance of ads for that product and its competitors often feels obvious and creepy. When behavioral advertisement becomes too pointed, the effect tends to backfire. When misused, behavioral advertising also risks reinforcing gender and racial stereotypes, such as targeting toy trucks to boys and dolls to girls.

Advertisers, however, believe behavioral ads to be far more effective than the general ad strategies that rely on television, radio, and print media. Many advertisers have learned to include just enough general promotion in part of the ads so as to keep the targeted ads from seeming like stalking. Because behavioral advertising allows companies to identify individuals by their affinities and traits, privacy advocates point out that different people will receive very different types of advertising, services, and even prices than someone else. A person's zip code, for example, already will change the cost of their car insurance. The same information could be used to charge people living in downtown or urban areas a premium, since the advertiser knows where the person lives and also knows that there are fewer retail outlets in those communities. Behavioral advertising has the potential to continue such disparities.

D. TARGETED MESSAGING, POLITICAL MANIPULATION, AND ANALYTICS

In addition to the concerns regarding behavioral advertising, there is also a concern that targeted advertising can be used to target individuals for specific messages. After all, that is precisely the purpose of advertising—to get a person to respond to the message in an ad to select a particular product or service. In 1973, artists Carlota Fay Schoolman and Richard Serra created a short film entitled *Television Delivers People*, which included the message:

"It is the consumer who is consumed. You are the product of T.V." The same sentiment has echoed often to refer to the consumption of the public's personal information by companies such as Google, Facebook, Amazon, and others involved in the commercial exploitation of advertising and data analytics.

The sale of a person's time on a website to advertisers is a very straightforward transaction. Every second spent on a website creates an opportunity for the website host to provide advertising directed at the person on the website. Ads are placed inside and alongside the feeds on social media sites and publisher media sites, before and after sessions in videogames, before, during, and after YouTube videos, and on search results to get to any of those other sites.

Beyond advertising, however, there is a more subtle business transaction between the sites and the data companies that treat the public as the product being sold. Instead of eyeballs to watch the advertisement, these analytic companies purchase the public's demographic, behavior, and preference data.

Companies turn the mountain of personal data into revenue in a few different ways. The first, and most laudatory use, is to improve the customer experience so that customers want to return to the site. The functionality of websites and mobile apps is constantly being reviewed and updated based on the usage data of the features on the site, the demographic information about the users, and the goals of the company. Content is lengthened or shortened, depending on the percentage of patrons scrolling to the end of the story. Videos are added, edited, or removed based on their viewership as measured at the beginning of the video, to see how many people opened the video, as well as at the end, to see how many people watched the entire video.

The behavioral data about how each individual navigates the site or app are compared to the goals of the corporate site owner. If the goal is to sell product, then if people linger on the videos but do not purchase products, the videos might actually be harmful to sales rather than helping promote sales. This idea would then be tested with design variations that provided the site with fewer videos to track the sales.

Such a site might also use demographic data, often as a surrogate for behavioral data. If a product is designed to attract thirty-year-old women who work, then the corporation will wish to track such women separately on the site regarding their behavior and purchasing activities. Built into such assumptions are often implicit biases regarding the ideal customer and target audience. Some companies are careful to test their assumptions before using them to make operational decisions, but many others rely on racial, gender, ethnic, religious, and geographic distinctions to make broad generalities and reinforce stereotypes through the use of their analytical tools and site design.

Typically, the demographic and behavioral data are not isolated to each site a person visits or each app a person uses. Instead, the software enables data-mining companies with the ability to track a person from site to site and app to app. As a person moves throughout each day, the total amount of information continues to accumulate, and the behaviors incorporate the interrelationship of the data to build additional value. Moreover, since people are networked through social media, content sharing tools, and geographical proximity, the data mapping can also extend beyond the individual to each individual's family, friends, coworkers, and acquaintances. The complexity of the data is overwhelming, but the power of modern computer systems can parse the data to identify trends and outcomes in the information.

Most individual companies cannot make use out of such granular information. Instead, they sell the information to data brokers. Data brokers combine the information from demographic, behavioral, and preference patterns on the Internet with information from credit card use and public records to create a very detailed profile of most Americans and commercialize that data for resale. The information profiles are then sold to retailers, advertising companies, and government agencies.

In a 2014 special report, *60 Minutes* reported that "the largest data broker is Acxiom, a marketing giant that brags it has, on average, 1,500 pieces of information on more than 200 million Americans."[8] Given the continuing growth of Internet usage, the scope of data has likely doubled once or twice since the report was filed. Data brokers then have the ability to commercialize the information. They sell the information to companies for the purposes of designing and selling new products and services. The data may also be used by insurance companies, health care companies, financing companies, and employers. In some cases, the use of this data would be legal, while in other cases, the misuse of the information could violate legal protections against discrimination.

Even where there are legal protections, however, the victim of discrimination may have a very difficult time demonstrating that an employer used data acquired from a data broker to exclude the person from an interview or to score the applicant lower than another person being considered. Amid the sea of data, the usage of the data is exceedingly difficult to track.

Some local, state, and federal government agencies purchase the data rather than undertake direct investigations. While generally legal, the ability to commercially purchase information that would otherwise require a search warrant or subpoena raises significant privacy concerns for some members of the public. The data brokerage business has evolved from a small credit-reporting industry into a multi-billion-dollar enterprise, creating both a revenue opportunity for popular websites and the backbone of consumer data aggregation. Data brokers fuel the sophisticated behavior tracking at the heart of the online economy and the erosion of individual privacy.

Political organizations also use the targeted information to try to manipulate public opinion. Messages are revised and changed so that a campaign may put out dozens or hundreds of versions of a message, each tweaked to a particular personality, race, gender, and geographic recipient.

> Today's political operatives develop highly detailed voter profiles, integrating demographic information, information about the economic, social, and political activities of potential voters, and detailed records of online and even offline behavior into a rich voter profile that can also reveal, through powerful data analytics, additional insight into thoughts, beliefs, and psychological characteristics. The resulting voter profiles can be combined with insights from psychological studies to develop persuasive messages that are tailored with respect not only to the content but also the form of the message (e.g., appearance, specific language, timing of the message), designed specifically to appeal or persuade based on specific recipient characteristics . . . These techniques can take advantage of cognitive limitations and vulnerabilities to shape consumer decisions.[9]

Members of the public will never know that their friends and neighbors are receiving different versions of political ads. Watchdog agencies and the press will have a very hard time fact-checking these messages, since they are sent somewhat privately to different groups. The microtargeting being conducted using these analytical tools harms transparency and undermines the ability of the government to ensure that elections are conducted in a free and fair manner. The same is as true for public interest campaigns as it is for candidates. Increasingly, these techniques are also being used to influence how consumers choose where to live, how to invest, and what to buy.

More than ever before, the people online are the product.

E. PROTECTION FROM UNWANTED INTRUSIONS

Privacy is often described as "the right to be let alone," but this phrase cannot begin to capture the nuance of privacy protection. Privacy means very different things to different people. Privacy laws include the restrictions on corporations' collection and use of personal information. Constitutional privacy protections limit states' power to criminalize personal decisions involving marriage, abortion, parenting, sex, and reproduction. Constitutional privacy protections also limit the power of the government to tap phones, conduct surveillance, or require self-incrimination in criminal trials.

Privacy is not protected under a single law or right in the Constitution. Instead, a wide range of statutes, common law rules, and constitutional protections combine to provide for the privacy protections available. Privacy protection against the government was fundamental to the Revolutionary War, as American colonists fought against the repressive acts of the British occupation. Constitutional protections from searches and seizures as well as the quartering of troops were both responses to the attacks on liberty by the British forces.

In the United States, the right to privacy has evolved slowly and sporadically. As the law developed, it focused on four common law forms of privacy violations:

(a) Unreasonable intrusion upon the seclusion of another;
(b) Appropriation of another person's name or likeness;
(c) Unreasonable publicity given to the other's private life; or
(d) Publicity that unreasonably places the other in a false light before the public.[10]

The federal government has never adopted a uniform right to privacy that covers all issues. Instead, different types of information are protected by state and federal law. Beginning in the 1970s, Congress enacted a series of laws to promote privacy of personal information and data in specific industries or economic sectors. Although that list is long, some of the most important laws include these:

• The Federal Privacy Act to protect against the misuse of federally collected public data.
• Family Educational Rights and Privacy Act (FERPA) to protect student records.
• Fair Credit Reporting Act (FCRA) to protect against the abuse and exploitation of consumer credit information.
• Gramm-Leach-Bliley Act, also known as the Financial Modernization Act of 1999 (GLBA), to require notice about the sharing of a financial institution's consumer data.
• Health Insurance Portability and Accountability Act (HIPAA), which includes the HIPAA Privacy Rule and the HIPAA Security Rule, to establish obligations for medical industry protection of personal and protected health information.
• Children's Online Privacy Protection Act (COPPA), to limit the collection and use of personal information regarding children under the age of thirteen.

FERPA is discussed in chapter 4, and COPPA is discussed in chapters 2 and 16.

At the federal level, general privacy enforcement is primarily conducted by the FTC. Various banking regulators have some additional role with regard to financial privacy, and the Department of Health and Human Service's Office for Civil Rights is responsible for enforcing the privacy and security rules under HIPAA. Nonetheless, it is the FTC that has taken the lead for federal privacy enforcement.

The FTC will investigate claims of privacy violations and has the choice on how it wishes to proceed if it finds a company has violated the terms of its own privacy policy or failed to adequately protect consumer data because of faulty data security measures. The FTC regularly brings administrative actions against companies for these types of failures. In most cases, the companies are willing to work with the FTC and enter into settlement agreements rather than face a protracted lawsuit or administrative hearing process. Many states have versions of consumer protection statutes similar to the Federal Trade Commission Act. This allows the attorneys general of the states also to enforce privacy violations. In some states, the laws allow for the individuals injured by the failure to adhere to the privacy policy also to bring lawsuits.

In addition, many states are also beginning to enact broader privacy protection law, particularly focused on the collection of digital information collected through cookies and other online tracking technologies. California, New York, and Illinois are leading the way in restricting how businesses can collect and use customer data without the consent of the customers. These state laws provide consumers the right to see what information is collected, to dispute inaccurate information, and in some cases to require companies to delete the data upon the request of the customer.

State privacy laws are rapidly changing, but the widespread concerns about the use of the public's personal data in behavioral advertising, artificial intelligence programs, and unwanted tracking have resulted in a growing demand for restrictions on the use of personal data by advertisers, employers, and others in the private sector.

F. PROTECTION FROM GOVERNMENT SURVEILLANCE

The word privacy is not used in the U.S. Constitution, but despite the term's absence, many of the provisions in the Bill of Rights have been interpreted to grant the right of privacy to U.S. citizens. The First Amendment's protections of religion and speech include protections against government compulsion and interference in writing and worship. The Fourth Amendment protects against unreasonable searches and seizures. The Fifth Amendment, which protects a person from being compelled to be a witness "against himself," also ensures that no person can be "deprived of life, liberty, or property, without due process of law." Finally, the Ninth Amendment reserved the unenumerated powers not granted in the Constitution to the people. It further provided that absence of a statement in the Constitution protecting of a particular right did not diminish or eliminate that right.

The most important constitutional limitation on the government's ability to conduct surveillance is found in the Fourth Amendment. The Fourth Amendment provides the "right of the people to be secure in their person, houses, papers, and effects, against unreasonable searches and seizures." Many state constitutions have similar protections.

The Fourth Amendment requires the government to obtain a warrant to search a person's home, car, or similar location based on probable cause. Probable cause for a search warrant requires that the facts and circumstances provide the basis for a reasonable person to believe that a crime was committed at the place to be searched, or that evidence of a crime exists at the location. A search warrant must both specify the place where the search will be conducted and the items to be seized.

The consequence of violating the Fourth Amendment results in the information obtained being excluded from use in the trial against the accused. Known as the "Exclusionary Rule," the policy discourages unlawful police practices because it frustrates the purpose for violating the constitutional rights of the target.

If a search does violate the Fourth Amendment, not only will the evidence be excluded from any subsequent trial, but it can also lead to a claim for civil liability. Individuals who have had their federal constitutional right violated may bring claims under the civil rights protection law, 42 U.S.C. § 1983, which imposes civil liability "upon any person who, acting under the color of state law, deprives another individual of any rights, privileges, or immunities secured by the Constitution or laws of the United States."

There are a number of exceptions to the warrant requirement. The warrantless search will be lawful if the police are given consent to the search by the person whose property they wish to search, if the items to be searched are in plain view, or if there are exigent circumstances. Exigent circumstances may exist if there is an imminent danger to a person, imminent risk of destruction of the items to be seized, or threat of a suspect's imminent escape.

1. The Reasonable Expectation of Privacy

The modern understanding of the Fourth Amendment was developed in *Katz v. United States* (1967) and the Wiretap Act of 1968. Prior to *Katz*, the protections against warrantless searches were primarily based on the physical conduct of a search. In the Communications Act of 1934, for example,

Congress protected phone calls from wiretaps by federal statute. The law was very effective at stopping private phone call interception, but it was not particularly well suited to the use of wiretaps and other eavesdropping by law enforcement. In addition, the statute was enforced inconsistently among different state courts.

In *Katz*, the Supreme Court fundamentally shifted the focus of the Fourth Amendment. The Supreme Court explained—

> we have expressly held that the Fourth Amendment governs not only the seizure of tangible items, but extends as well to the recording of oral statements overheard without any "technical trespass under . . . local property law." Once this much is acknowledged, and once it is recognized that the Fourth Amendment protects people—and not simply "areas"—against unreasonable searches and seizures it becomes clear that the reach of that Amendment cannot turn upon the presence or absence of a physical intrusion into any given enclosure.

The court then provided guidance on how the Fourth Amendment should be understood to apply to the protection of individuals rather than places. The majority opinion, however, did not provide the government or the lower courts a roadmap for future decisions. Instead, Justice Harlan's concurrence provided the summary essential to the future shape of the Fourth Amendment:

> My understanding of the rule that has emerged from prior decisions is that there is a twofold requirement, first that a person have exhibited an actual (subjective) expectation of privacy and, second, that the expectation be one that society is prepared to recognize as "reasonable." Thus a man's home is, for most purposes, a place where he expects privacy, but objects, activities, or statements that he exposes to the "plain view" of outsiders are not "protected" because no intention to keep them to himself has been exhibited. On the other hand, conversations in the open would not be protected against being overheard, for the expectation of privacy under the circumstances would be unreasonable.

The explanation provided by Justice Harlan eventually became the *Katz* test regarding the reasonableness of a warrantless search. In *Smith v. Maryland* (1979), the court summarized a decade of decisions applying *Katz*.

> Consistently with *Katz*, this Court uniformly has held that the application of the Fourth Amendment depends on whether the person invoking its protection can claim a "justifiable," a "reasonable," or a "legitimate expectation of privacy" that has been invaded by government action. This inquiry, as Mr. Justice Harlan aptly noted in his Katz concurrence, normally embraces two discrete questions. The first is whether the individual, by his conduct, has "exhibited an actual

(subjective) expectation of privacy," whether, in the words of the *Katz* majority, the individual has shown that "he seeks to preserve [something] as private." The second question is whether the individual's subjective expectation of privacy is "one that society is prepared to recognize as 'reasonable',"—whether, in the words of the *Katz* majority, the individual's expectation, viewed objectively, is "justifiable" under the circumstances.

The outline and examples in *Katz* served as the blueprint to adopt the Wiretap Act in 1968, which continues to govern the manner in which the government can use eavesdropping techniques regarding phones, email, and other communications platforms. In 1986, the law was expanded from wire and oral to all electronic communications. In 1998, it was further expanded to cover email and other forms of stored electronic communications. The Wiretap Act prohibits the interception of both oral and wire communications, but also provides a mechanism for seeking a court order to issue a wiretap or electronic surveillance.

There are exceptions to the prohibition on surveillance. For example, companies may record calls as part of their business operations. Telephone and communications companies have even greater latitude, provided the surveillance was necessary for the provision of the communications services. In addition, the law allows either party in a communication to consent to having that conversation monitored or recorded. Some states have more stringent laws, however, and in those states consent to record conversations is required from all parties to be lawful. Online platforms like Zoom provide icons to show that a call is being recorded to notify the participants that they are consenting to the recordings of the call by participating while it is being recorded.

2. Government Searches of Mobile Phones

While *Katz* and the Wiretap Act have provided a much better approach to the balance of the right to privacy and the government's interest in public safety, the advances in GPS tracking, satellite photography, data analytics, and mobile phones have led to a new challenge for Congress and the courts.

In a series of cases in the past decade, the Supreme Court addressed the growing risk to warrantless surveillance, culminating in *Carpenter v. U.S.* (2018). In *Carpenter*, the Supreme Court focused on the ability of law enforcement to track a person's movements simply by reading the movements of the person's cell phone over time. In the case, the government collected cell site location information (CSLI) of a suspect from two wireless telephone companies. The government was able to obtain 12,898 location points to detail the suspect's movements over 127 days—an average of 101 data points per day—with a single, simple request. The court rejected the government's position that the CSLI were merely corporate records and instead required that such extensive individual tracking required a valid search warrant.

Four years before *Carpenter*, the Supreme Court provided privacy protection to the search of a cell phone. In *Riley v. California* (2014), the Supreme Court held that a cell phone could not be searched, even as incident to an arrest. The phone may be seized pending the issuance of a search warrant, but it cannot be opened by the arresting officer to peruse through the content, unless the government has a search warrant or the search falls into one of the exceptions to the warrant requirement.

In *Riley*, the Supreme Court recognized the power of mobile devices.

Data on a cell phone can reveal where a person has been. Historic location information is a standard feature on many smart phones and can reconstruct someone's specific movements down to the minute, not only around town but also within a particular building.

The storage capacity of cell phones has several interrelated consequences for privacy. First, a cell phone collects in one place many distinct types of information—an address, a note, a prescription, a bank statement, a video—that reveal much more in combination than any isolated record. Second, a cell phone's capacity allows even just one type of information to convey far more than previously possible. The sum of an individual's private life can be reconstructed through a thousand photographs labeled with dates, locations, and descriptions; the same cannot be said of a photograph or two of loved ones tucked into a wallet. Third, the data on a phone can date back to the purchase of the phone, or even earlier.

An Internet search and browsing history, for example, can be found on an Internet-enabled phone and could reveal an individual's private interests or concerns—perhaps a search for certain symptoms of disease, coupled with frequent visits to WebMD. . . . Mobile application software on a cell phone, or "apps," offer a range of tools for managing detailed information about all aspects of a person's life. There are apps for Democratic Party news and Republican Party news; apps for alcohol, drug, and gambling addictions; apps for sharing prayer requests; apps for tracking pregnancy symptoms; apps for planning your budget; apps for every conceivable hobby or pastime; apps for improving your romantic life. There are popular apps for buying or selling just about anything, and the records of such transactions may be accessible on the phone indefinitely.[11]

Riley and *Carpenter* provide very clear statements that the modern tools for information tracking are not to be used to evade the constitutional and statutory protections from government surveillance.

3. Government Searches of Students

Students at school are entitled to limited constitutional protections from unlawful searches and seizures under the Fourth Amendment, but the standards are not the same as for adults. The rules were established in *New Jersey v. T.L.O.* (1985). Two fourteen-year-old female students were caught smoking in the bathroom by a teacher and brought to the vice principal's office. While in his office, T.L.O. denied smoking. The vice principal searched her purse. He found a pack of cigarettes but also found rolling papers. This led him to dig deeper, eventually finding a small amount of marijuana, a drug pipe, a list of student clients, and a large sum of cash.

The school called the student's mother and the police. While at the police station, T.L.O. admitted to selling drugs at school. The Supreme Court explained that the policy on searches needed to balance the rights of the students to their privacy and the schools with their obligation to maintain order.

> [T]he accommodation of the privacy interests of schoolchildren with the substantial need of teachers and administrators for freedom to maintain order in the schools does not require strict adherence to the requirement that searches be based on probable cause to believe that the subject of the search has violated or is violating the law. Rather, the legality of a search of a student should depend simply on the reasonableness, under all the circumstances, of the search.
>
> Determining the reasonableness of any search involves a twofold inquiry: first, one must consider whether the action was justified at its inception; second, one must determine whether the search as actually conducted was reasonably related in scope to the circumstances which justified the interference in the first place.
>
> Under ordinary circumstances, a search of a student by a teacher or other school official will be "justified at its inception" when there are reasonable grounds for suspecting that the search will turn up evidence that the student has violated or is violating either the law or the rules of the school. Such a search will be permissible in its scope when the measures adopted are reasonably related to the objectives of the search and not excessively intrusive in light of the age and sex of the student and the nature of the infraction.[12]

The policy established in *New Jersey v. T.L.O.* and subsequent cases makes clear that in the public school setting, a search will be permitted without a search warrant provided the search is reasonable. The same policies apply equally to law enforcement officers, safety officers, and school officials. Provided the search is reasonable, it will not violate the Fourth Amendment. The definition of reasonable is not well-defined under the law, but in general, the law requires that the school official or law enforcement officer has some concrete evidence that there is likely to be contraband in the object being searched. Mere hunches or general searches are not permitted.

For the search to implicate Fourth Amendment protections, it needs to be directed at a particular student. For example, the use of drug-sniffing dogs to conduct sweeps through schools, parking lots, and outdoor facilities is permitted. These generalized searches do not violate the Fourth Amendment for any particular individual student. Using a drug-sniffing dog to single out a particular student, in contrast, would generally require that the reasonable suspicion standard is met before the search should be allowed to proceed.

Courts have similarly allowed metal detectors to be used to protect schools. Both the metal detectors and drug-sniffing dogs are considered fall less intrusive than a physical search of a person's belongings and therefore do not trigger Fourth Amendment protections either for adults or for students.

For student lockers, the general rule is the same. If the locker is the property of the student, then the search of a particular student's locker requires that the search meet the reasonable suspicion standard. Some schools try to avoid even this requirement by claiming the lockers are the property of the school and subject to search at all times. These schools place the designation of lockers as school property in the student handbooks to help establish the school's right to search lockers on a random basis.

Schools sometimes use drug screening tests of athletes and other students as a condition of participation in extracurricular activities. These screening searches have been found not to be searches protected by the Fourth Amendment, in part because the choice to participate in the extracurricular activities are voluntary and the need to comply with drug-free competition rules create obligations to ensure the participants are meeting these policies.

The Fourth Amendment, however, only defines the minimum protections a person must receive from warrantless searches. States including Washington have interpreted their state law or otherwise provided additional protections against random drug testing for extracurricular activities.

Chapter 16

Protecting against Identity Theft and Fraud

A Nontechnical Introduction to Cybersecurity for the Family

A review of privacy basics is not complete without addressing the need to protect private information from unwanted exposure or access. With the tremendous growth of the Internet and social media, identity theft has also become an epidemic problem. In 2019, the FTC reported a record 3.2 million reports of fraud, including more than 650,000 cases of identity theft. The number of fraud cases reported to the FTC has doubled in the past decade.

The majority of these cases are credit card thefts, although in some situations, the thieves gain access to banking accounts, tax refunds, and even health care access. Imposters, posing as the victims, can run up large bills on credit cards and even swindle hospitals for surgeries and other medical treatment, all charged to the victim of the identity theft. After identity theft, the second most common form of consumer fraud is committed through imposter scams, in which a con artist will pretend to be a family member or other trusted person. The scammer then asks for money or personal information.

The FTC provides lists of different strategies used by these con artists, including "scammers claiming to work for or be affiliated with a government agency; scammers posing as a friend or relative with an emergency need for money; scammers posing as a romantic interest; scammers claiming to be a computer technician offering technical support; and scammers claiming to be affiliated with a private entity (e.g., a charity or company)." In other categories of fraud, scammers may offer low-cost vacations, renewal of car warranties, consolidation of student debts, or other offers that sound too good to be true. Identity theft and imposter scams are distinct crimes, but they are closely related.

To combat the threat of fraud and identity theft, each family must have a security and cybersecurity plan. The term cybersecurity often invokes an expectation that it refers to a set of processes, technologies, and methods to protect electronic systems and devices from unauthorized access through malicious attacks. Although a definition like this is not uncommon, it leaves out the much broader roles that legal rules, institutional practices, and user protocols add to the technical measures intended to protect information from becoming compromised.

A. THE ORIGINS OF DATA SECURITY: THE ENVELOPE

One of the earliest information security devices was the envelope, and it provided an excellent introduction, before the details became complicated with computer systems and technological solutions. Both in early common law and still today, the rules of privacy were very different for letters from postcards. When a letter was sent by mail, the sender had an expectation of privacy that the information in the letter would not be shared with third parties. This expectation was established by law, which made it illegal to tamper with the mail or to open a mailed letter without authorization. Unsealing a letter is not difficult, but the legal rules provided the primary protection of the letter. In contrast, a postcard had no legal protection of privacy, because the postcard exposed the contents to anyone who could see it. The law would not protect the contents of the postcard and the card's sender was on notice that there was no privacy available to the postcard.

In addition to the legal rules protecting the mail, there were also institutional or administrative rules to further this protection along with physical protection of the mails. Governmental mail services and commercial mail rooms adhere to strict procedures to collect, sort, and deliver mail and packages designed to minimize theft and ensure that the letters and parcels are not opened. These procedures help protect the mail and ensure that the law is enforced in a practical manner.

Finally, the user protocols for letters and parcels are also commonly understood. Before mailing a letter, the sender is taught to carefully seal the envelope or tape shut the package. People who regularly mail checks often buy heavier envelopes that are difficult to see through. And of course, most people deposit letters in postal mailboxes or their home mailbox to be sure the letter is not intercepted.

These same basic steps for data security apply in the electronic world as well. Cybersecurity laws and industry best practices require companies to ensure that the data they have collected are not stolen, destroyed, or misused by individuals within the company or by outside third parties. Cybersecurity requirements outline the steps needed to ensure the continued confidentiality, integrity, and availability of the data collected by each company.

There are many laws and regulations designed to ensure the protection of data stored and shared on computers, servers, networks, mobile devices, and other systems. Each organization with access to private information must have institutional, administrative protocols in place to protect the data from theft, destruction, manipulation, or other damage. There must be physical protections for the equipment to minimize the access to protected information by unauthorized individuals.

Protecting privacy means protecting the systems that store, transmit, and utilize protected information. This applies to the computers, mobile devices, networks, routers, servers, and other systems, whether connected to the Internet or which operate separately. It requires that software is up-to-date so that all known vulnerabilities, flaws, or errors in the software are corrected promptly. It requires that systems use passwords and other means to keep unauthorized individuals out of enterprise systems, and anticipate the techniques used by potential intruders.

B. PERSONALLY IDENTIFIABLE INFORMATION

Corporations, nonprofit agencies, and government offices gather a tremendous amount of information every day, but only a small fraction of it relates to protected information about individual consumers. This information is generally referred to as personally identifiable information (PII). The simplest examples are a person's name along with their username and password, but today most legal protections for PII are much more inclusive. In the medical industry, the information is referred to as personal health information (PHI), and this data is governed by HIPAA. As noted earlier, COPPA has a very long list of PII for minors under the age of thirteen. Under HIPAA, there are eighteen categories of PHI:

1. Names (last name and either first name or first name initial)
2. All geographical identifiers smaller than a state, except for the initial three digits of a zip code if, according to the current publicly available data from the U.S. Bureau of the Census: the geographic unit formed by combining all zip codes with the same three initial digits contains more than 20,000 people; and the initial three digits of a zip code for all such geographic units containing 20,000 or fewer people is changed to 000
3. Dates (other than year) directly related to an individual
4. Phone numbers
5. Fax numbers
6. Email addresses
7. Social Security numbers

8. Medical record numbers
9. Health insurance beneficiary numbers
10. Account numbers
11. Certificate/license numbers
12. Vehicle identifiers (including serial numbers and license plate numbers)
13. Device identifiers and serial numbers
14. Web Uniform Resource Locators (URLs)
15. Internet Protocol (IP) address numbers
16. Biometric identifiers, including finger, retinal, and voice prints
17. Full face photographic images and any comparable images
18. Any other unique identifying number, characteristic, or code except the unique code assigned by the investigator to code the data

The laws often define PII in slightly different ways, but they tend to include the items listed in COPPA and the health care regulations.

These types of data are only protected from publication and disclosure if the data are gathered as part of an interaction that falls into one of the federal or state categories for the protection of such information. Fortunately, the list of protected activities has grown significantly in recent years. At the federal level, this primarily includes student records, health records, and financial records, as well as data collected under COPPA for minors under thirteen. Most commercial websites do not differentiate the location of their users, so in addition to the federal laws, companies typically try to comply with the most stringent of the state laws. New York and California provide excellent examples.

In New York, the SHIELD Act provides that personal information is "any information concerning a natural person which, because of name, number, personal mark, or other identifier, can be used to identify such natural person." Private information, in contrast, is the personal information plus identification numbers such as state IDs, Social Security numbers, credit and debit account numbers (even without the PINs or access codes to those accounts), or other account numbers. Private information also includes a broad biometric category, not limited to fingerprint, voice print, retina, facial, and other unique physical representation or digital representation of biometric data. Finally, the private information category also includes "a user name or email address in combination with a password or security question and answer that would permit access to an online account." The SHIELD Act provides limited flexibility for small businesses, defined as those that have fewer than fifty employees; less than $3 million in gross annual revenue; or less than $5 million in year-end total assets.

In California, the law includes information gathered by operators that collect PII of California residents or individuals who visit a California operator's website. Known as the California Consumer Privacy Act, it only applies to companies with at least $25 million in annual revenue, 50,000 consumer households, or that operate by selling consumer's personal information.

At the same time, one of the greatest exclusions from PII are public records. As a result, information that is public because the government does not protect the information in real estate records, most court filings, and many department of motor vehicle databases, companies may have much greater access to personal information than the categories of PII might suggest.

If a company collects PII or PHI, then it must provide the consumer a privacy policy that explains what information is being collected, how it is being used, and the right to view and correct the information. The company must also take reasonable steps to ensure that the information collected is protected from theft, destruction, or misuse.

C. DATA PROTECTION—INTEGRITY, AVAILABILITY, AND CONFIDENTIALITY

When developing a company's system for assuring data protection, the company must generally focus on three aspects of the information. First, the company must ensure that there is data integrity, meaning that the data remains accurate and unchanged over time. Paper can fade and some backup tape systems tended to flake and decay. To be a reliable system, the physical material on which the data is recorded must be safe. Integrity also means that the data will not be changed. For example, although a student earns new grades each semester, once earned, the grades should never be altered. The student's cumulative grade point average (GPA) will be adjusted each term, but the GPA earned in each term should be a permanent and unchanging number. If there is no data integrity, then the information cannot be trusted.

To be usable, the information must also be available. Availability means that the system will be able to take advantage of the data for its processes. If a company stores backups of its data in remote locations, that may be a good practice for security purposes, but it reduces the availability of the data. In the same way, encryption may make data much more secure than having data be readable, but encrypted data generally has to be decrypted before it can be utilized.

Data integrity and availability are primary concerns for the company that collects the data. Data confidentiality is just as important to the consumer as to the company that collected the confidential data. New York's SHIELD Act (an acronym for "Stop Hacks and Improve Electronic Data Security Act") provides a useful example of the types of protections that the law requires for data confidentiality. These protections typically fall into three categories:

the physical safeguards to ensure the protection of the data and the medium on which it is stored; the administrative safeguards to ensure the company has policies and procedures to protect the information; and the technical safeguards which focus on encryption, firewalls, antivirus protection, and other efforts to reduce the risk to the data from hackers, ransomware, and unauthorized employees.

Physical Safeguards

Companies must plan their operations to ensure that the physical storage of personal and private information is secure from theft, misuse, loss, and manipulation. These obligations include the following:

- The physical facilities in which the data are stored.
- The manner of securing the data.
- The ability to limit who within the organization has access to the data.
- The process of destroying and disposing of data that should no longer be retained.
- A system for auditing or assuring that these physical systems have not been breached.

Administrative Safeguards

The administrative safeguards are the most critical and most overlooked aspect of information security. The regulations require that a senior-level security officer be identified as the person responsible for implementation of all data security efforts. If the company is small, the identified security officer can also fulfill other roles at the company, but every company must have a designated individual.

The person designated as the lead for data security will generally be one member of a team of employees focused on data security. Unauthorized access of information from either inside or outside the organization can be the basis for a security incident. Sometimes incidents are triggered by hackers but oftentimes incidents will occur because an employee attempted to gain unauthorized access to a company's information. A reasonable data security program will address both internal and external risks.

Training, auditing, updating, and recognizing the types of issues that the company can face are all part of the administrative safeguard obligations. Reasonable administrative safeguards also include an assessment of the manner used to select service providers that may be storing data, providing software, or otherwise accessing computer networks of the business.

Technical Safeguards

The technical safeguards are the computer systems, data minimization steps, audit controls, segregation of networks, firewalls, antivirus protection, installation of software patches, and similar steps that a company must take to stay abreast of its data security obligations. Technical safeguards focus on data at each of the storage, transmission, and processing steps. Encryption is essential in every stage where it is a feasible alternative.

Technical and physical safeguards together provide some strategies for data stored on mobile devices that are at greater risk of loss or theft. Encryption is the first step. In addition, companies should have systems to track the devices, to remotely remove the data, and to audit the disclosure of that data during the process.

D. HOUSEHOLD FUNDAMENTALS TO PROTECT PERSONAL INFORMATION

Although most laws focus on business enterprises, the same concerns for data privacy exist in the household. This is even more important during times when family members are working at home, particularly if they have access to information that is subject to state or federal regulation from their employers. Every family should have a data privacy plan and make sure that all members of the family are following the plan at all times.

The family plan for protecting personal information should follow the same three categories as is required by law for businesses. The physical safeguards include the steps to ensure that computers, laptops, and phones, as well as credit cards and checkbooks, are protected from loss and theft. The technical safeguards are the implementation and use of passwords, firewalls, encryption, and other tools to ensure that the family's important account and data information is always protected. The administrative safeguards are the household rules that every member of the family follows to protect and secure privacy information.

1. Technical Safeguards

When thinking about protecting personal information, most people begin with the technical safeguards. These are the basic steps that can reduce the risks from most identity theft and other forms of fraud.

- **Firewalls**: Every computer and device should have a firewall that limits the traffic into and out of the device. In the early days of the Internet, use of firewalls was one of the most talked about tools. Today, however, Windows-based computers and Apple's Mac computers have firewall software built directly into the operating systems. There is also firewall software included in most home routers as well. Many people continue to prefer a third-party vendor to add firewall protection, and some of these programs do offer additional protections. The most important step for the home user is to be sure the firewall remains turned on.

- **Updates**: There are millions of hacking attempts each day, and these are not all directed at large corporations. In the majority of successful outside attacks, passwords, firewalls, and other protections failed because a known vulnerability in the software was used to insert malicious software (malware). Computer and cell phone companies regularly issue updates to protect the users from these known vulnerabilities. The user must be sure that the updates are occurring, and the devices remain up-to-date with the required software patches and safeguards.
- **Device Encryption**: Every computer should have full disk encryption so that the data on the computer's hard drive cannot be accessed unless the user provides a password or PIN code. For Mac devices, the built-in full disk encryption is named FileVault. For Windows devices, the built-in full disk encryption is named Bitlocker. Users should be sure that the systems are running, and that the machine requires a password or PIN.
- **Passwords**: Enable a password on each device and for each account. Passwords are the single most important step in protecting accounts from hackers and scammers. If an account is not protected, it can be used by an intruder to add malware onto a device that can then steal credit card and other sensitive information. It is very difficult to memorize all these passwords, so users should consider using a password manager to collect and securely store the passwords.
- **Unique Passwords**: Every site and device should use a unique password. The password should be "strong," meaning that it is not obvious or standardized. Longer is better. Variations on phrases that are easier to remember work nearly as well as nonsense strings. A user won't forget: "Cry*havoc* andletslipthecatsofwar." The variation of cats for dogs in the phrase and the use of asterisks (*) around the second word will keep the phrase from being found in any phrase database.
- **Two-Step Verification of Passwords**: Wherever possible, use two-factor authentication, otherwise known as two-step verification. The most common form of two-factor authentication is the use of a person's cell phone to verify that an attempted use of a log in was made by that person. Most systems allow trusted devices to avoid two-factor authentication, so the site will trust a password sent from a user's registered home computer or cell phone, but it will require verification if it is used anywhere else.

- **Internet Encryption**: Use HTTPS, designated with the lock icon, to help reduce the unencrypted information a user is sending. The HTTPS protocol provides encryption of the traffic being sent to and from a website, so it significantly helps reduce third parties from stealing or intercepting the information. At the same time, the lock icon and HTTPS is not a seal of approval that a site is legitimate; it is only a technical specification that it uses encryption. Scammers are increasingly using HTTPS as well as the legitimate sites. Still, sites without HTTPS are much worse than those that have it, so be sure to look for the lock icon. Just don't treat the lock as a guarantee that a site is legitimate.
- **File Encryption**: In addition to the encryption on a device, any files that have confidential data should also use file-level encryption. This ensures that when the file is transmitted online, such as to a cloud-based backup, the file cannot be read by malware while it is being sent or as a result of a data breach at the cloud storage facility.

2. Physical Safeguards

To protect the personal information for an individual or family, the family members should adopt common-sense protections for the physical security of all confidential information and all devices or equipment that can store confidential information.

- **Passwords**: Use passwords on all devices, even those in the home. Cell phones and laptop computers are constantly being lost or stolen. One should never assume that a device won't be lost.
- **Calls**: Never provide confidential information over the phone. Instead, always find an independent method for verifying the caller. Adhering to this rule will protect a household from most consumer fraud.
- **Emails**: Never click on links from an unrecognized address. Scammers often conduct phishing attacks by sending emails that look like they are coming from popular vendors, such as credit card companies, major retailers, or government agencies. Rather than clicking on the links in the email, log onto the sites directly. If the email was legitimate, the information will be available in the customer's account. If the email was a scam, the request will not be there. By hovering over the link, the full address will appear. Even if an email looks legitimate, hover over the link to be sure it is directing the user to the correct location.
- **Websites**: Be cautious when using unknown websites, particularly if the site is for the purchase of goods or services. Using services like Yelp or Angie's List will help verify smaller vendors and ensure that other users are familiar with the companies. For other local vendors, check that the

website offers a phone number and address to contact the store. If a household member really needs to buy something from an untrusted source, only use a credit card or gift card. The gift card cannot be charged beyond its face value, further limiting the risk of the credit card number being stolen.

- **Social Media**: Do not post any personal information. This admonition includes the types of PII described earlier, as well as any information that is confidential to the family or that might otherwise embarrass the individual or the family. Sending a message to a friend seems private, but that message might be seen or intercepted. Cell phones and computers also make it much easier to resend a picture or post that was intended to be kept private. Examples abound of intimate and graphic pictures intended to be shared only with a partner ending up on social media.
- **Destroy Unnecessary Personal Information**: Paper documents with credit card numbers, social security numbers, driver's license data, prescription information, or other personal information should be shredded or destroyed before being recycled. The same is true of junk mail that includes offers for credit cards and loans. Shred or rip up all the unwanted mail before discarding. If a household doesn't own a shredder, then manually ripping the account information off the document and shredding that information will achieve the same result. For old credit cards, the cards should be cut into pieces, making sure the microchip has been cut apart. The card pieces should be discarded using two or more garbage receptacles so the card cannot be reproduced.
- **Erase Unnecessary Personal Information**: For digital information, there is no physical destruction. Instead, the data must be properly erased to be eliminated. Once information is no longer needed, it should be destroyed. This requires that the files are deleted, and the drives are properly erased. Deleting data does not erase the data from the drive. To erase the data, a software program must be used that writes over the "empty" space on a drive to make it unrecoverable. This should also be done on cell phones and all devices before those devices are recycled. If the household has a printer with digital scanners or internal hard drives, those devices must also have the content on the drives deleted and thoroughly erased before they are recycled.
- **Manage Wallets and Purses**: Limit the information each member of the household carries. Avoid carrying a social security card and limit the number of credit cards. Make a copy of the credit cards (ideally with the middle digits blocked out) including the information on the back. This photocopy of the card backs makes it much easier to contact the card issuers in the case of a loss or theft of the cards.
- **Use Locks and Passwords**: Some houses are Fortresses of Solitude while others are more like Grand Central Station. The amount of physical security

should be appropriate to the number of household members and strangers regularly in the home. Generally speaking, a house is safer if the doors to the house and vehicles are locked. Wallets and purses should be kept in secure, private locations. Confidential papers should be kept in filing cabinets, and if the house has frequent visits from vendors or other strangers, then those cabinets should be locked. Computers and cell phones should always be password protected to protect them from strangers being able to access them.

3. Administrative Safeguards for the Home

Most households have one family member who becomes the resident Information Technology (IT) guru. Many families also often have one family member responsible for paying the bills. In the same way, each household should have one person who takes on the responsibility to be the family's chief security officer (CSO). Understanding how to implement information privacy practices is not technically difficult, but it is important that the steps are completed each time.

- **Make Privacy a Priority**: In business, the purpose of creating cybersecurity regulations with administrative safeguard policies was to ensure that senior management was paying attention to privacy and security. The same is true for the household. The designated CSO should develop a household security plan and be sure that all family members adhere to the plan.
- **Take Stock**: A privacy plan starts with an audit of the information that needs to be kept secure. A credit report provides an excellent tool to know what outstanding credit cards have been issued to the home. The plan should identify the credit cards, loan documents, safety deposit box information (including the location of the keys), social security card information, and driver's licenses.
- **Monitor**: The three major credit reporting agencies each provide a free annual credit report. Use the credit report to check on any changes. Each credit card company, bank, and loan agency provides a monthly statement. The family CSO should be sure that these are reviewed each month to be sure there are no unexpected charges or changes. Medical statements should be reviewed in the same manner.
- **Train**: Each member of the family should be trained to follow the physical safeguards and to use the technical safeguards listed above. Children often start using tablets and cell phones before elementary school. As they mature, they should be taught how to follow the privacy and security guidelines in an age-appropriate manner.

- **Manage**: Every device in the household that connects to the Internet can be a source of data breach. This includes all the computers, tablets, routers, and cell phones, but it also includes the IoT devices, such as child monitors, nanny-cams, refrigerators, toasters, and light bulbs. Every device should be checked to be sure the software is updated and that a unique password has been assigned.
- **Additional Considerations**: Households increasingly rely on monitoring devices such as Google Assistant, Alexa, Siri, Bixby, and other services that eavesdrop on the home. Employees monitoring these services have acknowledged having eavesdropped on marital fights, drug deals, and confidential business transactions. Families should carefully consider whether the convenience of these devices outweighs the risk of continuous eavesdropping built into these machines.

E. TRACKING DEVICE USAGE AND THE BALANCE BETWEEN TRUST AND VERIFY

Establishing a household approach for fraud protection and cybersecurity is an essential part of modern life. At the same time, however, parents must understand that the tools used to protect the household privacy and security can also be used to pry into the personal lives of the family members. In corporate America, information technology (IT) staff are bound by employer rules and federal laws that create liability for exceeding their authority to spy on other employees.

The tracking falls into a few different categories. One set of apps is designed to simply track the location of a mobile phone or device. Google's Find My Device and Apple's Find My iPhone both provide this function, as do many other apps.

Another set of features allows parents to access transcripts of their children's content on social media, texts, and messaging apps. Some will also log the search activities of the user. Many will limit the amount of time a device can be used online, and some will limit the apps and websites that can be visited by the user. Others will even record calls.

Many of these apps promise to operate silently in the background. This makes it very hard for the user to know when the monitoring is occurring.

For the household, it is important to establish the expectations of the household and to make age-appropriate rules to respect adolescent privacy while also assuring safety and security. Many of the tracking tools are only legal with the consent of the person being tracked. In the case of a minor, that consent can come from the parent or guardian, giving the parents the authority to use the devices.

While it is legal to install tracking software on a child's device, it is very important that the parents have done so with the understanding of the children. Parents will have a much easier time using the information if their children know in advance that there are limits on their computers and cell phones. If a teen first learns that a parent has access to their device or has been reading their messages during a time of crisis, it will be much harder to use that information to resolve the underlying problems.

Of the various tracking tools, device tracking is probably the least controversial. Cell phones are very expensive and easily lost or stolen. Installing features to track the phone in case of loss is a very practical step to protect the equipment. Parents also have a general expectation that their children will be truthful about where they go.

For tweens and younger teens, parents will likely find that the fears of what could occur online will outweigh their children's interest in privacy. As teens age, however, the importance of privacy becomes paramount. A parent's insistence on using tracking technologies is likely to have a long-term, negative effect on the relationship between the parent and child.

The need for tracking software may change, however, if there have been instances of harassment, bullying, sexual exploitation, or severe disciplinary problems with the older teen. Even in these situations, however, it is better to use the tracking tools as part of an agreed-upon strategy for the parents and teen to reestablish trust and to reduce the use of tracking as the teen demonstrates appropriate behavior.

Parenting advice is highly split regarding the appropriateness of tracking teens' online behavior. The app companies tend to paint a picture of a highly dangerous Internet populated by trolls and predators in every chatroom and on every text chain. As discussed in more detail in chapter 7, however, the challenges adolescents face from anxiety, depression, harassment, and abuse are not primarily triggered from their online activities. Instead, the challenges adolescents face manifest equally both online and offline.

Undoubtedly, there are concerns that could be learned earlier if a parent uses direct access to a teen's texts or social media accounts. But that also interferes with the teen's ability to address those issues. Parental monitoring of a teen's social interactions would likely increase issues of anxiety and depression, making it harder for the child to cope with the situation. Parental monitoring will also interfere with the teen's ability to receive confidential counseling and medical treatment.

Parents will also have a very different set of concerns and contextual knowledge regarding the content. If a parent overreacts to a situation, that conduct could make the situation far worse. In addition to demonstrating a lack of trust for the teen, parents could easily embroil themselves in situations that could have been mitigated by the teens who were involved.

As with any tool, the monitoring apps and tools should be used when they provide a practical solution to a real problem that cannot be solved in other ways. The tools provide a practical solution to allowing young children and tweens limited access to mobile phones and online content. They become less effective for older teens and should be used thoughtfully and in consultation with those teens.

Chapter 17

Summary

Building Balance Online and Offline

A. CONTROLLING THE ONLINE ENGAGEMENT

As highlighted throughout the book, the Internet and its associated technologies have become the backbone of global culture, economic productivity, innovation, and human interaction. The choice to unplug completely from the Internet would be as profound as Henry David Thoreau's sojourn on Walden Pond. Thoreau lasted only two years in isolation.

Parents seeking to raise healthy, happy, and productive children in the twenty-first century should not seek to isolate themselves from modern technology, but neither should they let social media and the demands of the Internet control their family life. As suggested throughout the book, the key to raising a healthy family is to establish a structure in the family norms that keep the online experience a balanced part of the family's daily, weekly, and annual routines.

Prioritize what is important for the family as a whole, and for each member of the family. Keeping in touch with friends is likely to be a priority, whereas simply scrolling through social media feeds will be much lower down on the list. Build a schedule around those priorities. The schedule does not need to be rigid with timetables and checkboxes, but it should have significant priorities spelled out.

1. Establishing Routines

What happens first in the morning? Does the day start by getting washed and dressed, feeding and walking the pets, having breakfast, and preparing for school and work? Or does the day start by grabbing the cell phone and checking for texts, emails, tweets, and other messages? Grounding the morning routine in what needs to be done before what arrived on the cell phone will establish the pattern for the entire day. In 2014, Admiral William H. McRaven gave a famous commencement speech to the University of Texas at Austin, in which he discussed how the graduates could change the world. He explained how Navy SEAL training began with making beds.

> If you did it right, the corners would be square, the covers pulled tight, the pillow centered just under the headboard and the extra blanket folded neatly at the foot of the rack—that's Navy talk for bed.
>
> It was a simple task—mundane at best. But every morning we were required to make our bed to perfection. It seemed a little ridiculous at the time, particularly in light of the fact that were aspiring to be real warriors, tough battle-hardened SEALs, but the wisdom of this simple act has been proven to me many times over.
>
> If you make your bed every morning you will have accomplished the first task of the day. It will give you a small sense of pride, and it will encourage you to do another task and another and another. By the end of the day, that one task completed will have turned into many tasks completed. Making your bed will also reinforce the fact that little things in life matter. If you can't do the little things right, you will never do the big things right.[1]

Admiral McRaven's point was that each completed successful task provides a structure for adolescents (and all the family members) who struggle to balance the competing demands of life.

The same approach should also apply to other key milestones in the day. Healthy families prioritize family dinner as an opportunity to get all members of the family to sit down together, listen to each family member's stories of the day, discuss what people are reading and watching, and spend time focused only on each other. With hectic schedules and competing obligations, many families can only manage such uninterrupted dinners a few nights per week, but these times together make an important difference in the family and should be scheduled as frequently as possible.

Bedtime routines are nearly as important as morning routines. Most adolescents benefit from getting off their devices at least an hour before bed. Using the last hour of the day for reading, music, and quiet activities can improve sleep considerably while reducing tension and anxiety. Some families find mindfulness exercises and similar relaxation techniques are also helpful as part of the evening routines.

2. Being Watchful But Not Controlling

As this book acknowledges, the dangers online are real, but in most cases, they are also remote. There are billions of people using the Internet and online technologies, most on a daily basis. Adolescents need to be online for school, to connect with their peers, and to experience the modern world. Developing coping skills to manage the challenges of the online experience were much the same as developing coping skills in the rest of their children's lives.

> Children who felt their parents showed them unconditional love and support, were involved in their lives and respected their choices and opinions are most likely to be resilient online, and thus more likely to benefit from positive outcomes online . . . whilst parental strategies of restriction and monitoring may have some utility in directly shielding young people from potential harms, they could have the unintended negative effect of undermining resilience and constructive engagement online.[2]

As children mature, they must be provided with an increasing amount of their own responsibility to address and judge the risks associated with online activity. By engaging and supporting the children, the parents can both ensure that the children are developing their online skills and support their children's emotional and cognitive development.

3. Master the Literacies and Competencies of the Information Age

Modern technology is continually adapting at a dizzying pace. All members of the household need to keep current with the impact of modern technologies by mastering the information literacy, digital literacy, privacy literacy, cultural competency, and others to be sure that as individuals, they do not become manipulated by the media and information trying to influence the public every day. At the dinner table, when the family is talking about what they have read during the day, parents should be sure to help the children assess the trustworthiness of the content they read. Did they read something published in a reputable newspaper, or did they merely see a headline from an unattributed source? When shopping, were there customer reviews, and were those reviews from a reputable source with enough responses that the scoring appeared trustworthy? Adolescents are very critical of traditional advertising, but they are less critical of promoted social media posts or manipulated customer reviews. Building critical reading skills includes developing a healthy skepticism for the first thing one reads. Everything on the Internet should be viewed using the adage "trust, but verify."

Basic security techniques and privacy management should also be a requirement for every member of the household. Every device should have some password protection, and financial information should be protected with two-factor authentication. Members of the household should regularly be updating the privacy settings on their social media accounts to be sure that each member of the household is only sharing the information that is supposed to be public.

Parents also need to support their children's use of technology so that the adolescents can develop their digital literacy skills. To participate in modern education and the digital economy, teens need to be able to read, write, shoot video, edit content, and even do some simple programming. Spending time online creating new content, playing creative games, and developing a digital set will help the teens stay abreast of modern technology, provide opportunities for engagement with peers, and prepare them for jobs in the expanding digital economy.

4. Managing Stress, Anxiety, and Mental Health

As noted throughout the book, the Internet and digital technology come with many risks. In many situations, however, those risks are tied to factors associated with stress, anxiety, and mental health concerns. Adolescents who exhibit these issues become magnets for bullying and harassment both online and in person. These are the students who may exhibit instances of self-harm. Because of their anxiousness, these are the teens who may be more willing to bend to online pressure and flash themselves, starting a cycle of bullying, shaming, and abuse.

All teens struggle through adolescence at some level. Middle school and high school are very stressful environments for everyone. Nonetheless, parents need to watch for potentially destructive behaviors in an effort to anticipate incidents of bullying, harassment, exposure, criminality, or other activities that reflect underlying issues of mental health, anger management, or deep anxiety.

Most of the examples of bullying, harassment, hacking, and other harmful online activity escalated over time. When a situation arises, parents should take decisive action to seek professional help and try to keep the situations from spiraling out of control. Certainly, there are situations that cannot be anticipated, and problems that arise without any warning signs, but in most cases, early warning signs of depression, anger, and anxiety can put parents on alert that their teen is in trouble and the trouble could manifest itself in their online activities.

B. MAKE THE MOST OF ONLINE EDUCATION

Online education has provided a lifeline for students across the globe during the COVID-19 pandemic, but online education is not for everybody. Online courses work best for students who are highly self-disciplined and self-motivated. Prior to the pandemic, most were used in collegiate settings or for professional education, rather than in the K-12 environment.

The lessons of 2020 have helped educators rethink online education and how best to adapt it for younger students. For students of all ages, the immediacy and relevance of the material make it much easier to learn than abstract information that will rarely, if ever, be used. Educators and parents can help transform online learning into a more immediate and relevant learning environment by connecting the online lessons with active learning exercises, as well as by having students engage with their classmates to study, do projects, and be responsible for their outcomes.

Traditional schools are very tightly structured with time periods, breaks, lunch, study halls, and afterschool activities. This structure has a hidden agenda designed to help students stay on track during their lessons. If the online courses do not provide a similar structure, parents can work with their children to add the structure to help break up the day and build small deadlines into the student's work flow. The small deadlines create motivation to finish assignments, and they provide the promise of an end to each session. A series of small time blocks enables students to have small successes and complete small goals, which, like making the bed every morning, grows to be larger achievements over time.

The most effective version of K-12 education is blended education, taking the best aspects of in-person schools and combining them with improvements offered through online education. Parents should take advantage of LMS systems to stay informed about their children's progress and the work their children are doing in school. The LMS also provides an excellent resource for communicating with the teachers and administration. In some districts, the LMS is also used to connect the parents with each other, further expanding the resources for the children.

C. TAKING ADVANTAGE OF THE INTERNET

The modern technological age is truly a marvel. Through YouTube videos, adolescents can learn new hobbies and explore new worlds easier than ever before. Wikipedia, the free online encyclopedia, boasts over 6 million articles in English alone, and 320 languages in addition to English.[3] The Khan Academy provides free tools to students, parents, and teachers to democratize education. As it explains, "[w]e tackle math, science, computing, history, art history, economics, and more, including K-14 and test preparation (SAT, Praxis, LSAT) content. We focus on skill mastery to help learners establish strong foundations, so there's no limit to what they can learn next!"[4]

The Internet has connected global commerce, allowed virtually every museum in the world to welcome online visitors, and opened access to the world's literature at the touch of a button. Most people use their cell phone to connect to the world every day, often all day.

The suggestions and skills promoted in this book are intended to help embrace the modern world and enable parents and their children to take the greatest advantage of what the Internet has to offer without falling prey to the challenges that exist online. Most of the challenges are self-inflicted, the risk of overindulging in too much of a good thing.

By treating the Internet, cell phones, online commerce, and the wonders of the digital age as improvements in access and efficiency, households can take full advantage of what these tools have to offer. The Internet is the great elixir of the modern age. Like any wonder drug, the package comes with a simple label: Use With Caution.

Appendices

1. HISTORY OF TECHNOLOGIES
THAT RUN THE WORLD

A. DARPA and the Internet's Origins

The modern information age was built upon a series of technological innovations that included the personal computer, the graphical interface design, the Internet, and the publishing power of the World Wide Web. While mobile technology, Bluetooth and wireless connectivity, and many other technologies played a part in the emergence of the modern information age, it is the development of these four fundamental changes that ushered in the digital age.

The Internet truly began with the space race triggered by the Soviet Union's launch of the Sputnik satellite in 1957.[1] With the surprise launch of the first man-made satellite, civil and military officials in the United States scrambled to retake the initiative to develop technologies needed to win the space race and the Cold War. Within a year, the Department of Defense created the Defense Advanced Research Projects Agency (DARPA), though the word "Defense" was not added to the agency title until years later.[2]

DARPA became involved in many fields of scientific research in support of the broader space program, including the development of weather satellites, optical navigation, information processing, and military technologies. It pioneered early technology for the computer mouse, time-sharing computers, and networking systems. In 1965, DARPA partner labs developed "packet switching," a protocol to distribute discrete units of information that could be disassembled and reassembled as the packets moved across a communications network, solar system, or battlefield.[3] Packet switching enables information to be sent, received, and reassembled very efficiently even if there are significant disruptions to the communications medium.

Expanding on the packet switching innovations, in 1969 DARPA researchers launched the ARPANET, first connecting computers at UCLA and the Stanford Research Institute. The network quickly grew in capacity and partners. By 1972, researchers added email to the information and file-sharing systems.[4]

At the heart of the ARPANET was a shift from the traditional development of communication systems. Unlike the proprietary nature of the telegraph and telephone lines or the government regulation of airwave spectrum, packet switching allowed anyone adopting the technical protocols to add data into the system. For the first time, information could move from anyone to anyone, rather than having to be routed through the central switchboard, like that of the telephone company.

The technical shift also served as a philosophical shift. Different organizations and systems could each operate their own particular networks, but by utilizing a common packet switching technology these various networks would communicate together as an "internetworking architecture." The system was designed to be as open as possible, providing maximum usefulness to any compatible network system. Despite the philosophy, however, there were many technologies under development, and there were often technical incompatibilities.

In the early 1970s, DARPA researchers began to approach the problem to standardization and resiliency by building a Transmission Control Protocol (TCP) and the Internet Protocol (IP), which together are known as TCP/IP. Vinton Cerf began to work with Robert E. Kahn and together they developed the open-architecture interconnection protocol to upgrade and expand the ARPANET.[5] Cerf used the term "internet" in 1974 as shorthand for the process of internetworking, or connecting multiple computer networks. The TCP/IP standard emerged during the 1980s, although there remained competing and incompatible standards for many, many years. The Internet Engineering Task Force (IETF), an open standards organization, was formed in 1986 to build consensus and establish protocols for the Internet, which helps but does not eliminate the emergence of competing technologies problems with interoperability of Internet devices.

As early as 1975, efforts began to provide commercial access to the ARPANET. Telenet was the first commercial adaptation of the system made available. It initially operated in seven cities, offering connections among government agencies and those businesses that paid monthly service fees. Telenet also provided a free public dial-up service. Telenet expanded over the next decade, covering hundreds of cities. Eventually, Telenet was acquired by GTE and then Sprint, where it was rebranded SprintNet, where it remains as a component of Sprint's Internet network.

Following the popular film *War Games*, the Department of Defense grew increasingly distrustful of the ARPANET's mix of military and academic uses.[6] Efforts to regulate traffic on the ARPANET were simply ignored by the academic users. Instead, the Defense Communications Agency, which had been given the duty to supervise the ARPANET, split the system into two systems, separating military use from academic research. The military shifted to MILNET, leaving ARPANET to the academic users.

The National Science Foundation stepped in to support the transition of the ARPANET into a commercial setting. It launched the NSFNet, which it eventually connected to the MCI Mail system. It supported the growth of nonprofit networks including CERFnet and UUNet and connections with a growing list of Internet service providers (ISPs) such as PSINet and CompuServe. Like Telenet, commercial enterprises were able to follow the Internet protocols and provide their own commercial resources to build out the networks. By the late 1980s, much of the modern Internet had begun. In 1990, ARPANET was officially decommissioned, and its sister network run by the National Science Foundation was shut down in 1995.[7]

B. The Computer Chip and PC

The expanded growth of the Internet was not the only technology needed to start the modern information age revolution. The early development of the Internet was based upon the assumption that the network would connect military, government, and university mainframe computers, allowing these behemoth machines to interact with people at more and more institutions. The true information revolution came from the power to the people, in the form of the personal computer.

The modern computer age can be traced back to IBM, though there was a century of development of inventions that precede this starting point, particularly those at Bell Labs.[8] In the same year DARPA was launching its efforts to join the space race, IBM adopted technologies that transformed computing and opened the modern marketplace. IBM switched from the vacuum tube to the transistor, greatly reducing the size of its machines. To store its information, it invented the magnetic disk to store information. Finally, IBM introduced the high-speed chain printer, which could take advantage of the storage and speed of the solid state computer to support the demands of the printer. Together, these technologies transformed computing from very large, complex computing machines to the robust general application devices that could be sold to businesses around the country.

By the 1960s, IBM took the next step, consolidating its various computer designs with different circuitry into a universal machine that integrated its transistors into a circuit board. Although there was competition among computer companies, IBM had as much as 70 percent of the market share for mainframe computers, dominating the industry. In the following decade, although IBM continued to control the mainframe marketplace, competitors began to chip away at IBM's lead by shipping smaller, "mini-computers" for those customers who could not afford the expensive room-sized IBM machines.[9]

The efficiency of the integrated circuits continued to improve, which helped fuel the increased performance of both mini-computers and handheld calculators. The calculator business provided a much more dynamic and demanding marketplace, pushing companies such as Fairchild Semiconductor, Texas Instruments, and Intel to make increasingly sophisticated computer chips comprised of embedded circuitry needed for large computing tasks. In 1972, Intel expanded its calculator chips into an 8-bit general-purpose central processing unit, and it began to promote its chip not just for calculators but also for computer hobbyists. During the next decade, dozens of small computer companies came out with computer kits and home computers.[10]

Apple Computers began as one of the first attempts to commercialize the hobby computer, primarily based on the innovative circuit boards invented by Steve Wozniak, who, along with Steve Jobs, had founded the company. Moving past a simple kit to a true computer, Apple began with its first successful product, the Apple II, in 1976, a full five years earlier than the IBM PC.[11]

As the small machines become more powerful, their use also started to expand. In 1979, Dan Bricklin produced the first computer spreadsheet program, VisiCalc, which ran on the Apple II.[12] The introduction of VisiCalc provided the impetus for businesses to see the home computers as an essential business tool. With the power of VisiCalc, the hobby computer was transformed into an essential tool for both business and home use. Although the Apple II was a great success for the company, it was not a breakthrough product. The VisiCalc accounting software was critically important to the sales of the Apple II, but the hobbyist ethos of Apple was at odds with the corporate demand for spreadsheet technologies. Other companies were trying to fill this gap. Collectively, the growth of Commodore, Tandy, Apple, and the other small computer companies was becoming an annoyance to the mainframe industry of IBM.

Some of the senior leadership at IBM recognized that the home computer business was becoming a risk to its market dominance, but most employees could not imagine the hobby market replacing the mainframe business. In 1980, Bill Lowe was given the go-ahead to redesign the IBM line of micro-computers into a personal computer. Lowe promised to deliver a new machine within a year, a feat considered impossible at the very conservative and slow-moving IBM.[13]

Lowe's success was IBM's greatest triumph and worst defeat. Few of the engineers within IBM had the time to waste on the personal computer side project. Nor was Lowe willing to use experimental technologies that could put his ambitious agenda at risk. Instead, Lowe assembled the central processor from Intel, operating software from a tiny start-up named Microsoft, and the keyboard, disk drives, and even the printers from other manufacturers. The retail price for the machine was $1,565, as compared to the $9 million price tag on some of IBM's mainframes of the 1960s.

IBM released the IBM PC on August 12, 1981. The IBM machine was an extraordinary success, ushering in an entirely new understanding of the personal computer for business, education, and eventually home use. Though much more expensive than the hobby computers of the previous decade, the IBM PC instantly standardized computing. In the first few years of the IBM PC launch, it generated billions of dollars in revenue and redefined both business computing and home computing.

Unfortunately for IBM, Bill Lowe's strategy backfired for the company. All of the hardware and software that made up the PC came from other vendors. There were no proprietary components patented by IBM in the makeup of the hardware, and Microsoft did not have any exclusive relationship with IBM, so it could sell the same operating software to IBM's competitors as it sold to IBM.[14]

This was not even the first such decision by IBM to forego the PC market. Earlier, it rejected a proposal to develop the IBM Selectric electric typewriter as ASCII compatible, which would have enabled the Selectric to be used as a printer solution for the PC. IBM dismissed this proposal as well.[15] Instead, the introduction of the IBM PC led to the rapid expansion of the computer clone industry, the collapse in sales of IBM Selectrics (which were discontinued in 1986), and the eventual withdrawal of IBM from the PC and laptop computer markets.

Given the ambivalence of IBM in its new home computer industry, it did not embrace the market and seek additional innovation. Instead, the PC hardware market fragmented while the software continued to be supplied by Microsoft, which struggled to remain fully operable with the wide range of products and devices on the market.

In contrast to the IBM PC, the Apple II remained a great success for the company. Nonetheless, the home use market was much smaller than the business use market. Apple's attempt to make the Apple III, introduced as business computer, met with very poor sales and technical problems that resulted in the product's recall.

In the battle for dominance of the personal computer, the ultimate winner was Microsoft, which was able to sell the operating software to the entire PC-compatible market. Microsoft also expanded its products to provide a spreadsheet and word processor, programs so central to the use of business and home computing that even Apple was forced to rely on Microsoft software for much of its sales.

Because of the chip specifications of the IBM PC, the other winner in the personal computer industry was Intel, maker of the original 8088 chip that powered the first IBM PC. In each succeeding iteration of computers, they have become faster and more capable, allowing the software to become vastly more sophisticated in what it can do.

As early as 1965, Gordon Moore, the co-founder and CEO of Fairchild Semiconductor and then the co-founder of Intel, observed that the number of components that could be placed on an integrated circuit would double approximately every two years, resulting in exponential growth of computing power.[16] The prediction became known as Moore's Law. Moore's original prediction was that this rate of growth was sustainable for at least a decade. In fact, more than half a century later, this observation remains true of the computer industry, driving voracious expansion of capacity to process information.

More generally, the idea behind Moore's Law is that the scale of the technology decreases without increasing power consumption. The improvements in computer chip density have been accompanied by a myriad of improvements in the other microchips and technologies that drive modern equipment. There are certain physical limits to the miniaturization of circuits because the circuits are approaching the size limitations created by the atoms that make up the circuits. Nonetheless, additional innovations suggest that while the technical nature of Moore's Law will reach physical capacity, quantum computing and other innovations will continue the overall capacity of computer and computer networks to expand for years to come.

C. Shift to the Graphical Interface

Despite the market dominance by the PC and the importance of Microsoft software, Apple continued to be the more innovative company. IBM was struggling with its internal ambivalence toward the PC market and its lack of innovation in the small business computing sphere. It was losing market share in both computer sales and typewriter sales due to the competition from the PCs. The emerging PC clone manufacturers were not as sophisticated or innovative as Apple had been with its proprietary technologies.

For its next breakthrough products, Apple actually returned to some of the original DARPA-supported research. With the support of DARPA, Xerox Corporation had developed the first graphical user interface (GUI) and first accompanying computer mouse in the 1960s. Steve Jobs allowed Xerox to make a substantial investment just prior to its public sales of securities, guaranteeing Xerox a substantial profit. In exchange, the deal allowed Apple to gain access to Xerox research.[17] Jobs visited the Xerox Palo Alto Research Center (PARC), where he discovered the mouse and the GUI. Jobs immediately saw the potential for a point-and-click-based interface that eliminated the typing requirements that discouraged many computer users. Xerox, in contrast, primarily sold its imaging and computing equipment to business users in the data entry fields. Those industries tended to see a mouse as a distraction that slowed a person's typing speed rather than as a benefit to improve efficiency.[18]

Apple initially released its GUI computer as the Apple Lisa, a modestly successful product. With the growth of the PC market, Apple needed to reinforce its distinction between its computers and the boring, corporate PCs. The Macintosh (Mac) was sold emphasizing MacPaint as the killer app on the machine, and also incorporated an iconic design to the machine, bold colors, and a brilliant marketing campaign. The Mac created a population of truly devoted users and provided important financial support for the company.

Among the personal computing marketplace, the need for standardization and interoperability meant that none of the PC makers were taking risks on innovation. This left Microsoft as the corporate parent for the PC environment. Recognizing the popularity of the mouse and GUI, Microsoft released Windows in 1985 as its answer to the Mac. The initial Windows product had little market impact, but its successor in 1987 began to add significant features that mimicked the Mac GUI. Finally, in 1990, Microsoft released Windows 3.0, which became the breakthrough product. Microsoft bundled Solitaire and Minesweeper to encourage users to pick up the mouse. Windows 3.0 sold over 10,000,000[19] units and remained available for over a decade, until 2001.

Propelled by Apple and popularized by Microsoft, the GUI interface made the use of the Internet much more practical and popular. Computers were now more than spreadsheets and word processors. They had evolved into story-telling devices with sound and pictures.

D. World Wide Web

The expansion of a graphical interface for the personal computer paralleled development of the graphical capabilities for the Internet. Since the 1980s, aspects of the Internet supported email, file transfers, and many other tools. Hobbyists used the Internet for text-based chats and simple games. Corporations and organizations used the tools to share data and improve efficiency.

For the growth of the modern Internet, however, the next key improvement was the development of the World Wide Web, or simply the Web, the user interface that served to both democratize and commercialize the Internet. In

1989, English scientist Tim Berners-Lee began to develop the World Wide Web project for CERN (the European Organization for Nuclear Research), the particle physics laboratory in Geneva. Berners-Lee wrote the software for the first web browser in 1990, which was publicly released the following year.[20]

To create the World Wide Web, Berners-Lee essentially adapted and reinvented three discrete technologies. The first was the uniform resource locator (URL), which is often referred to as a web address. A URL combines the identification of the domain name, file path (or folder), and file name. The second was the development of the publishing language Hypertext Markup Language (HTML), which programs the computer to provide the visual layout of a website. The third invention was the Hypertext Transfer Protocol (HTTP), which generates a request for content to be displayed or otherwise used in the web browser. HTML webpage coding drives the ability of each webpage to find the source at another site's web page, making it foundational to the interconnectedness of the web.

The HTTP request is made by the computer using the packet switching technology embodied in the TCP/IP protocols, allowing the information to flow in small, fast packets from the user's device to the local ISP and from there through the various computer networks until the request is received by the network hosting the information. The information is sent back the same way.

Although Berners-Lee invented the web browser, the browser was truly popularized by the release of the Mosaic browser in 1993. Mosaic was the first popularly successful effort to bring a GUI to the web, combining text and images into integrated web pages. Mosaic opened the Internet to widespread use by people from all fields.[21]

Mosaic was developed by Marc Andreessen at the National Center for Supercomputing Applications at the University of Illinois at Urbana–Champaign through funding supplied by the High Performance Computing Act of 1991, originally known as the Gore Bill, named after its author and chief sponsor, then senator Al Gore. The Gore Bill led to the creation of the National Information Infrastructure (NII), which Gore referred to as the "Information Superhighway." The NII went on to support many of the innovations that gave the United States dominance over the Internet and supported its widespread growth.[22]

Competition among browsers quickly emerged. Andreessen founded a new company, Netscape, and wrote an entirely new web browser to compete with his earlier effort. Netscape Navigator quickly surpassed Mosaic in popularity. Looking to become relevant on the Internet, Microsoft licensed the Mosaic software, updating and rebranding the software Internet Explorer. Netscape later launched Mozilla as a replacement for Netscape.

The market power of Microsoft and the integration of the Internet Explorer with the Windows Operating System enabled Microsoft to quickly dominate Internet use. Microsoft was successfully sued by the Department of Justice for antitrust violations related to its marketing strategies involving the Internet Explorer browser. At the same time, Apple introduced the Safari browser, Google launched the Chrome browser, and other companies offered additional choices. Netscape spun the Mozilla browser into a nonprofit organization, the Mozilla Foundation, making the code open-source software.

By harnessing the power of the personal computer using graphical interfaces and a graphical web browser, the modern Internet was born. The personal computer, the Internet protocols that connect computer networks with efficient packet switching, and the GUI on the computer, and the graphical web browser combine to make the modern Internet. Additional protocols and operating systems for phones and mobile devices extend the online environment much further, but these remain the essential building blocks for the modern telecommunications world.

There are many innovations that have been integral to the modern communications environment in addition to these four developments. The exponential growth in computing power has helped provide similar growth in memory storage, visualization software, communications technologies, wireless transmission, and many more building blocks essential to the information age. Together, these changes have enabled the culture and economy to move into the information age, creating a fundamental shift in how we do business and how we live.

E. eCommerce and Product Sales

None of the companies doing business on the Internet, the nonprofit organizations trying to standardize the Internet, or the users of the Internet set out to change the culture in their society. The early pioneers of the Internet understood it as an academic endeavor that should be free of commercial activity. As Apple, Microsoft, and other commercial endeavors became involved, however, the early academic orientation was quickly overwhelmed by the opportunity to sell and advertise online. There are only three ways to make money on the Internet. A business can use the technology to sell goods and services, a business can sell advertising space, and/or a business can sell information to those who wish to sell advertising or goods and services.

Amazon.com, the third largest retailer in the United States (behind Walmart and CVS Health), opened its online operations in 1995 as an online bookstore. Amazon was just one of many online retailers that were experimenting with a business-to-consumer (B2C) model of providing immediate, direct, national sales to the public. The same year, the online classified advertisement service, Craigslist, was founded, providing free simple ads for goods and services of all kinds onto the Internet.

Also in 1995, eBay was launched under its original name, AuctionWeb. The site immediately grew in popularity. The year after it launched, a popular craze surrounding Beanie Babies stuffed toys became widely popular, exceeding the ability of Ty Warner's ability to manufacture the toys. The public took to eBay, which reports having sold $500 million worth of Beanie Babies in 1996.

Although there were many other B2C operations, in the first few years of the web, most vendors were using websites to promote their products or provide information. The addition of shopping carts and direct retail took many years for most retailers. While some companies embraced online sales directly, it was highly disruptive of their traditional face-to-face sales, so many companies were slow to adopt a direct-to-consumer shopping experience.

In contrast, from the beginning industry understood the benefits of business-to-business (B2B) transactions. In the B2B transaction, the companies develop a product catalog and ordering system that allows the corporate networks to talk to each other directly (or that requires the supplier to adopt the computer system used by the major purchaser). The transactions then link the goods producer directly to the retailer. For example, a food cannery can use tracking information to know the amount and type of each can of vegetables sold on a weekly, or even daily, basis. The buyer can look at the suppliers' available materials, including the cost of the goods and the cost of shipping. Using either a professional supply manager or an automated system of supply management, orders for new goods and supplies are processed based on the needs of the purchaser as they arise. This might be weekly, daily, or hourly depending on the nature of the business.

Tracking allows the purchaser to know precisely what goods are on hand, what is in shipment, and what is available. The effect dramatically reduced the need for warehousing purchases and significantly improved the efficiency of the systems. Retailers such as Walmart used these systems to dramatically reduce its warehouse requirements and improve the guarantee that stock would be on the shelves at each of its stores. Target and other major retailers quickly followed suit.

The integrated purchasing systems and interoperable networks also improved efficiency in the manufacturing sector. In automobile manufacturing, for example, the computers know the consumption rate of every nut and bolt, so the vendors know how many parts to ship and when to ship them. The transactions are much smoother, storage of supplies is reduced, and significant costs of creating and tracking orders are eliminated.

Over time, both B2B and B2C have become ubiquitous. PayPal was founded in 1998 to help finance online transactions as an alternative to credit cards and the use of electronic deductions from checking accounts. The explosion of individual retailers and wholesalers providing goods online made the process of finding the right goods or services more difficult rather than easier. In 2004, nearly a decade after the launch of Amazon, eBay, and Craigslist, Yelp was launched to create a public review system to identify the best restaurants, doctors, and other services in each community.

The success of Yelp highlighted the importance the public places in the aggregated review information provided by real users of goods and services. Angie's List provided a similar service by offering customer reviews of home improvement services as early as 1995. But because Angie's List was a paid subscription service, it did not reach the same scale or influence as that of Yelp. Amazon had pioneered customer reviews from the time the company began. As the company expanded from books to music to general goods, the reviews became an increasingly important aspect of its business model. For businesses today, positive customer ratings and reviews are an essential element of successful sales.

F. Technology Today

Although the Internet was built on the innovations that led to the miniaturization of computer chips, the networking of computers, the packet switching communications, and the graphical nature of webpage design, dozens if not hundreds of other innovations have been built upon these first four steps to create the modern, interconnected world. Although email was one of the original services provided by the early Internet, continued improvements in email, text messaging, instant messaging, and video conferencing have dramatically reduced the distance between people. In much the same way, online commerce has reinvented modern business.

The improvements in computer chips have led to much greater capabilities in computer software, including word processing, spreadsheets, photo and video editing, and many other tools and games. This also led to improvements in video and audio compression, opening the way for iPods, smartphones, and tablets. These technologies have also expanded the range of medical devices available for health care testing while reducing the cost for many of these services, greatly expanding access to health care for millions of people around the world.

The global positioning system (GPS) allows people to plan their routes, track shipments, and greatly improve the knowledge of the movement of goods and people. Wireless, Bluetooth, Radio-Frequency Identification (RFID), and similar technologies that enable devices to communicate without wires, allowing for machines to connect GPS with wireless to control drones and allow appliances and other devices to become networked. They also allow for toll booth passes and cashless monetary systems.

The combination of these systems allows for the development of the "Internet of Things (IoT)," an awkward acronym for interconnected parts or devices that use these technologies to communicate with each other. IoT devices are used for real-time monitoring of water usage for irrigation, movement of farm animals for herd management, controls of electrical systems to improve efficiency, fleet management for shipping, taxi services, and ride-sharing companies, safety protocols on airplanes and trains, and much more. IoT also has a consumer use, facilitating cashless payments, crowd management at amusement parks, electronic keys at hotels, and the auto-billing system in the hotel mini-bar.

Machine learning, big data, and artificial intelligence take advantage of the trillions of data points created through all these systems and the people who use them. These tools improve health data analysis and enable smart cars, chatbots for automated customer service, photo and video augmentation, virtual reality rendering, and many additional tools.

All these advances continue to be built upon the core technologies that enabled the emergence of the Internet and the many-to-many communication that now includes machines and their component parts as well as people and communities.

2. UNDERSTANDING THE INFORMATION ECONOMY

A. Removing the Middleman from the Global Economy

In October 1997, Philip Evans and Thomas Wurster published "Strategy and the New Economics of Information"[23] and later expanded the thesis for their book, *Blown to Bits*.[24] They studied how the Internet's informational flow fundamentally reshaped the relationships between consumers and retailers, and among businesses. Evans and Wurster explain that information is the "glue" that holds corporate supply chains and consumer relationships together. By controlling the flow of information, companies tend to keep the supply chains linked. Unglue information content from the delivery mechanism for that content, and old business alliances unravel. As the Internet has allowed consumers to get information from a multiplicity of sources—including each other—the dominance of the manufacturer and supplier has dwindled.

The second phenomenon identified by Evans and Wurster was the inverse relationship between "richness" and "reach" that existed for information before the advent of the Internet. Rich content is highly interactive, readily customizable, and able to flow in large amounts. Historically, rich content had very limited reach. For example, a teacher who can spend one-on-one time with students provides very rich content. The teacher's instruction is customized to the experience and needs of each student in the classroom, providing a great deal of feedback, and responding to the students' actions to continually adjust the instruction to the pace and understanding of the student.

In contrast, the reach for such a class would be very limited. Once the size of the student body increases, the competing demands of the students makes it impossible to tailor the information. As the reach of content grows inside the classroom, the richness declines. Larger classes are invariably less rich than smaller classes.

The third factor impacting the relationship between richness and reach is scalability. Prior to the computer age, the process of creating and disseminating content was very challenging and time consuming. Information has a production cost and a distribution cost. Improvements in computer hardware, software, and networking have reduced the cost of production modestly, and at the same time, they have dramatically reduced the cost of distribution.

The music industry provides an excellent example of these changes. For most of the twentieth century, radio and records dominated the music industry. Prior to the twentieth century, most music was performed live. This started to change in the 1800s with the popularity of the player piano, which brought high-quality commercial music into the home, but player pianos were very expensive. Still, by the turn of the twentieth century, as many as 10 percent of homes had a player piano. Then the phonogram and the radio changed everything.

Records were recorded in commercial studios and then pressed for sale, first on lacquer, and then on vinyl discs. Radio stations played the music to promote the sale of the records, and the musicians played at concerts and shows, touring the country for live events and making appearances on radio or television to promote the sales of the records. When a consumer bought a record, most of money went to cover the cost of pressing the album, shipping it to retailers, and paying to promote the sales. The record companies that had invested in the costs of recording as well as in the costs of distribution first recovered its expenses, and then if there was money left, the recording artists received royalties for their work on the record.

The public paid a great deal of money for a vinyl record that held 22 minutes of music on each side of the album. The compact disc became very popular because it improved the ease of use for music. CDs were much more portable than LPs and significantly more resilient to weather and scratching. (They were not, however, indestructible, to the disappointment of many.) CDs added some consumer convenience, but they did not change the structure of the music industry.

The two technologies that completely disrupted the music industry were the MP3 and the iPod. The MP3 was an audio encoding protocol designed to minimize sound quality loss, while significantly reducing the data size of music files.[25] In 1995, licensed companies and hackers disseminated versions of the MP3 code that enabled it to be used to rip CD files and compress them into the MP3 format. Winamp was released in 1997, providing free CD ripping software that let consumers convert their CD collections into files that could be stored on computers and played on digital devices. MP3 music does not match the acoustic fidelity of vinyl records, but the convenience of MP3s is unmatched. Soon a number of peer-to-peer sharing sites such as Napster appeared, allowing the public to download and swap music for free.

For the record companies, the unauthorized file sharing created a new threat. Instead of cheaper music made less expensive by the elimination of pressing and distribution costs, millions of music fans moved to the peer-to-peer music sites for free, pirated music. The recording industry's income plummeted.

Recognizing the transformation in the music industry, Steve Jobs had Apple design a device to capture the change. In 2001, Apple released the iPod, a device designed to hold 1000 songs in your pocket.[26] The iPod reshaped both the music and the computing industries. Still, the music industry struggled to compete with free, even though the cost of music declined significantly.

The peer-to-peer file-sharing systems reflected the ultimate break in the relationship between richness and reach. Using Napster or Grokster, a music fan could find millions of songs and select the songs important to that person. The reach was nearly infinite as was the richness, and the transaction costs were lower than any lawful transaction in music.

For most of the music industry, most of the jobs for making and distributing CDs and records were eliminated. To compete with free, unauthorized downloads of music, the industry shifted to streaming services like Spotify that operate much like customizable radio stations. Unlike radio, however, which primarily offered music to promote record sales, the streaming services share ad revenue and subscriber revenue with the music industry to fund the production of new music.

In much this same manner, the Internet and related technologies have eliminated jobs and middlemen in every industry. Rather than requiring a salesperson to explain how to use a product, the company can post a series of "frequently asked questions" (FAQs) or instructional videos to help the purchaser with information. Product specifications and manuals are all available on a company's website, so the number of people needed to be in the field supporting the sales of goods and services has dwindled dramatically.

The change in the relationship between richness and reach of content and the reduction of transaction costs for distribution of information are more analogous to the invention of the automobile and air conditioning than to radio and television. Automobiles and trucks expanded the ability to deliver goods across the country in a fundamentally different way than had any technology that went before them. Similarly, air conditioning changed where people could work and live year-round, shifting the demographic movement of people and jobs throughout the industrialized world. The Internet has followed the same path, changing how jobs can be done and where the work can occur.

In the decades following Evans and Wurster's initial article, many newspapers have faltered, and retail giants have lost much of their market share. International production of goods has increased dramatically because many of the barriers to overseas manufacturing are mitigated through the use of videoconferencing and other Internet technologies.

At every level of the economy, including manufacturing, distribution, and retail, the marketplace has fundamentally changed, redefining jobs and reducing the number of people needed to make products and deliver services. These changes have been fueled by the efficiency and reach of rich content available through the Internet.

B. The Medium Is the Message—How the Internet Influences Culture

Well before the Internet revolution, writer Marshall McLuhan was chronicling the burgeoning impact of the nascent information age. He proposed that it is the "medium that shapes and controls the scale and form of human association and action."[27]

> Electronic circuitry has overthrown the regime of "time" and "space" and pours upon us instantly and continuously the concerns of all other men. It has reconstituted dialogue on a global scale. Its message is Total Change, ending psychic, social, economic, and political parochialism. The old civic, state, and national groupings have become unworkable . . . You can't *go* home again.[28]

In the electronic age of mass communication, McLuhan understood the world to be contracting into a single, national village, bound together by the three broadcast television networks, an English language that played on the television without much regional inflection, as well as a national highway system designed, in part, to unify and standardize the goods and services bought and sold throughout the nation.

There were differences of course among communities, and the urban flight to the suburbs underscored continuing tensions regarding race, class, and religious communities within the nation. But at the same time, the three national television networks brought visions of Civil Rights marches and Vietnam War protests into the living rooms of America. In 1965, CBS News correspondent Morley Safer aired a report from Vietnam showing Marines' use of flamethrowers to burn down a village even though no enemy troops were found during the invasion. Three years later, CBS news anchorman Walter Cronkite presented an even more powerful series of live reports from Vietnam.[29] Upon his return, in an opinion piece at the end of his broadcast, Cronkite explained that, in his opinion, "the bloody experience of Vietnam is to end in a stalemate," he said, because "it is increasingly clear to this reporter that the only rational way out then will be to negotiate, not as victors, but as an honorable people who lived up to their pledge to defend democracy, and did the best they could."[30] Within weeks, President Johnson announced that he would not seek reelection to the U.S. presidency. Because Walter Cronkite was the most influential journalist on the most successful of the three television networks, his emerging understanding of the Vietnam conflict galvanized the nation.

There were many other examples. The power of television and radio and the centralization of media ownership more generally created a national narrative that had very little room for regionalism. It also tended to silence the large, non-majority populations, whitewashing Americana into a world first defined by *Father Knows Best* and, in a somewhat more self-reflective era, by *All in the Family*. Educational television shows like *Mister Rogers' Neighborhood* and *Sesame Street* created a national preschool educational curriculum far more expansive and accessible than a typical public school program.

This vision for America was first captured in the theater by British playwright Israel Zangwill's *The Melting Pot*, which focused on the immigrant experience of the Russian Jews and Cossack families, in which America was a crucible, divinely created to burn away the old hatreds of European barbarism and tribalism and replace it with a new country where old hatreds had no place. The play idealizes this vision.

> Ah, what a stirring and a seething! Celt and Latin, Slav and Teuton, Greek and Syrian—black and yellow—Jew and Gentile—Yes, East and West, and North and South, the palm and the pine, the pole and the equator, the crescent and the cross—how the great Alchemist melts and fuses them with his purging flame! Here shall they all unite to build the Republic of Man and the Kingdom of God.[31]

The metaphor of the crucible, of course, starts with a flame that burns away much of what is there, as well as combining what is left into something new. There is much to criticize in this metaphor, which at its worst can lead to a totalitarian demand for uniformity described in George Orwell's *1984*. The Melting Pot metaphor may have been used to stifle minority voices and devalue the importance of cultural identity, but as Zangwill understood about the horrors of war, pogrom, and bloodshed in Europe, those differences were often used as pretext for what today is known as ethnic cleansing.

Nonetheless, although the Melting Pot metaphor provides a vision of shared values that is limited and flawed, it reflects the power of the twentieth century's mass media, for better or worse. Radio and television tied the country together under the majority's understanding of our shared culture and idealized common values.

C. From Mass Media to the Media of the Masses

Unlike the centralized influence of radio, television, and even print media, the ability of every audience member to also be a content provider fundamentally reshapes politics, culture, and economic transactions.

The nature of the packet switching technology enables any person on the network to send signals as well as receive signals. This creates a fundamental difference from mass media, which is inherently hierarchical, broadcasting information only outward from a central point of origin. Radio and television viewers could not send signals back through their home devices to the broadcasters. Internet users, however, can easily send messages back to the broadcasters, and they regularly do through likes, comments, forwarding, and reposting. Internet users can also communicate to each other, horizontally among themselves.

Mass media provided a one-to-many centralized version of communications. The telephone system provided a one-to-one network. Anyone on the system could dial another party. But it was a closed connection that did not invite other people into the call. The Internet, in contrast, provides a many-to-many network. Each content consumer on the Internet is also a content creator. Some of the content is as simple as a thumbs up. Other posts are comparable to feature-length movies, studio-recorded albums, or epic novels. Packet switching allows for everyone to have access to all of it.

Traditional media is not forgotten, but it now provides one set of voices among a cacophony of billions. If the medium is the message, then it follows that the message of the twenty-first century has reverted to tribalism and identity focus. At its best, the Internet creates opportunities for community empowerment. Traditionally overlooked communities and marginalized people have an opportunity to be heard, and more importantly, an ability to share their own stories together. People overlooked and underrepresented by the Hollywood media have an opportunity to share their own voices and be heard. This has forced traditional media companies to look past simple, willfully blind representations of the public to see the much more varied and diverse nation for what it is.

Unfortunately, the dark side of community empowerment is tribalism and isolation. Depending on where one stands culturally and socially, the use of the many-to-many communications platforms have made it easier than ever for terrorist organizations to recruit and radicalize adherents, to promote racial tensions, and to promote fear-inspired movements to isolate and even take up arms against those who are somehow different. Isolationism fueled by the tribalistic and populist appeals made so effective on the Internet have led to attacks on immigrants, the vote for Britain to leave the European Union (known as Brexit), and the increase in regional conflicts across the globe.

The many-to-many model of the Internet also changes the normative expectations regarding the accuracy of the information being broadcast to the public. In the pre-Internet era, there were norms requiring factual accuracy for journalism and a legal duty to monitor the content of broadcasts by licensed radio and television outlets. Those obligations never extended to the general public, only to licensed broadcasters and standards of practice for the daily newspapers.

Today, newspapers, radio, and television play a small role in the news and information the public read, hear, and watch. Since anyone can say anything, there are a lot of opinions and many factually inaccurate stories. Making matters worse, human nature tends to encourage people to react to the outrageous far more quickly than to the reasonable. Thus, extreme headlines and other salacious content tend to catch the public's eye far more quickly than thoughtful, considered content. The term "clickbait" was coined to capture the nature of extreme, sexual, or outrageous headlines that motivate people to click on the hyperlink just to see what it could be. Even though most people doubt the veracity of the content, many are still willing to look.

Added to the problem that anyone can post content, no matter how inaccurate it might be, even the professional publishers struggle to keep pace with a news cycle that operates 24/7. Algorithms that promote content operate continuously. Newspapers are no longer printed once or twice per day. Instead, the news sites are being updated constantly. Efforts to provide thoughtful, accurate, and carefully fact-checked content are eroded by a publication cycle that cannot wait for the fact-checking to take place.

None of these changes were the intent of the packet switching technology at the heart of the Internet, but by creating a platform for many-to-many communications of information that travels virtually instantly, the medium now drives a culture that suffers from inaccurate information used to promote tribal alliances rather than shared common agendas. On the positive side, the many-to-many communications system has dramatically democratized the creation and dissemination of arts, culture, and information. Individual influences from all points on the globe, all walks of life, and all genders, races, ages, and backgrounds are now front and center in creating the narratives that shape the future. In the years to come, the challenge will be to capture the best that many-to-many has to offer while improving informational and digital literacy to assure that the public is benefited rather than harmed from the information revolution.

List of Acronyms

Abstinence Only Education (AOE)
American Academy of Pediatrics (AAP)
Americans with Disabilities Act (ADA)
Archive of Our Own (AO3)
Better Business Bureau (BBB)
Business-to-Business Commerce (B2B)
Business-to-Consumer Commerce (B2C)
Cell Site Location Information (CSLI)
Centers for Disease Control and Prevention (CDC)
CERN, the European Organization for Nuclear Research
Chief Security Officer (CSO)
Children's Online Privacy Protection Act (COPPA)
Code of Federal Regulations (CFR, C.F.R., or Fed. Reg.)
Computer Fraud and Abuse Act (CFAA)
Creative Commons (CC)
Cyber Civil Rights Initiative (CCRI)
Defense Advanced Research Projects Agency (DARPA)
Digital Millennium Copyright Act (DMCA)
Electronic Frontier Foundation (EFF)
End User License Agreement (EULA)
Entertainment Software Rating Board (ESRB)
European Union (EU)
Fair Credit Reporting Act (FCRA)
Family Educational Rights and Privacy Act (FERPA)
Federal Communications Commission (FCC)
Free and Appropriate Public Education (FAPE)
Frequently Asked Questions (FAQs)

Gay-Straight Alliance (GSA)
General Social Survey (GSS)
Grade Point Average (GPA)
Global Positioning Systems (GPS)
Gramm-Leach-Bliley Act or Financial Modernization Act of 1999 (GLBA)
Graphical User Interface (GUI)
Health Insurance Portability and Accountability Act (HIPAA)
Human Resources Department (HR)
Hypertext Markup Language (HTML)
Hypertext Transfer Protocol (HTTP or HTTPS)
Individualized Education Plan (IEP)
Individuals with Disabilities Education Act (IDEA)
Information Technology (IT)
International Standards Organization (ISO)
Internet Content Rating Association (ICRA)
Internet Engineering Task Force (IETF)
Internet of Things (IoT)
Internet Protocol (IP)
Learning Management System (LMS)
Lesbian, Gay, Bisexual, Transgender and Queer or Questioning (LGBTQ)
National Center for Missing & Exploited Children (NCMEC)
National Information Infrastructure (NII)
National Telecommunications and Information Administration (NTIA)
Peer-To-Peer File Sharing (P2P)
Personal Health Information or Protected Health Information (PHI)
Personal Identification Number (PIN)
Personally Identifiable Information (PII)
Post-Traumatic Stress Disorder (PTSD)
Proceedings of the National Academy of Sciences (PNAS)
Prosecutorial Remedies and Tools Against the Exploitation of Children
    Today Act of 2003 (PROTECT Act)
Quick Response Matrix Barcode (QR code)
Radicalization Awareness Network (RAN)
Radio-Frequency Identification (RFID)
Screen Actors Guild - American Federation of Television and Radio Artists
    (SAG-AFTRA)
Service Set Identifier (SSID)
Sexual Health Education (SHE)
Sexually Transmitted Disease (STD)
Social Security Number (SSN)
Stop Hacks and Improve Electronic Data Security Act (New York's SHIELD
    Act)

Terms of Service Agreement (TOS)
The Onion Router (TOR) Browser
Transmission Control Protocol and Internet Protocol (TCP/IP)
Xerox Palo Alto Research Center (PARC)
Uniform Resource Locator (URL)
Virtual Private Network (VPN)
Web Accessibility Initiative (WAI)
Web Content Accessibility Guidelines (WCAG)
World Wide Web Consortium (W3C)

Notes

CHAPTER 1

1. John DeFrain & Sylvia M. Asay, Strong Families around the World: An Introduction to the Family Strengths Perspective, *Marriage & Family Rev.*, Aug. 1–2, 2007: 41, doi: 10.1300/J002v41n01_01.

2. *Id.*

3. *Id.* (bullets rearranged).

4. Terry Clark-Jones, Qualities of a Healthy Family, *Mich. S. U. Extension*, Apr. 2, 2018, https://www.canr.msu.edu/news/traits_of_a_healthy_family.

5. *Id.*

6. U.S. Adults Added 1 Hour of Digital Time in 2020, *Insider Intelligence*, Jan. 26, 2021, https://www.emarketer.com/content/us-adults-added-1-hour-of-digital-time -2020.

7. Todd Spangler, U.S. Households have an Average of 11 Connected Devices—And 5G Should Push that Even Higher, *Variety*, Dec. 10, 2019, https://va riety.com/2019/digital/news/u-s-households-have-an-average-of-11-connected-devic es-and-5g-should-push-that-even-higher-1203431225/.

8. Abigail Miller, Structure Can be More Important than Warmth for Teenagers to Develop into Functioning Adults, Child Psychologist Claims, *Daily Mail*, Aug. 1, 2017 (*citing* Dr. Lisa Damour), https://www.dailymail.co.uk/health/article-4748022/ Kids-need-rules-need-affection-parents.html.

9. Fred Rogers, *You Are Special*, reprinted in Frederic and Mary Ann Brussat, *Book Review of You Are Special, Words of Wisdom for All Ages from a Beloved Neighbor by Fred Rogers* (2018), https://www.spiritualityandpractice.com/book-reviews/view/28548/you-are-special.

10. How to Set Boundaries with Family: The Definitive Guide, *MedCircle*, Oct. 13, 2020, https://medcircle.com/articles/how-to-set-boundaries-with-family/.

11. *Insider Intelligence*, supra note 1.6.

12. Earlier variations on the Golden Rule include "Love your neighbor as yourself: I am the LORD" from Leviticus 19:18; an Egyptian proverb "that which you hate to be done to you, do not do to another"; and a passage from the Mahābhārata that "one should never do something to others that one would regard as an injury to one's own self. In brief, this is dharma. Anything else is succumbing to desire." *See* Mahābhārata 13.114.8 (Critical edition).

13. *William Davidson Talmud*, Shabbat 31a, https://www.sefaria.org/Shabbat .31a.4?lang=bi&with=all&lang2=en.

14. *Matthew* 7:12 (*quoting* Leviticus 19:18 and *paraphrasing* Leviticus 19:34).

15. Dave Kerpen, Powerful Leadership: Do Unto Others As They Would Want Done, *Inc.*, June 11, 2013, https://www.inc.com/dave-kerpen/powerful -leadership-do-unto-others-as-they-would-want-done-to-them.html.

16. How to Set Boundaries with Family: The Definitive Guide, *MedCircle*, Oct. 13, 2020, https://medcircle.com/articles/how-to-set-boundaries-with-family/.

17. Jeff Thompson, Is Nonverbal Communication a Numbers Game?, *Psychology Today*, Sept. 20, 2011, https://www.psychologytoday.com/us/blog/beyond-words/20 1109/is-nonverbal-communication-numbers-game.

18. *Id.*

19. Skills Employers Want in College Graduates, *West. Mich. U. Career and Student Emp. Svs.*, https://wmich.edu/career/students/transferableskills (last visited April 26, 2021).

20. *Id.* (*citing* What is Career Readiness?, *National Association of Colleges and Employers,* https://www.naceweb.org/career-readiness/competencies/career-read iness-defined/.)

CHAPTER 2

1.   Victoria Rideout & Michael B. Robb, The Common Sense Census: Media Use by Kids Age Zero to Eight, 2020: 1, https://www.commonsensemedia.org/sites/ default/files/uploads/research/2020_zero_to_eight_census_final_web.pdf.

2.   *Id.* at 3.

3.   Media and Young Minds, *Pediatrics*, Nov. 2016; 138(5): e20162591, doi: https://doi.org/10.1542/peds.2016-2591.

4.   What Does Too Much Screen Time Do to Children's Brains?, *NewYork-Presbyterian Health Matters* (*quoting* Jennifer Cross), https://healthmatters.nyp.org/ what-does-too-much-screen-time-do-to-childrens-brains/ (last visited April 25, 2021).

5.   *Id.*

6.   *See id.* (Dr. Cross explained "I believe YouTube is generally bad for young children. . . . The largely unregulated nature of the site allows children to watch almost anything; at best there is little educational value, and at worst it can be violent or inappropriate content.)

7.   Warren Buckleitner, What Should a Preschooler Know About Technology?, *Scholastic*, https://www.scholastic.com/teachers/articles/teaching-content/what-sho uld-preschooler-know-about-technology/.

8. Media Use in School-Aged Children and Adolescents, *Pediatrics*, November 2016; 138(5): e20162592, doi: https://doi.org/10.1542/peds.2016-2592.

9. *Id.*

10. Media Use in School-Aged Children and Adolescents, *supra* note 2.1 *quoting* Lenhart A. Teens, Social Media & Technology Overview 2015, *Pew Internet and American Life Project*, 2015.

11. The Common Sense Census: Media Use by Tweens and Teens, *Common Sense*, 2015; 13.

12. Lily Rothman, The Scathing Speech That Made Television History, *Time*, May 9, 2016 (*quoting* Newton Minnow), https://time.com/4315217/newton-minow -vast-wasteland-1961-speech/.

13. Morgan Neville, Won't you be my Neighbor (*Tremolo Prod's* 2018) (Documentary Film), *quoting* Fred Rogers.

14. Mizuko Ito, Candice Odgers, Stephen Schueller, Social Media and Youth Wellbeing: What We Know and Where We Could Go, *Connected Learning Alliance*, 2020, https://clalliance.org/wp-content/uploads/2020/06/Social-Media-and-Youth -Wellbeing-Report.pdf.

15. Adolescent Mental Health, *World Health Organization*, Sept. 28, 2020, https ://www.who.int/news-room/fact-sheets/detail/adolescent-mental-health.

16. Mizuko Ito, *supra* note 2.14 at 3.

17. *See* Normal Teenage Behavior or Mental Health Issue? Know When to Seek Help, *Georgetown Behavioral Health Institute*, Feb. 2, 2018, https://www.georgeto wnbehavioral.com/blog/normal-teenage-behavior-or-mental-health-issue.

18. K. A. Aschbrenner, J. A. Naslund, E. F. Tomlinson, A. Kinney, S. I. Pratt and M. F. Brunette, Adolescents' Use of Digital Technologies and Preferences for Mobile Health Coaching in Public Mental Health Settings, *Front. Public Health*, 2019; 7: 178, doi: 10.3389/fpubh.2019.00178, https://www.ncbi.nlm.nih.gov/pmc/articles/P MC6614191/.

19. Mizuko Ito, *supra* note 2.14 at 12.

20. *Id.* at 8.

21. *Id.* at 14, *citing* Hanckel et al.

22. The Cost of Coming Out: LGBT Youth Homelessness, *Lesley Univ.*, https:// lesley.edu/article/the-cost-of-coming-out-lgbt-youth-homelessness

23. *See*, e.g., Wesley C. Davidson & Jonathan L. Tobkes, Parenting a Gay Child, *Psy. Today*, July 29, 2016, https://www.psychologytoday.com/us/blog/when-your-child-is-gay/201607/parenting-gay-child. Additional Psychology Today articles can be found listed at https://www.psychologytoday.com/us/blog/when-your-child -is-gay.

24. Internet Content Rating Association, *Wikipedia*, https://en.wikipedia.org/ wiki/Internet_Content_Rating_Association (last visited April 27, 2021).

25. 15 U.S.C. §§650–6605 (2021).

26. *See* 144 Cong. Rec. S12741 (Oct. 7, 1998) (statement of Sen. Bryan). *See* Prepared Statement of The Federal Trade Commission, An Examination Of Children's Privacy: New Technology and the Children's Online Privacy Protection Act, before the Subcommittee On Consumer Protection, Product Safety, And Insurance,

Committee On Commerce, Science, And Transportation, United States Senate (April 29, 2010), https://www.commerce.senate.gov/services/files/5DDCFC53-0C6A-480D -B621-37552E7DDC59.

27. Children's Online Privacy Protection Rule, 16 C.F.R. Part 312 (2013).

28. 16 C.F.R. § 312.2 (definition of "Website or online service directed to children," paragraph [1]).

29. Google and YouTube Will Pay Record $170 Million for Alleged Violations of Children's Privacy Law, *FTC Press Release*, Sept. 4, 2019, https://www.ftc.gov/ news-events/press-releases/2019/09/google-youtube-will-pay-record-170-million-al leged-violations.

30. Complying With COPPA: Frequently Asked Questions, *FTC*, https://ww w.ftc.gov/tips-advice/business-center/guidance/complying-coppa-frequently-asked-questions-0 (last visited April 27, 2021).

31. *Id.*

32. Hilarie Cash, Cosette D. Rae, Ann H. Steel, & Alexander Winkler, Internet Addiction: A Brief Summary of Research and Practice, *Curr Psychiatry Rev.* 2012; 8(4): 292–298. doi:10.2174/157340012803520513, https://www.ncbi.nlm.nih.gov/p mc/articles/PMC3480687/.

33. Joshua Breslau, Eyal Aharoni, Eric R. Pedersen, & Laura L. Miller, A Review of Research on Problematic Internet Use and Well-Being: With Recommendations for the U.S. Air Force, *RAND Corp.*, 2015, https://www.jstor.org/stable/10.7249/j.ctt14bs4q1.

34. *Id.* at chap. 4 at 4.

35. Cash, *supra* note 2.32 citing K. U. Petersen, N. Weymann, Y. Schelb, R. Thiel, R. Fortschr Thomasius, Pathological Internet Use—Epidemiology, Diagnostics, Co-Occurring Disorders and Treatment, *Neurol Psychiatr.* May 2009; 77(5): 263–271.

36. *See id.*

CHAPTER 3

1. McDougal v. Fox News Network, *LLC*, Case No. 1:2019cv11161 (S.D.N.Y. 2020), https://cases.justia.com/federal/district-courts/new-york/nysdce/1:2019cv111 61/527808/39/0.pdf?ts=1601047194.

2. *Id.*

3. A. W. Geiger, Key Findings about the Online News Landscape in America, *Pew Research Center*, Sept. 11, 2019, https://www.pewresearch.org/fact-tank/2019 /09/11/key-findings-about-the-online-news-landscape-in-america/.

4. Robert Mueller, III, Report On The Investigation Into Russian Interference In The 2016 Presidential Election, *U.S. Dept. of Justice*, March 2019 (report of Special Counsel submitted to the Attorney General pursuant to 28 C.F.R. § 600.8[c]), https:// www.justice.gov/archives/sco/file/1373816/download.

5. *See* Microsoft, Digital Literacy, https://www.microsoft.com/en-us/digitall iteracy.

6. https://beinternetawesome.withgoogle.com/en_us/.

7. *Id.*

CHAPTER 4

1. Mary Steward, Understanding Learning Theories and Critique 8, in *Lynne Hunt & Denise Chalmers, Teaching in Focus*, 2013.

2. Paul Stevens-Fulbrook, 15 Learning Theories in Education (A Complete Summary), *TeacherOfSci*, Apr. 18, 2019, https://teacherofsci.com/learning-theories -in-education/.

3. Personal Privacy in an Information Society, The Family Educational Rights and Privacy Act—The Origins of FERPA, *U.S. Dept. Health & Human Scvs.*, July 12, 1997, https://aspe.hhs.gov/report/personal-privacy-information-society/family-edu cational-rights-and-privacy-actthe-origins-ferpa.

4. Family Educational Rights and Privacy Act (FERPA), https://www2.ed.gov/ policy/gen/guid/fpco/ferpa/index.html.

5. 34 C.F.R. §99.31 (2021).

6. 34 C.F.R. §99.36 (2021).

7. What is a "Law Enforcement Unit Record"?, *U.S. Dept. of Ed*, https://student privacy.ed.gov/faq/what-%E2%80%9Claw-enforcement-unit-record%E2%80%9D# :~:text=(34%20CFR%20%C2%A7%2099.8(b,and%20eligible%20students%20b y%20FERPA. (citing 34 C.F.R. §99.8(b)(1) (2021)).

8. What is a "Law Enforcement Unit"?, *U.S. Dept. of Ed.*, https://studentprivacy .ed.gov/faq/what-%E2%80%9Claw-enforcement-unit%E2%80%9D#:~:text=Under %20FERPA%2C%20%E2%80%9Claw%20enforcement%20unit,enforce%20any% 20local%2C%20state%2C%20or (citing 34 C.F.R. §99.8(a)(1) (2021)).

9. *Id.*

CHAPTER 5

1. Remote Learning Recommendations During COVID-19 Emergency, *Illinois Dept. of Ed.* 17–18, Mar. 27, 2000, https://www.isbe.net/Documents/RL-Recomm endations-3-27-20.pdf.

2. The Effects of Online Learning on a Teen's Mental Health, *High Focus Centers*, Nov. 20, 2020, https://highfocuscenters.pyramidhealthcarepa.com/the-ef fects-of-online-learning-on-a-teens-mental-health/.

3. Kristen Setera, FBI Warns of Teleconferencing and Online Classroom Hijacking During COVID-19 Pandemic, *FBI Boston Press Release*, Mar. 30, 2020, https://www.fbi.gov/contact-us/field-offices/boston/news/press-releases/fbi -warns-of-teleconferencing-and-online-classroom-hijacking-during-covid-19-p andemic.

4. *See* Giuliana Santini, *Children Are At Risk Of Being Exposed To More Than Just COVID-19*, manuscript on file with the author, Apr. 29, 2021.

5. Aubri Juhasz, As Esports Take Off, High School Leagues Get in the Game, *NPR*, Jan. 20, 2020, https://www.npr.org/2020/01/24/798172352/as-esports-take-off -high-school-leagues-get-in-the-game.

6. Thomas Armstrong, Mindfulness in the Classroom: Strategies for Promoting Concentration, Compassion, and Calm, *Association for Supervision & Curriculum Development*, 2019: 1.

7. *Id.*

8. *Id.* at 31.

9. Gina Levete, Addressing Inner Needs, in *Meditation in Schools: Calmer Classrooms*, edited by Clive Erricker, and Jane Erricker, 2001.

CHAPTER 6

1. Rehabilitation Act of 1973, 29 U.S.C. §794 (2021).

2. Erin Myers, ADA Compliance in the Classroom, *Rev.* Mar. 13, 2020, https://www.rev.com/blog/ada-compliance-in-the-classroom.

3. *Id.*

4. Individuals with Disabilities Education Act (IDEA), *Am. Psy. Ass'n*, https://www.apa.org/advocacy/education/idea.

5. *Id.*

6. Web Content Accessibility Guidelines (WCAG) 2.1, *W3C Recommendation*, June 5, 2018, https://www.w3.org/TR/WCAG21/.

7. Web Accessibility, University of Oregon, https://communications.uoregon.edu/accessibility.

8. *Id.*

9. National Telecommunications and Information Administration, *Digital Nation Data Explorer*, June 10, 2020, https://www.ntia.doc.gov/data/digital-nation-data-explorer#sel=homeInternetUser&demo=scChldHome&pc=prop&disp=chart (89,317,301 of families with children [73.1 percent] had Internet at home.).

10. Andrew Perrin & Erica Turner, Smartphones Help Blacks, Hispanics Bridge Some—But Not All—Digital Gaps with Whites, *Pew Research Center*, Aug. 20, 2019, https://www.pewresearch.org/fact-tank/2019/08/20/smartphones-help-blacks-hispanics-bridge-some-but-not-all-digital-gaps-with-whites/.

11. *Id.*

12. *Id.* Data for those with Asian ethnicity was not broken out in the study.

13. Carlos Iglesias, The Gender Gap in Internet Access: Using a Women-Centred Method, *World Wide Web Foundation*, Mar. 10, 2020, https://webfoundation.org/2020/03/the-gender-gap-in-internet-access-using-a-women-centred-method/.

14. Columbia Center for Teaching and Learning, https://ctl.columbia.edu/files/2020/02/Guide-for-Inclusive-Teaching-at-Columbia_Accessibility-Revisions_15-January-2020_FINAL.pdf.

CHAPTER 7

1. *See Nathaniel Hawthorne, The Scarlet Letter*, 1850.

2. What It Means to Get 'Canceled,' *Merriam-Webster*, https://www.merriam-webster.com/words-at-play/cancel-culture-words-were-watching.

3. Clifton Smart, Balancing Rights and Responsibilities When Our Values are Offended, *Missouri State Presidential Updates*, June 2, 2020, https://blogs.missouristate.edu/president/2020/06/02/balancing-rights-and-responsibilities-when-our-values-are-offended/.

4. Jonathan A. Segal, Legal Trends—Social Media Use in Hiring: Assessing the Risks, *SHRM*, https://www.shrm.org/hr-today/news/hr-magazine/pages/0914-social-media-hiring.aspx.

5. Jon M. Garon, *A Short and Happy Guide to Privacy and Cybersecurity*, 202: 81.

6. *See* Pickering v. Board of Education, 391 U.S. 563 (1968); Denis Sweeney, Social Media Screening of Homeland Security Job Applicants and the Implications on Free Speech Rights, *Naval Postgraduate School*, March 2019 (Master's Thesis), https://www.hsdl.org/?view&did=825218.

7. Students for Fair Admissions, Inc. v. Pres. and Fellows of Harvard College, 980 F.3d 157, 185 (1st Cir. 2020).

8. *Id.* at 186 *quoting* Fisher v. U. of Texas at Austin, 136 S. Ct. 2198, 2211 (2016).

9. *See N.Y. Times* College Admissions Scandal Coverage, https://www.nytimes.com/news-event/college-admissions-scandal.

10. *See* Types of Educational Opportunities Discrimination, *U.S. Dept. of Justice*, Mar. 25, 2021, https://www.justice.gov/crt/types-educational-opportunities-discrimination#:~:text=The%20Civil%20Rights%20Act%20of,housing%2C%20employment%2C%20and%20education.&text=Additionally%2C%20the%20Equal%20Educational%20Opportunities,%2C%20color%2C%20and%20national%20origin.

11. Clay Calvert, Rescinding Admission Offers in Higher Education: The Clash Between Free Speech and Institutional Academic Freedom When Prospective Students' Racist Posts Are Exposed, *In Discourse, UCLA L. Rev.*, Oct. 25, 2020, https://www.uclalawreview.org/rescinding-admission-offers-in-higher-education-the-clash-between-free-speech-and-institutional-academic-freedom-when-prospective-students-racist-posts-are-exposed/.

12. *Id.*

13. Aaron Krolik, The Slander Industry, *N.Y. Times*, Apr. 24, 2021, https://www.nytimes.com/interactive/2021/04/24/technology/online-slander-websites.html.

CHAPTER 8

1. Brian Kisida & Daniel H. Bowen, New Evidence of the Benefits of Arts Education, *Brookings*, Feb. 12, 2019, https://www.brookings.edu/blog/brown-center-chalkboard/2019/02/12/new-evidence-of-the-benefits-of-arts-education/.

2. *Id.*

3. *See Kerry Thomas & Janet Chan, Handbook of Research on Creativity*, 2013: 21.

4. 17 U.S.C. §102(a) (2021).

5. *See id.* at §102(b).

6. Creative Commons "CC BY": License, https://creativecommons.org/about/c clicenses/.

7. *See* 17 U.S.C. §107.

8. *Id.*

9. More Information on Fair Use, U.S. Copyright Office, https://www.copyrigh t.gov/fair-use/more-info.html.

10. *See* 17 U.S.C. §512.

11. 47 U.S.C. §230 (2020).

12. Section 230 of the Communications Decency Act, Electronic Frontier Foundation, https://www.eff.org/issues/cda230/.

13. Jon M. Garon, Constitutional Limits on Administrative Agencies in Cyberspace, *Belmont L. Rev.* 499 (2020); *citing* Zeran v. Am. Online, Inc., 129 F.3d 327, 331 (4th Cir. 1997).

14. 47 U.S.C. §230 (c)(2).

CHAPTER 9

1. 42 U.S.C. §710 (2020).

2. *Id.*

3. *Id.*

4. John Santelli et al., Abstinence and Abstinence-Only Education: A Review of U.S. Policies and Programs, *J. Adolescent Health*, 2006; 38(72): 77.

5. *Id.*

6. *See* https://www.cdc.gov/healthyyouth/whatworks/what-works-sexual-health -education.htm.

7. *Id.*

8. Report of the APA Task Force on the Sexualization of Girls, *Am. Psy. Ass'n*, 2007, www.apa.org/pi/wpo/sexualization.html.

9. *Id.*

10. *Id.*

11. Stefanie E Davis, Objectification, Sexualization, and Misrepresentation: Social Media and the College Experience, *SM+S*, July–Sept. 2018, https://doi.org/10 .1177/2056305118786727.

12. Help Us Stop Body Shaming in its Tracks, *Girl Scouts*, https://www.girlscou ts.org/en/raising-girls/happy-and-healthy/happy/body-shaming-girls.html (last visited April 26, 2021).

13. Hudaisa Hafeez, et al., Health Care Disparities Among Lesbian, Gay, Bisexual, and Transgender Youth: A Literature Review, *Cureus*, Apr. 20, 2017, doi: 10.7759/cureus.1184.

14. *Id.*

15. *Id.*

16. *Id.* (internal citations omitted).

17.   Caitlin Ryan, A Practitioner's Resource Guide: Helping Families to Support Their LGBT Children, *SAMHSA*, citing Andrew Boxer & Gilbert Herdt, Children of Horizons: How Gay and Lesbian Teens are Leading a New Way Out of the Closet, 1993, http://store.samhsa.gov/product/A-Practitioner-s-Resource-Guide-Helping -Families-to-Support-Their-LGBT-Children/PEP14-LGBTKIDS.

18.   https://www.childwelfare.gov/topics/systemwide/diverse-populations/lgbtq/ lgbt-families/.

19.   https://www.cdc.gov/lgbthealth/youth-resources.htm.

20.   https://www.hopkinsmedicine.org/health/wellness-and-prevention/tips-for -parents-of-lgbtq-youth.

21.   *See* Ogi Ogas, & Sai Gaddam, A Billion Wicked Thoughts: What the Internet Tells Us About Sex and Relationships, 2012.

22.   Julie Ruvolo, How Much of the Internet is Actually for Porn, *Forbes*, Sept. 7, 2010, https://www.forbes.com/sites/julieruvolo/2011/09/07/how-much-of-the-interne t-is-actually-for-porn/?sh=6ec02cc25d16.

23.   Lizzie Enfield, The Fine Line Between Art and Pornography, *BBC*, Sept. 17, 2020, https://www.bbc.com/culture/article/20200917-the-fine-line-between-art-and- pornography.

24.   *Id.*

25.   Nudity and Pornography, *Nat. Coalition Against Censorship*, https://ncac.or g/issue/nudity-pornography.

26.   Alan McKee, Catharine Lumby & Kath Albury, *The Porn Report*, 2008.

27.   How Much Pornography are Americans Consuming?, *Austin Institute for the Study of Family and Culture*, https://relationshipsinamerica.com/relationships-and-se x/how-much-pornography-are-americans-consuming.

28.   Kimberly J. Mitchell, Janis Wolak, & David Finkelhor, Trends in Youth Reports of Sexual Solicitations, Harassment and Unwanted Exposure to Pornography on the Internet, *J. Adolescent Health*, 2007; 40: 116, http://www.sciencedirect.com/s cience/article/pii/S1054139X06002266.

29.   Reno v. American Civil Liberties Union, 521 U.S. 844 (1997).

30.   *See* Ashcroft v. American Civil Liberties Union, 535 U.S. 564 (2002).

31.   Miller v. California, 413 U.S. 15, 24–25 (1973); Smith v. United States, 431 U.S. 291, 300–302, 309 (1977); Pope v. Illinois, 481 U.S. 497, 500–501 (1987).

32.   *See* Joseph Price, Rich Patterson, Mark Regnerus & Jacob Walley, How Much More XXX is Generation X Consuming? Evidence of Changing Attitudes and Behaviors Related to Pornography Since 1973, *J. Sex Res.*, Jan. 2016; 53: 12.

33.   *Id.*

34.   New York v. Ferber, 458 U.S. 747, 759 (1982).

35.   *See* 18 U.S.C. §2256 (2021).

36.   *See* 18 U.S. Code §2252 (2021).

37.   U.S. v. Williams, 553 U.S. 285, 290 (2008).

38.   *See* Anne Cohen, How Do You Direct A Child In A Movie About Sexual Abuse?, *Refinery29*, https://www.refinery29.com/en-us/2018/05/200084/the-tale-true -story-sexual-abuse-director-jennifer-fox.

39.   National Center for Missing & Exploited Children, Reporting Child Sexual Exploitation, https://www.missingkids.org/content/dam/missingkids/pdfs/NCMEC _0022-20_CSAM%20Brochure_Digital.pdf.

40.   www.nctsn.org/resources/sexual-health-and-traumaDigital.

41.   www.hotline.rainn.org/online.

42.   Anna T. Prescott, James D. Sargent, & Jay G. Hull, Metaanalysis of the Relationship Between Violent Videogame Play and Physical Aggression Over Time, *PNAS*, Oct. 1, 2018, https://doi.org/10.1073/pnas.1611617114.

43.   *Id.*

44.   *See*, e.g., Andrew K. Przybylski & Netta Weinstein, Violent Videogame Engagement is not Associated with Adolescents' Aggressive Behavior: Evidence from a Registered Report, *Royal Society Open Science*, Feb.13, 2019; 6, https://ro yalsocietypublishing.org/doi/10.1098/rsos.171474.

45.   Violent Videogames and Young People, *Harvard Mental Health Letter*, Oct. 2010, https://www.health.harvard.edu/newsletter_article/violent-video-games-and-y oung-people.

46.   Brown v. Entertainment Merchants Association, 564 U.S. 786 (2011).

47.   Patricia E. Vance, Beyond the Box: ESRB Ratings for Downloadable Videogames, *ESRB*, Dec. 16, 2020, https://www.esrb.org/blog/beyond-the-box-esrb -ratings-on-digital-storefronts/.

48.   *Id.*

49.   Wes Fenlon, PC Piracy Survey Results: 35 Percent of PC Gamers Pirate, *PC Gamer*, Aug. 26, 2016, https://www.pcgamer.com/pc-piracy-survey-results-35-per cent-of-pc-gamers-pirate/.

50.   *Id.*

CHAPTER 10

1.   Joey L. Blanch & Wesley L. Hsu, An Introduction to Violent Crime on the Internet, *U.S. Attorneys' Bulletin*, 63, May 2016 (issue dedicated to Cyber Misbehavior), https://www.justice.gov/usao/file/851856/download.

2.   Monica Anderson, A Majority of Teens Have Experienced Some Form of Cyberbullying, *Pew Research Center*, Sept. 27, 2018, https://www.pewresearch.o rg/internet/2018/09/27/a-majority-of-teens-have-experienced-some-form-of-cyberbu llying/.

3.   *Id.*

4.   *Id.*

5.   *Id.*

6.   What is Stalking, *U.S. Dept. of Justice*, https://www.justice.gov/ovw/ stalking.

7.   Blanch & Hsu, *supra*, note 10.1.

8.   Get Help Now, *Stopbullying.gov*, https://www.stopbullying.gov/resources/g et-help-now.

9.   Virginia v. Black, 538 U.S. 343, 359 (2003).

10. Chaplinsky v. New Hampshire, 315 U.S. 568, 574 (1942).
11. 18 U.S.C. § 2261A(2) (2018).
12. *See*, e.g., Matter of Welfare of A. J. B., 929 N.W.2d 840 (Minn. 2019).
13. John D. Ferrero, Will The Jessica Logan Act Aid in the Prevention of Bullying?, *Stark County Prosecutor's Office*, https://www.starkcountyohio.gov/Sta rkCounty/media/StarkCounty/StarkCountMain/Prosecutor/PUBLICATIONS-Jessica -Logan-Act-Prev-Bullying.pdf.
14. *Id.*
15. Tinker v. Des Moines Indep. Cmty. Sch. Dist., 393 U.S. 503, 509 (1969).
16. *Id.* at 509 (1969) (citations omitted).
17. Bethel Sch. Dist. No. 403 v. Fraser, 478 U.S. 675, 683 (1986), *quoting* Tinker, 393 U.S., at 508.
18. Morse v. Frederick, 551 U.S. 393 (2007).
19. *Id.* at 397 (2007).
20. Hazelwood Sch. Dist. v. Kuhlmeier, 484 U.S. 260 (1988).
21. *Id.* at 273.
22. Mahanoy Area Sch. Dist. v. B. L. by and through Levy, __ U.S. __, 141 S. Ct. 2038 (2021).
23. *Id.* at 2042–2043.
24. *Id.* at 2044–2045 *quoting* Tinker, 393 U.S., at 506; Kuhlmeier, 484 U.S., at 266 (internal quotation mark omitted).
25. *Id.* at 2045 *citing* Frederick, 551 U.S., at 409; Kuhlmeier, 484 U.S., at 271.
26. *Id.*
27. *Id.* at 2046. The Opinion explains the attribution of the last quote in the section as follows: Although this quote is often attributed to Voltaire, it was likely coined by an English writer, Evelyn Beatrice Hall.
28. 590 U.S. ___, 40 S. Ct. 1731 (2020).
29. *Id.*
30. *See* https://www.stopbullying.gov/resources/laws/federal.
31. *See id.*
32. *Id.*
33. *Id.*

CHAPTER 11

1. Justin W. Patchin & Sameer Hinduja, Digital Self-Harm Among Adolescents, *J. Adolescent Health*, 2017; 61, doi: 10.1016/j.jadohealth.2017.06.012.
2. *Id.*
3. Ryan C. Meldrum, Justin W. Patchin, Jacob T.N. Young & Sameer Hinduja, Bullying Victimization, Negative Emotions, and Digital Self-Harm: Testing a Theoretical Model of Indirect Effects, *Deviant Behavior*, 2020, https://doi.org/10.1 080/01639625.2020.1833380.
4. Patchin & Sameer Hinduja, *supra* note 11.1.
5. Meldrum, et al., *supra* note 11.3.

6.   Elizabeth Englander, Digital Self-harm: Frequency, Type, Motivations, and Outcomes, *MARC Research Reports*, 2012; 5, http://vc.bridgew.edu/marc_reports/5.

7.   Patchin & Sameer Hinduja, *supra* note 11.1.

8.   *Id.* (citation omitted).

9.   danah boyd, Digital Self-Harm and Other Acts of Self-Harassment, *apophenia*, https://www.zephoria.org/thoughts/archives/2010/12/07/digital-self-harm-and -other-acts-of-self-harassment.html (Dr. boyd prefers not to capitalize her name or that of her site).

10.   Patrick McGeehan, Conviction of Ex-Rutgers Student Is Thrown Out in Roommate's Suicide, *N.Y. Times* at A15, Sept. 10, 2016, https://www.nytimes.com/2 016/09/10/nyregion/conviction-thrown-out-for-rutgers-student-in-tyler-clementi-case .html (the criminal conviction of the roommate on bias intimidation was later overturned by a New Jersey court of appeals).

11.   https://www.cybercivilrights.org/.

12.   Ruobing Su, Tom Porter, and Michelle Mark, Here's a Map Showing which US States Have Passed Laws against Revenge Porn—and Those Where It's Still Legal, *Business Insider*, Oct. 30, 2019, https://www.businessinsider.com/map-states -where-revenge-porn-banned-2019-10.

13.   Jennifer Leach, What to do if You're the Target of Revenge Porn, *FTC Blog*, Jan. 11, 2018, https://www.consumer.ftc.gov/blog/2018/01/what-do-if-youre-target -revenge-porn.

14.   U.S. v. Williams, 553 U.S. 285, 298 (2008).

15.   *Id.*

16.   Howard N. Snyder, Sexual Assault of Young Children as Reported to Law Enforcement 10, *National Center for Juvenile Justice*, 2000, https://www.bjs.gov/ content/pub/pdf/saycrle.pdf.

17.   Isabel Grant & Janine Benedet, The "Statutory Rape" Myth: A Case Law Study of Sexual Assaults against Adolescent Girls, *Canadian J. Women and the Law*, 2019; 31: 266, doi: 10.3138/cjwl.31.2.03.

18.   *Id.* (internal citations omitted).

19.   Gisela Priebe, Kimberly J. Mitchell & David Finkelhor, To Tell or Not To Tell? Youth's Responses to Unwanted Internet Experiences, *Cyberpsychology: Journal of Psychosocial Research on Cyberspace*, 2013; 7: 6, doi: 10.5817/CP2013-1-6.

20.   Janis, Wolak, Lindsey Evans, Stephanie Nguyen & Denise Hines, Online Predators: Myth versus Reality, *New Eng. J. Pub. Pol'y*, 25, http://scholarworks.umb .edu/nejpp/vol25/iss1/6.

21.   *Id.*

22.   *Id. See also* Christine Elgersma, Parents, Here's the Truth About Online Predators, *CNN with Common Sense Media*, Aug. 3, 2017, https://www.cnn.com/ 2017/08/03/health/online-predators-parents-partner/index.html#:~:text=ask%20to %20meet%3F-,The%20facts%3A,who%20are%20most%20often%20targeted.

23.   *See* Deborah C. England, Teen Cyberbullying and Harassment, *NOLO*, https ://www.criminaldefenselawyer.com/resources/teen-cyberbullying-and-harassment .htm (providing articles for each state on cyberbullying).

24. Choosing whether or not to report severe episodes of online harassment to law enforcement can be a difficult decision, *Pen America*, https://onlineharassmentf ieldmanual.pen.org/reporting-to-law-enforcement/.

CHAPTER 12

1. What is Violent Extremism?, *FBI*, https://www.fbi.gov/cve508/teen-website/ what-is-violent-extremism.
2. https://www.unodc.org/e4j/en/terrorism/module-2/key-issues/radicalization -violent-extremism.html.
3. Online Radicalization to Violent Extremism: Awareness Brief, *International Association of Chiefs of Police*, 2014, *citing* Majority and Minority Staff of the Senate Committee on Homeland Security and Governmental Affairs, Zachary Chesser: A Case Study in Online Islamist Radicalization and Its Meaning for the Threat of Homegrown Terrorism (Washington, DC: United States Senate, 2012), www.hsgac. senate.gov/imo/media/doc/CHESSER%20FINAL%20REPORT%281%29.pdf.
4. Murder and Extremism in the United States, *ADL*, Feb. 2020: 11.
5. A Dark & Constant Rage: 25 Years of Right-Wing Terrorism in the United States, *ADL*, 2017.
6. Ines von Behr, Anaïs Reding, Charlie Edwards & Luke Gribbon, Radicalisation in the Digital Era, *Rand Corp*. Ix, 2013 (spelling adapted to U.S. style).
7. *Id.* (spelling adapted to U.S. style).
8. Countering Online Radicalization in America: Executive Summary, *National Security Program*,
9. Why Do People Become Violent Extremists?, *FBI*, https://www.fbi.gov/ cve508/teen-website/why-do-people-become-violent-extremists.
10. *Id.*
11. Alice Oppetit, *et al.*, Do Radicalized Minors Have Different Social and Psychological Profiles From Radicalized Adults?, *Psychiatry*, Sept. 10, 2019, https:// doi.org/10.3389/fpsyt.2019.00644.
12. Rachel Briggs & Sebastien Feve, Policy Briefing: Countering the Appeal of Extremism Online, *Inst. Strategic Dialogue*, 2014; 6, https://www.dhs.gov/sites/defa ult/files/publications/Countering%20the%20Appeal%20of%20Extremism%20On line-ISD%20Report.pdf (*citing* Arthur, C. Anwar al-Awlaki Videos Available on YouTube, *Guardian*, Nov. 2, 2010.
13. Emilia Aiello, Lidia Puigvert & Tinka Schubert, Preventing violent radical-ization of youth through dialogic evidence-based policies, *International Soc.*, 2018; 33: 534, doi:10.1177/0268580918775882.
14. *Id.*
15. *Id.* (Internal citations omitted).
16. School Shootings This Year: How Many and Where, *Education Week*, April 27, 2021, https://www.edweek.org/leadership/school-shootings-this-year-how-many-and-where/2021/03.

17. Emily Shapiro, Dissecting the distinctive profile of school shooters: There's always a trail of what they're about to do, *ABC News*, Feb. 22, 2018, https://abcnews.go.com/US/dissecting-distinctive-profile-school-shooters-trail/story?id=53197511 (*quoting* FBI agent and ABC News contributor Brad Garrett).

18. *Id.*

CHAPTER 13

1. Aditi Kumar and Eric Rosenbach, The Truth about the Dark Web, *Finance & Development*, Sept. 2019; 56: 22, https://www.imf.org/external/pubs/ft/fandd/2019/09/the-truth-about-the-dark-web-kumar.htm.

2. Jose Pagliery, FBI Hackers Took Down a Child Porn Ring, *CNN Business*, Jan. 25, 2016, https://money.cnn.com/2016/01/25/technology/fbi-child-porn/index.html.

3. Senior Advisor of the "Silk Road" Website Pleads Guilty in Manhattan Federal Court, *U.S. Drug Enforcement Agency*, https://www.dea.gov/press-releases/2020/01/30/senior-advisor-silk-road-website-pleads-guilty-manhattan-federal-court.

4. Aditi Kumar and Eric Rosenbach, The Truth about the Dark Web, *Finance & Development*, Sept. 2019, https://www.imf.org/external/pubs/ft/fandd/2019/09/the-truth-about-the-dark-web-kumar.htm.

5. *See* Metro-Goldwyn-Mayer Studios Inc. v. Grokster, Ltd., 545 U.S. 913, 924 (2005); A & M Records, Inc. v. Napster, Inc., 239 F.3d 1004 (9th Cir. 2001); In re Aimster Copyright Litigation, 334 F.3d 643, 645–646 (7th Cir. 2003).

6. *See* Sony BMG Music Ent. v. Tenenbaum, 719 F.3d 67 (1st Cir. 2013); Capitol Records, Inc. v. Thomas-Rasset, 692 F.3d 899 (8th Cir. 2012).

CHAPTER 14

1. Steve Morgan, Cybercrime to Cost the World $10.5 Trillion Annually by 2025, *Cybercrime Mag.*, https://cybersecurityventures.com/hackerpocalypse-cybercrime-report-2016/.

2. Thomas J. Holt, Jordana N. Navarro & Shelly Clevenger, Exploring the Moderating Role of Gender in Juvenile Hacking Behaviors, *Crime & Delinquency*, 2019 (internal citations omitted); doi: 10.1177/0011128719875697.

3. What is Hacking, *Malware Bytes*, https://www.malwarebytes.com/hacker/.

4. *Intel Bug Bounty Program Terms*, https://www.intel.com/content/www/us/en/security-center/bug-bounty-program.html.

5. EC-Council Code of Ethics, https://www.eccouncil.org/code-of-ethics/.

6. Roger A. Grimes, 11 Signs Your Kid is Hacking—and What to do About It, *InfoWorld*, July 5, 2016, https://www.infoworld.com/article/3088970/11-signs-your

-kid-is-hacking-and-what-to-do-about-it.html. *See also*, Roger A. Grimes, Malicious Mobile Code: Virus Protection for Windows, 2001.

7. *Id.*

8. *Id.*

9. Thomas J. Holt, Jordana N. Navarro & Shelly Clevenger, Exploring the Moderating Role of Gender in Juvenile Hacking Behaviors, *Crime & Delinquency*, 2019 (internal citations omitted); doi: 10.1177/0011128719875697.

10. *Id.*

11. *Id.*

12. *Id.*

13. *Id.*

14. https://twitter.com/NCA_UK/status/1228092570422718464. *See* Charlie Osborne, UK Police Deny Responsibility for Poster Urging Parents to Report Kids for Using Kali Linux, *ZDNet*, Feb. 14, 2020, https://www.zdnet.com/article/uk-police-distance-themselves-from-poster-warning-parents-to-report-kids-for-using-kali-linux/.

15. Holt, Navarro, & Clevenger, *supra* note 14.9.

16. Neil J. Rubenking & Ben Moore, The Best Password Managers for 2021, *PC Mag.*, Dec. 21, 2020, https://www.pcmag.com/picks/the-best-password-managers.

CHAPTER 15

1. U.S. Ecommerce Grows 44.0% in 2020, *DigitalCommerce360*, Jan 29, 2021, https://www.digitalcommerce360.com/article/us-ecommerce-sales/.

2. BBB Research Shows Spike in Online Purchase Scams Since COVID Started, *Better Business Bureau*, Oct. 27, 2020, https://www.bbb.org/article/news-releases/23276-bbb-research-shows-spike-in-online-purchase-scams-since-covid-started.

3. *Id.*

4. Before You Shop, USA.Gov, https://www.usa.gov/before-you-shop (last visited April 5, 2021).

5. BBB, supra note 15.2.

6. IAB Releases Internet Advertising Revenue Report for 2020, *IAB*, Apr. 07, 2021, https://www.iab.com/news/iab-internet-advertising-revenue/.

7. *Id.*

8. Steve Kroft, The Data Brokers: Selling your personal information, *60 Minutes*, Mar. 9, 2014, https://www.cbsnews.com/news/the-data-brokers-selling-your-personal-information/.

9. Jacquelyn Burkell & Priscilla M Regan, Voter Preferences, Voter Manipulation, Voter Analytics: Policy Options for Less Surveillance and More Autonomy, *Internet Pol'y Rev.*, 5: 4, doi: 10.14763/2019.4.1438 (internal citations omitted; spelling modified for U.S. English).

10. Restatement (Second) of the Law of Torts §652A.

11. Riley v. California, 573 U.S. 373, 394–395 (2014).

12.   *Id*. at 341–342 (internal quotations and citations omitted).

CHAPTER 17

1.   Admiral William H. McRaven, Make Your Bed, *James Clear*, https://jamescl ear.com/great-speeches/make-your-bed-by-admiral-william-h-mcraven (commencement address for The University of Texas at Austin, May 17, 2014).

2.   Andrew K. Przybylski, et al., *A Shared Responsibility—Building Children's Online Resilience*, 2014: 4, https://parentzone.org.uk/sites/default/files/Building% 20Online%20Resilience%20Report.pdf.

3.   Wikipedia, *Wikipedia*, https://en.wikipedia.org/wiki/Wikipedia (last visited April 29, 2021).

4.   About, *Khan Academy*, https://www.khanacademy.org/about (last visited April 29, 2021).

APPENDICES

1.   *See* About Darpa, *Darpa*, https://www.darpa.mil/about-us/about-darpa (last visited May 1, 2021).

2.   *Id.*

3.   *See* Vint Cerf, A Brief History of the Internet & Related Networks, *Internet Society*, https://www.internetsociety.org/internet/history-internet/brief-history-int ernet-related-networks/ (last visited May 1, 2021); From Arpanet to the Internet, *Science Museum* (UK), Nov. 2, 2018, https://www.sciencemuseum.org.uk/objects -and-stories/arpanet-internet.

4.   Katie Hafner, *Where Wizards Stay Up Late: The Origins of the Internet*, 1998: 142–143.

5.   *See* Barry M. Leiner, *et al.*, Brief History of the Internet, *Internet Society*, 1997: 4–6, https://www.internetsociety.org/wp-content/uploads/2017/09/ISOC-H istory-of-the-Internet_1997.pdf

6.   Giovanni Navarria, How the Internet was Born: From the ARPANET to the Internet, *The Conversation*, Nov. 2, 2016, https://theconversation.com/how-the-inte rnet-was-born-from-the-arpanet-to-the-internet-68072.

7.   A Brief History of NSF and the Internet, *Nat. Sc. Found.*, Aug. 13, 2003, https://www.nsf.gov/news/news_summ.jsp?cntn_id=103050.

8.   Gerald W. Brock, *The Second Information Revolution*, 2003: 83–84.

9.   *See* Andrew Pollack, The Daunting Power of I.B.M., *N.Y. Times*, Jan. 20, 1985 at 127 (Sec. 3), https://timesmachine.nytimes.com/timesmachine/1985/01/20 /227232.html?pageNumber=127.

10.   *See* Doing it Yourself, *Computer History Museum*, https://www.computer history.org/revolution/personal-computers/17/296 (last visited May 1, 2021).

11.   *See* Steven Levy, *Hackers: Heroes of the Computer Revolution Paperback*, 2010: 215, 253.

12. Dan Bricklin & Bob Frankston, Inventors of the Modern Computer: VisiCalc, *Inventors*, http://www.landley.net/history/mirror/timelines/inventors/html/aa01019 9.htm#:~:text=Dan%20Bricklin%20%26%20Bob%20Frankston&text=VisiCalc %20was%20the%20first%20computer,new%20level%20in%20application%20softw are (last visited May 1, 2021).

13. Jimmy Maher, The Complete History of the IBM PC, Part One: The Deal of the Century Bill Gates, Mysterious Deaths, and the Business Machine that Sparked a Home Revolution, *Ars Technia*, June 30, 2017, https://arstechnica.com/gadgets/2017 /06/ibm-pc-history-part-1/

14. Jeff Lindsay & Mike Hopkins, From Experience: Disruptive Innovation and the Need for Disruptive Intellectual Asset Strategy, *J. Product Innovation Mgmt.*, 2010; 27: 283, 284; Jon M. Garon, *The Enterpreneur's Intellectual Property & Business Handbook*, 2018: 121–122.

15. Garon, *Enterepreneur's Business Handbook* at 122 *quoting The Selectric Typewriter*, IBM 100: *Icons of Progress*, http://www03.ibm.com/ibm/history/ib m100/us/en/icons/selectric/.

16. 50 Years of Moore's Law, *INTEL*, http://www.intel.com/technology/moo reslaw/index.htm (last visited May 1, 2021).

17. James Ellis, The Story of Steve Jobs, Xerox and Who Really Invented the Personal Computer, *Newsweek*, Mar. 19, 2016, https://www.newsweek.com/silicon -valley-apple-steve-jobs-xerox-437972.

18. *Id.*

19. Windows 3.0, *Wikipedia*, https://en.wikipedia.org/wiki/Windows_3.0#:~:te xt=Windows%203.0%20sold%2010%20million,by%20Windows%203.1%20in%20 1992 (last visited May 1, 2021).

20. History of the World Wide Web, *Wikipedia*, https://en.wikipedia.org/wiki/ History_of_the_World_Wide_Web (last visited May 1, 2021).

21. Mosaic (web browser), *Wikipedia*, https://en.wikipedia.org/wiki/ Mosaic_(web_browser) (last visited May 1, 2021).

22. *Id.*

23. Philip B. Evans & Thomas S. Wurster, Strategy and the New Economics of Information, *Harv. Bus. Rev.*, Sept.–Oct. 1997; 75: 70, 71.

24. *Philip Evans & Thomas S. Wurster, Blown to Bits*, 1999.

25. *See* Joel Rose & Jacob Ganz, The MP3: A History of Innovation and Betrayal, The Record, *MPR*, Mar. 23, 2011, https://www.npr.org/sections/therecord /2011/03/23/134622940/the-mp3-a-history-of-innovation-and-betrayal.

26. Apple Presents iPod, *Apple*, Oct. 23, 2001, https://www.apple.com/new sroom/2001/10/23Apple-Presents-iPod/ (press release).

27. Marshall McLuhan, *Understanding Media 9*, 1964.

28. Marshall McLuhan & Quentin Fiore, *The Medium Is the Massage: An Inventory of Effects*, 1967: 16.

29. Joel Achenbach, Did the News Media, Led by Walter Cronkite, Lose the War in Vietnam, *Wash. Post*, May 25, 2018.

30. *Id.*

31. Israel Zangwill, *The Melting-Pot Act IV*, 1908.

Bibliography

Armstrong, Thomas, *Mindfulness in the Classroom: Strategies for Promoting Concentration, Compassion, and Calm, Association for Supervision & Curriculum Development*, 2019.

Brown, Peter, Henry Roediger III, and Mark McDaniel, *Make it Stick: The Science of Successful Learning*, 2014.

Christensen, Clayton M., Michael Horn, and Curtis Johnson, *Disrupting Class, Expanded Edition: How Disruptive Innovation Will Change the Way the World Learns*, 2010.

Dhoest, Alexander, The Persistence of National TV: Language and Cultural Proximity in Flemish Fiction, in *After the Break: Television Theory Today*, Valck, Marijke de, and Jan Teurlings, ed., Vol. 51, 2013.

Evans, Philip & Thomas S. Wurster, *Blown to Bits*, 1999.

Evans, Philip B. & Thomas S. Wurster, Strategy and the New Economics of Information, 75 *Harv. Bus. Rev.*, Sept.–Oct. 1997: 70, 71.

Federal Trade Commission, *Consumer Sentinel Network, Data Book 2019*, https://www.ftc.gov/system/files/documents/reports/consumer-sentinel-network-data-book-2019/consumer_sentinel_network_data_book_2019.pdf.

Federal Trade Commission, *Endorsement Guidelines*, https://www.ftc.gov/sites/default/files/attachments/press-releases/ftc-publishes-final-guides-governing-endorsements-testimonials/091005revisedendorsementguides.pdf.

Fuchs, Christian, *Internet and Society: Social Theory in the Information Age*, 2008.

Garon, Jon M., *A Short & Happy Guide to Privacy and Cybersecurity Law*, 2020.

Gopnik, Alison, *The Gardener and the Carpenter: What the New Science of Child Development Tells Us About the Relationship Between Parents and Children*, 2016.

Hafner, Katie, *Where Wizards Stay Up Late: The Origins of the Internet*, 1998.

Horn, Michael & Heather Staker, *Blended: Using Disruptive Innovation To Improve Schools*, 2014.

Janning, Michelle Y., *Contemporary Parenting and Parenthood: From News Headlines to New Research*, 2018.

Jenson, Kristen A., *Pictures Bad Pictures: Porn Proofing Today's Young Kids*, Rev. ed., 2018.

Klobuchar, Amy, *Antitrust: Taking on Monopoly Power from the Gilded Age to the Digital Age*, 2021.

Leiner, Barry M., et al., Brief History of the Internet, *Internet Society*, 1997, https://www.internetsociety.org/wp-content/uploads/2017/09/ISOC-History-of-the-Internet_1997.pdf.

Mascolo, Michael, *8 Keys to Old School Parenting for Modern-Day Families*, 2015.

Media and Young Minds, Policy Statement of the American Academy of Pediatrics, *Pediatrics*, Nov. 2016: 138, https://pediatrics.aappublications.org/content/138/5/e20162591.

Nicolas, Guerda, Anabel Bejarano, & Debbiesiu L. Lee, *Contemporary Parenting: A Global Perspective*, 2015.

Senior, Jennifer, *All Joy and No Fun: The Paradox of Modern Parenthood*, 2014.

Index

About the Author

Jon M. Garon is a professor of law and director of the Intellectual Property, Cybersecurity, and Technology Law program at Nova Southeastern University Shepard Broad College of Law, teaching Constitutional Law, Privacy, Contracts, Entertainment Law, and many other courses. As an educator, parent, and counselor, he has written and trained individuals to understand how best to address the challenges and opportunities in the online environment for entrepreneurs and creative artists. With the new importance of online education and the millions of parents who find themselves thrust into the online environment, Professor Garon seeks to provide essential guidance and coaching to make the move online understandable and manageable for all.

He is a nationally recognized authority on education, information privacy, technology regulation, free speech entertainment law, and copyright. He has published over 50 books, book chapters, and academic articles, and has presented at more than 300 programs. A Minnesota native, he received his bachelor's degree from the University of Minnesota in 1985 and his juris doctor degree from Columbia University School of Law in 1988.

Professor Garon served as dean for the NSU Shepard Broad College of Law from 2014 to 2020. Prior to joining Nova Southeastern University in 2014, Garon was the inaugural director of the Northern Kentucky University Salmon P. Chase College of Law, Law + Informatics Institute, serving from 2011 to 2014. He served as dean and professor of law at Hamline University School of Law in St. Paul, Minnesota, and as interim dean of the Hamline Graduate School of Management from 2005 to 2006. Before Hamline, Professor Garon taught Entertainment Law and Copyright at Franklin Pierce Law Center in Concord, New Hampshire, and Western State College of Law in Orange County, California.